The Kingdom of God in 20th-century Interpretation

THE KINGDOM OF GOD IN 20TH-CENTURY INTERPRETATION

Edited by Wendell Willis

HENDRICKSON
PUBLISHERS
PEABODY, MASSACHUSETTS 01961-3473

Copyright © 1987
Hendrickson Publishers, Inc.
P. O. Box 3473
Peabody, Massachusetts, 01961–3473
Printed in the United States of America
ISBN 0–913573 82–5

Contents

Foreword

I am grateful for the courtesy of being invited to contribute a few comments to this timely and valuable project dealing with a topic that has so long interested me. While earlier work of my own is cited in these pages, it is piquant that at this date I should be afforded an opportunity to look back on the wider changing fronts of the enterprise here surveyed.

I can point up this piquancy by noting that I had courses with C. H. Dodd at Oxford in 1922–1923 dealing with the teaching of Jesus, as well as with Streeter and R. H. Lightfoot. There also I served briefly as amanuensis for Albert Schweitzer when he lectured in 1922 at Mansfield College. These now ancient contacts with the vicissitudes of kingdom of God discussions, along with later encounters with Bultmann and Kümmel at Marburg remind me of many of the issues canvassed in these chapters.

I am also happy to find among the contributors to the present volume the names of a number of friends whom I knew at Harvard in their student years, including Eldon Epp, Ramsey Michaels, Karl Donfried and Everett Ferguson as well as others with whose work in this field I had been acquainted.

What is immediately striking about the present survey is that a major theme, "God as king," with its variants, including the term "the kingdom of God," can be identified and studied, in its various contexts, from its ancient antecedents through so many centuries in the texts, a theme and a term whose usage has continued to have such import down to the present day. When we speak of continuities in culture or myth there are few motifs whose study can be so rewarding. Despite all the vicissitudes of "royalty" in human societies, its attribution to God in this great stream of global culture and tradition has been so rooted as to flourish in radically changing situations.

Indeed, much of the interest in these particular historical studies attaches to shifting usages and implication of the common ground-theme in the successive phases of the life of Israel and the Church.

In this long history we have to do with the changing parameters of Israel's experience related both to crises in the life of the people and to external influences. Such matters as the scope of God's reign, the particular rivals and limits to his sway, and the identification of his sovereignty with particular institutions of the nation, all have their variables.

The dialectics of theocratic/universal and present/future show their differing phases. Of particular importance is the emergence of those visionary versions of the kingdom associated with the Haesmonean crisis which we speak of as apocalyptic.

As in the literature of the Christian movement the actual term, "the kingdom of God," may at times recede in its incidence. Those who contribute here to the portrayal of Judaism at the time of Christ, however, are satisfied that in announcing "the Kingdom of God" Jesus would have been readily understood. Again in the New as in the Old Testament writings the kingdom language differs in form and frequency as well as in particular reference. Ramsey Michaels points to the same dialectics I have mentioned above: The kingdom is both present and future, with more or less emphasis in one case than another; similarly, the basic God-centeredness of the kingdom can shift toward Christ-centeredness in some writings. Again God's kingdom can be identified not only with that of his Son but also with the life of the Spirit in the Christian fellowship. These variables, however, shade off into each other. But God is King, and it ultimately is his kingdom which comes. In this respect it is appropriate that in the last book of the Bible we should find so momentous an image as that of the Great White Throne.

With regard to varying usages of Kingdom language in the New Testament period my attention was arrested at a number of points.

There appears to be no inclination among these writers to question the basic authenticity of Mark's account of the opening of Jesus' ministry. The formulation in 1:15 may, indeed, be that of the evangelist, but the core announcement of Good News that the kingdom of God was at hand can be viewed as historical. Dissent with this old consensus in some quarters today seems to me to be based on a mistaken view of "apocalyptic" which is then used as a test of Jesus, rightly dissociating him from such perspectives.

Much attention has lately been drawn to the kind of "realized eschatology" that is evoked in the Gospel of Thomas and to the kingdom language here used especially in connection with Jesus' parables. This early and probably extra-Synoptic vein of Jesus' sayings is, indeed, interesting because it shows how early a divergent sapiential and proto-Gnostic view of the kingdom could arise. Although Wisdom/Kingdom in Thomas is community-oriented, yet (like the *basilikos* attributes and "royalty" featured in Philo and much Hellenistic *paideia*) it was not one which involved the sect or school in a fateful wrestling with the public and cultural actualities of the age—in Galilee, Jerusalem, and the provinces—as in the case of the Synoptic tradition.

In his chapter on the School of St. John, Robert Hodgson offers a striking example of how the term, the Kingdom of God, all but disappeared in one of the main branches of the School. He persuasively shows that the corruption of the term and idea by the Sethian wing made it tabu in the situation. Of course the term is rare in the Fourth Gospel itself, and eschatology here is transformed. But with his categories of eternal life, light, and truth, this evangelist does not forfeit in any way the celebration of the New Age and the travail of its advent.

In view of the topic of this volume I would like to presume on the license given me here to urge again certain views of my own about eschatology in the New Testament. However the meaning of the kingdom of God fluctuates as between reign and realm, future and present, transcendent and embodied, its older antecedents in Israel properly implied what we would call political dimensions in the Gospel. These had to do not only with God's sovereignty but with power-status, social roles, and liberation, at least in an underground way, vis-à-vis the structural authorities of the times, whether in Palestine or the provinces.

In this connection it may be noted that while the approach of the present volume is mainly exegetical and biblical-theological, confining itself largely to the canon, yet this approach balances somewhat two current foci of early Christian study. The sociological approach and that pursuit which is given to the trajectories of saying-forms should enrich the present angle of approach. But this latter should help provide criteria for the others. As regards the costly confrontation of the kingdom with the stubborn patterns and tyrannies of the age, I have already suggested one example of such an input.

My concern in interpreting the imminent eschatological proclamation of Jesus is that its full force and import should not be misread as some kind of apocalyptic fanaticism or literalized scheme. Jesus' message following on John the Baptist represented a dynamic transcendental witness to the New age breaking in, and he used the term, kingdom of God, as evoking archaic motifs of the wars of Yahweh and the hostility of Satan and the demons, all in relation to the calling of Israel in a time of crisis. I have always stressed that the inevitable imminence of the kingdom should be understood in terms of what should be a commonplace with sociologists of religion, namely, those horizons which accompany all analogous movements stirred by Utopia-Millennium fervors as in the case of the English Puritans.

The first phase, especially Jesus' own mission, was visionary and powerful like all such initial phases. The evangelists reflect something of its dramatic overtones in such features as the Temptation, the Transfiguration and the dramatis personnae that includes Satan, Moses, Elijah, and the Son of Man. Such a messenger in such a time crystallized and provoked controversy just as the later followers disturbed the order of the world.

Of course the incandescent phase of the gospel gave way to more pragmatic ones in the sequel. Visionary and even ecstatic phenomena continued. But even from the beginning visionary intensity could be linked with worldly realism of its own kind. Jesus' parables were no less at home with his apocalyptic horizons than was Jeanne d'Arc's shrewdness with her angels.

As time passed the churches adapted themselves to their distance from the original phase. We speak of the "delay of the parousia." But this obscures the transitions. What is interesting is the ways in which the various early Christian communities perpetuated the power and impact of the original impulse in varying situations.

I have spoken of the case of the Fourth Gospel. One could say that the kingdom language in Luke–Acts has lost much of its tension. The eschatological horizon has receded, and the age of the Spirit fills the nearer view. But in its own way Luke–Acts dramatizes in Christian terms that turn of the ages which (as Dieter Georgi has recently shown) answered to the cultural hungers of Vergil and Horace.

As several of the contributors to this book have noted, Norman Perrin joined me in my view of the kingdom language of Jesus. The kingdom for him was a "tensive" symbol, not a literal or "steno" one. But I agree with two of these writers that Norman made a mistake in then viewing the symbol of the kingdom as intemporal. This threw him in with those who are identified with a "realized eschatology" as Kümmel recognized, in an existential version. But the futurist aspect of Jesus' symbol should not be thus forfeited. It is inseparably linked with that confrontation with Satan and the principalities and powers which involve the gospel in history. Paul finds a powerful figure for this worldly aggression of the eschatological kingdom when he likens his role to that of one led by Christ in a triumphal procession.

Amos N. Wilder
Hollis Professor of Divinity, Emeritus
The Harvard Divinity School

Acknowledgments

I want to take this opportunity to express my gratitude to all those who have shared in bringing this project to completion over the past two years. This begins with the contributors; of those originally invited to participate only two have been lost, and both had legitimate reasons to withdraw from the project. As editor I have found those whose work is included to have been an unusually cooperative group. Virtually all deadlines were met, or were only missed by a little. That significantly lightened the load of editing and spared me the task of harassing persons more experienced and knowledgeable than myself. Special gratitude goes also to Amos Wilder, who took the time and effort to offer some of his own reflections in a foreword. It was truly an honor to have one whose voice has done so much to shape the present understanding of the Kingdom of God share in this volume.

Thanks are also given to the staff of Hendrickson Publishers. I am especially grateful to Patrick Alexander for his conscientious work in style editing that accounts for the attractiveness of the volume. Beyond this he has helped in other ways to make our writings appear better than they were upon submission.

The origin of this collection of essays is an interesting story in its own right, and I wish to recount it to thank some and encourage others. In the spring of 1985 the New Testament section of the Central States Society of Biblical Literature was chaired by Dr. Charles Hedrick. He conceived and carried off the plan of having a thematic presentation around the topic of "The Kingdom of God." Of the papers herein contained, seven originally appeared in that format. It was also Charlie who first encouraged the publication of the papers, and thus while his name is not included in the authors, he is godfather to the book. I think this approach of doing a thematic meeting, especially on a status questions topic, commends itself to the academic community as a worthy means of allowing common reflection on important topics—first in person, and later in press.

Because of this origin, however, it is the case that the essays have some duplications and missed connections. Each author wrote (and rewrote) independently of the others. Since this topic is one where competent people have been unable to reach consensus for over a century, I have sought to impose no strict uniformity on the writers—either in style or position. This is a resource volume, not an autopsy report, after all.

Finally, I want to extend thanks to my secretary, Mrs. Arlene Blakely, who has helped immensely with correspondence, proofreading, and typing in the production of the volume. I thank also my wife and family for support during the distractions that are necessary in any publishing endeavor.

1 The Discovery of the Eschatological Kingdom: Johannes Weiss and Albert Schweitzer

Wendell Willis

Adjunct faculty, Department of Religious Studies
Southwest Missouri State University

Introduction

THE LATE NORMAN PERRIN'S last work, *Jesus and the Language of the Kingdom*, marks a major shift in this century in the interpretation of Jesus' teaching of the kingdom of God.[1] If this approach is the new phase of kingdom interpretation, then we have come full circle in less than a century from the previous major shift to an apocalyptic interpretation. So this may be an apposite time to consider two books which, in hindsight, marked the previous shift by their discovery of the eschatological Jesus, preacher of the apocalyptic kingdom of God.

The two books are Johannes Weiss's *Jesus' Proclamation of the Kingdom of God*[2] and Albert Schweitzer's *The Mystery of the Kingdom of God*[3] published in 1892 and 1901 respectively. I chose this book of Schweitzer, rather than his more famous *The Quest for the Historical*

1. Norman Perrin, *Jesus and the Language of the Kingdom* (Philadelphia: Fortress, 1976).

2. Johannes Weiss, *Jesus' Proclamation of the Kingdom of God* (Philadelphia: Fortress, 1971, first published 1892). Unless otherwise stated, all references to Weiss come from this work. In the second, much enlarged edition of the work (*Predigt* 2) published in 1900, Weiss is less absolute in his eschatological thesis and more openly avows Ritschlian theology. Perrin, *Jesus and Language*, 66, says "In retrospect one can see that the whole modern interpretation of Jesus and his teaching stems from these sixty-five pages."

3. Albert Schweitzer, *The Mystery of the Kingdom of God* (New York: Schocken, 1914, first published 1901). Unless otherwise stated, all references to Schweitzer come from this work.

Jesus,[4] because it is in *Mystery* that Schweitzer first sets forth the thesis he later defended in *Quest*.

One of the most remarkable—and frankly discouraging—features of these two books is that both are the work of their authors' youth. Weiss, son of the famous NT scholar Bernard Weiss, published *Proclamation* at the age of 29. Schweitzer's *Mystery* was a portion of his doctoral dissertation on the Lord's Supper: *Das Abendmahl–Das Messianitäts und Leidensgeheimnis*, published as his initial effort in theological studies, when he was 26.[5] His better known *Quest* was published five years later in reaction to the poor reception which his first work received.[6]

To appreciate the significance of Weiss's and Schweitzer's works one must recall that at the end of the last century theology dominated biblical studies. Many of the famous "Lives of Jesus" were written by scholars whose main field was theology. The theological establishment of the day was social liberalism, articulated, for example, by Albert Ritschl (1822–1889), who argued that the kingdom of God was "this-worldly, monistic and ethical in character,"[7] a picture ultimately derived from Kantian ethical idealism. Both Weiss and Schweitzer wrote to critique this picture, but Weiss did so with reluctance,[8] for his conclusions were at odds with his honored teacher (and father-in-law!)—Albert Ritschl. Schweitzer, however, eagerly attacked representatives of the establishment, casting doubts not only on their results, but also their highly prized "objectivity."

The Ritschlian theological foundations had begun to show cracks before Weiss wrote. Wilhelm Hermann, an outstanding pupil of Ritschl,

4. Albert Schweitzer, *The Quest for the Historical Jesus* (New York: Macmillian, 1968, first published 1910). As Martin Werner, "Albert Schweitzers Antwort auf die Frage nach dem historischen Jesus," in *Eherfurcht vor dem Leben: Albert Schweitzer* (Bern: P. Haupt, 1954) 13, notes, this is one of the very few pre–World War I books to reappear after World War I in a new edition. Probably *Quest* is much more influential in America because it was translated into English in 1910, four years before the first translation of Schweitzer's first work, *Mystery*.

5. John Reumann, "The Problem of the Lord's Supper as Matrix for Albert Schweitzer's 'Quest for the Historical Jesus,'" *NTS* 27 (1981) 476. He notes (p. 479) that Schweitzer had reached his conclusions in 1897, prior to his study of the life of Jesus. Thus it was not his study of modern research which led Schweitzer to question its reconstructions, but rather he reviewed modern interpretations to show that his construction in *Mystery* was much superior to the "Lives" he critiques.

6. W. G. Kümmel, "Die 'konsequente Eschatologie' Albert Schweitzers im Urteil der Zeitgenossen," in *Heilsgeschen und Geschichte: Gesammelte Aufsatze* (Marburg: N. G. Elwert, 1965) 331f.

7. Gösta Lundström, *The Kingdom of God in the Teaching of Jesus* (Richmond: John Knox, 1963) 6f., points out that it was Ritschl and his pupils who established the "kingdom of God" as the focus of theology in the nineteenth century.

8. Weiss withheld publication of his study until 1892, three years after the death of Ritschl. He says that he was encouraged to publish it in 1891 with the appearance of similar, but independent, studies by Otto Schmoller and Ernst Issel. See D. L. Holland, "History, Theology and the Kingdom of God: A Contribution of Johannes Weiss to Twentieth-century Theology," *Biblical Research* 13 (1968) 56.

attacked social liberalism with his radically individualistic and experiential interpretation of the kingdom as the rule of God in one's heart.[9] The eschatological factor, already anticipated by H. S. Reimarus and David F. Strauss in their attempts to show the mythological character of the Gospels, was set out in the works of Wilhelm Baldensperger (1895), Otto Schmoller (1893), and Ernst Issel (1891).[10] Richard Kabish in 1893 showed apocalyptic influences in Paul as well as Jesus.[11] But even with these dissenting tremors, the foundation of Ritschlian liberalism held strong at the turn of the century, as is evidenced by the response to Weiss and Schweitzer.

Schweitzer was a totally unrecognized Straussberg instructor whose *habilitationschrift* had no reason to be noticed—and it was not![12] When Walter Lowrie translated the work into English in 1914, he noted that it had received little attention in Germany, and was not even publicly noted in English-speaking journals.[13] M. Rade, editor of the influential *Die christliche Welt*, wrote in 1907 that he had read *Mystery*, but did not introduce it to his readers whom it might confuse![14]

The appearance of Weiss's *Proclamation*, however, created a notable crisis in liberal Protestantism. It was critically reviewed by Hermann Gunkel (1892) and attacked by Wilhelm Bousett in an 1893 monograph with the provocative title: "Jesu predigt in ihren Gegensatz zum Judentum."[15] The attention given to Weiss's work may have been due to the fame of his father (and father-in-law), for it was not at all influential in British and American scholarship.[16] In fact, the eschatological interpretations of Weiss and Schweitzer did not really carry the day in NT scholarship until after World War I when the collapse of liberal world optimism caused by the "Great War" made it more understandable to speak of an "otherworldly" gospel.[17]

9. Lundström, 10, 35.

10. Ibid., 27–34. W. G. Kümmel, "Ein Jahrhundert Erforschung der Eschatologie des Neuen Testaments," TLZ 107 (1982) 83f. Also see Kümmel, "Konsequente Eschatologie," 328f., for a review of the rise of the eschatological interpretation.

11. W. G. Kümmel, "Futuristic and Realized Eschatology in the Earliest Stages of Christianity," JR 43 (1963) 304.

12. Kümmel, "Jahrhundert Erforschung," 85.

13. Schweitzer, Mystery, 18. Lundström, 78–80, reviews the British response, including that Sanday and F. C. Burkitt originally praised Schweitzer's position. Sanday, however, later publicly regretted his enthusiastic endorsement. See also Kümmel, "Konsequente Eschatologie," 335.

14. Cited by Kümmel, "Konsequente Eschatologie," 333f. He also quotes Jülicher: "Sie ist dogmatische, nicht historische, Kritik." ("This is dogmatic, not historical, criticism.")

15. Ibid., 329f. Also, Weiss, Proclamation, 4.

16. Weiss, Proclamation, 34f.

17. Kümmel, "Konsequente Eschatologie," 338. In the field of theology, of course, Karl Barth addressed his nein to liberal optimism about the coming kingdom of God erected by humanity.

Because both Schweitzer and Weiss, in contrast to the liberal consensus, stressed the eschatological view of Jesus and the kingdom, there has been a tendency to equate their views and achievements, and even to suggest a dependent relationship.[18] But, surprisingly, Schweitzer gives no indication that he even knew of Weiss's book.[19]

Comparison of Interpretations of the Gospels

Jesus' Teachings on the Kingdom

Weiss's book focuses on Jesus' idea of the kingdom of God and especially opposes the views of Jesus' teaching as set forth by Ritschl, Kaftan, and the liberal establishment.[20] Weiss argues that since Jesus did not closely define his own meaning of the kingdom of God, he certainly assumed that his hearers would understand him correctly without such an explanation. Therefore Jesus actually "adopted this concept primarily and predominantly in the sense in which it was understood by his contemporaries and without correcting it."[21] Jesus' teaching of the kingdom is distinguished from other apocalyptics only in that while he followed their traditional interpretations he did so "with modesty, reserve and sobriety."[22]

Weiss distinguishes six characteristics of Jesus' teaching on the kingdom of God:[23] (1) It is radically transcendent and supramundane.[24] (2) It is radically future and in no way present. (3) Jesus was not the founder or inaugurator of this kingdom, but he waited for God to bring it.[25] (4) The kingdom is in no way identified with Jesus' circle of disciples. (5) The kingdom does not come gradually by growth, or development.[26] (6) The ethics that the kingdom sponsors are negative and world-denying.[27]

18. E.g., Floyd Filson, *Jesus Christ, the Risen Lord* (Nashville: Abingdon, 1941) 103, n. 12, says: "Schweitzer was indebted to others for much of what he said. Johannes Weiss . . . was his most important predecessor." Cf. Perrin, *The Kingdom of God in the Teaching of Jesus* (Philadelphia: Westminster, 1963) 29f., who speaks of Schweitzer's work as "a development of Johannes Weiss's interpretation of the kingdom of God." Similarly, Stephen Neill, *The Interpretation of the New Testament 1861–1961* (London: Oxford, 1964) 198.

19. Richard Hiers, "Eschatology and Methodology," *JBL* 85 (1966) 174.

20. See Lundström 5f. for his discussion of Ritschl's definition of the kingdom. See also Weiss, *Proclamation*, 32, for the editor's review of Weiss's discussion of Kaftan.

21. Weiss, 102.

22. Ibid., 104.

23. Holland, 57f.

24. Weiss, 133, "The Kingdom of God as Jesus thought of it is never something subjective, inward, or spiritual, but is always the objective Messianic Kingdom. . . ."

25. Weiss, 78.

26. Weiss, 73f., notes that in the Lord's Prayer, ἐλθέτω ἡ βασιλεία σου does not mean "'May your Kingdom grow,' 'May your kingdom be perfect,' but rather 'May thy kingdom come'; for the disciples, the βασιλεία is not yet here. . . ."

27. Weiss, 134.

Schweitzer shares most of these six views regarding Jesus' teaching on the kingdom, for he agrees that Jesus drew from Jewish apocalyptic. He explicitly rejects any conception of "growth" in the kingdom,[28] of it representing a "moral outlook,"[29] and he insists that it is sharply different from the present age.[30]

Both scholars emphasize, against liberal theology, that the kingdom cannot be equated with ethical conduct. Schweitzer's well-known designation of Jesus' preaching as "interim ethics" is intended to make clear that Jesus proclaimed demands to enter the kingdom, not the morality of the kingdom.[31] Thus the Beatitudes "define the moral dispositions which justify admission into the kingdom."[32] While Weiss did not anticipate Schweitzer's phrase "interim ethics," his interpretation of the Beatitudes is virtually identical with Schweitzer's when he says that they picture righteousness *for* the kingdom, not *of* the kingdom.[33]

Similarly, both stress the call to "repentance" as the focus of Jesus' ethics for the kingdom.[34] The newness of the kingdom is the motive for repentance. For Weiss, the lack of repentance on the part of the people is the major obstacle for the coming of the kingdom.[35] But, while Schweitzer agrees that the morality demanded by the kingdom (which he too called "repentance") precedes the kingdom, he does not think that its lack is the hindrance to the coming of the kingdom. Rather, what is missing, according to Schweitzer, is the tribulation.[36]

28. Schweitzer, 101. Both Schweitzer and Weiss reject those interpretations of the parables which describe a growth of the kingdom. Rather, the parables are to be taken with a wholistic point of view. Weiss, 63; Schweitzer, 109f. Both argue that the interpretation of the parable of the Sower in Mk 4 is secondary and added by the early church to Jesus' parable.

Thus Schweitzer also thinks that Jesus spoke of the kingdom of God as did his contemporary Jews (i.e., in apocalyptic terms). He repeats this view in *The Kingdom of God and Primitive Christianity*, 90f., saying that since Jesus did not explain how he understood the kingdom of God, he must have assumed the common view of his hearers was correct.

29. Schweitzer, 102: "The Kingdom of God is super-moral."

30. Ibid., 74f. In his later *Kingdom of God and Primitive Christianity*, 98–101, Schweitzer speaks of the ethics of Jesus in more traditional terms, stressing the "inwardness of the heart," yet he does not reject his earlier views about the eschatological basis of Jesus' ethics (93f.).

31. Ibid., 76.

32. Ibid., 96. On the understanding of "interim ethics" see also Richard Hiers, "Interim Ethics," *Theology and Life* 9 (1966) 220–33.

33. Weiss, 71, 132. Hiers and Holland in a footnote, *Proclamation*, 113, n. 79, note that in *Predigt 2* (134ff.), Weiss admitted that he may have overstated the world-denying aspect of Jesus' teaching. But he continued to insist that for Jesus, ethics were preparatory for the kingdom. See Hiers, "Eschatology and Methodology," 173; Lundström, 40f.

34. Weiss, 105f.: "Repent, *because* the Kingdom of God has drawn near." Schweitzer, 94, says that this teaching derives from the prophetic meaning of repentance. "It is moral renewal in prospect of the accomplishment of universal perfection in the future."

35. Weiss, 86. Perrin, *Kingdom of God*, 22, says that Jesus demands "a superhuman effort from those who would fulfill the conditions for entering into the kingdom."

36. Schweitzer, 125f., 233–36. See Richard H. Hiers, *Jesus and Ethics* (Philadelphia:

Finally, in regard to Jesus' teaching about the kingdom, how do Weiss and Schweitzer deal with those Gospel passages which seem to speak of a present kingdom? Schweitzer does not seem to be concerned about that difficulty.[37] Weiss is more thorough on this point, and explains the "present" sayings as due either to Jesus' proleptic enthusiasm resulting from the success of his exorcisms,[38] or as arising from Jesus' two-storied world in which heavenly events have an exact parallel on earth and therefore something can occur in heaven that has not yet taken place on earth.[39]

The "Son of Man" and the Kingdom

Weiss and Schweitzer agree that Jesus selected the expression "Son of Man" as a self-designation in preference to other messianic titles available to him.[40] Schweitzer does not discuss the origin and meaning of the term in Judaism, but really looks to Daniel for the sole background to Jesus' meaning.[41] Weiss also notes Daniel's importance, but in addition considers passages from Enoch and 4 Ezra.[42] Both scholars use the apocalyptic, coming-judge image as the criterion to evaluate sayings in the Gospels about the "Son of Man" that are attributed to Jesus. Thus those sayings are authentic that refer to the "Son of Man" either in connection with Jesus' passion or the parousia.[43] Both scholars agree that those passages in which "Son of Man" equals "I" are inauthentic and are due rather to the Gospel writers' later putting this designation in Jesus' mouth, since they knew that he was the Son of Man.[44] Weiss explains some of the

Westminster, 1968) 43, concerning Jesus' anticipation of the "testing" as a prelude to the kingdom.

37. Schweitzer, 246–48. He basically neglects those passages which speak of a present kingdom. This is notable with respect to Mt 10:7, since Mt 10 and 11 are so vital to his reconstruction.

38. Weiss, 78, "When an awareness of victory came over him." Lundström, 37, says that it was "only a subjective experience on the part of Jesus." Cf. Hiers, "Eschatology and Methodology," 172.

39. Weiss, 74.

40. Ibid., 115f.; Schweitzer, 190.

41. Schweitzer, 195, 199. "All those passages are historical which show the influence of the apocalyptic reference to the Son of Man in Daniel; all are unhistorical in which such is not the case."

42. Weiss, 116f. Although both Weiss and Schweitzer worked in the heyday of "history of religions" research, they gave surprisingly little attention to Jewish eschatology. Schweitzer made use only of Daniel, and Weiss little more. In Quest Schweitzer made use of Psalms of Solomon, Enoch, 2 Baruch and 4 Ezra. Weiss devotes a long section to Jewish apocalyptic in the second, enlarged edition of Predigt, 1–35. T. F. Glasson, "Schweitzer's Influence—Blessing or Bane?" JTS 28 (1977) 300f., argues that Judaism knew of no such awaited "Son of Man" from heaven.

43. Weiss, 126; Schweitzer, 193, 236f.

44. Weiss, 122; Schweitzer, 195f.

nonfuturistic uses of the title (e.g. Mk 2:10, 28) as due to a Hebraism by which Jesus simply meant "man," but which Mark understood as a messianic claim.[45]

The future sayings about the Son of Man are taken by both Weiss and Schweitzer to be a claim that Jesus makes about his future role. "Since Jesus is now a rabbi, a prophet, he has nothing in common with the Son of Man, except the claim that he will become the Son of man"—so Weiss.[46] It is a claim for the future, either in this life, or after his death.[47] Schweitzer also holds that in his ministry Jesus is not yet the Son of Man but he recognizes that he will be in the future.[48] Schweitzer sees in this designation, not an open claim, but a hidden secret. To all outsiders (even John the Baptist) Jesus claims only an absolute solidarity between himself and the Son of Man.[49] Even the disciples did not perceive Jesus to be the Son of Man until after he revealed it to them in the transfiguration.[50]

"Son of Man" was a proper designation only of the Messiah who comes on the clouds as judge, an understanding shared by Jesus' friends and foes alike. It never occurred to anyone, according to Schweitzer, that Jesus thought of himself as the Son of Man.[51] That he did hold this self-evaluation is the messianic secret that Jesus revealed only to three disciples (Peter, James, and John). Later, Peter confided in the rest of the Twelve; consequently, Judas told the "secret" to the high priest, who used this as the basis for his call for Jesus' execution.[52]

Thus there is a subtle difference between Weiss's and Schweitzer's understanding of Jesus as the Son of Man designate. For Weiss it is a claim that Jesus makes for his future; for Schweitzer it is a secret known only to those to whom Jesus revealed it. This difference is to be explained by the fact that Weiss, on the one hand, is concerned with Jesus' teaching, in which the Son of Man sayings are clearly aimed to the future. To Schweitzer, on the other hand, Jesus knows himself fully as Son of Man, but keeps it hidden. So again one can see that Schweitzer is really affirming Mark's conception of the messianic secret!

45. Weiss, 123f.; Schweitzer, 198, sees this passage as secondary and nonhistorical.
46. Weiss, 82, cf. 118.
47. Ibid., 119f.
48. Schweitzer, 192f.
49. Ibid., 136f. In *Kingdom of God and Primitive Christianity*, 109f., he repeats the view that the disciples first became aware that Jesus viewed himself as the Son of Man at the transfiguration.
50. Ibid., 138. To explain this confession, Schweitzer reverses the confession at Caesarea Philippi and the transfiguration. This is because the disciples could not have guessed that Jesus claimed to be "Son of Man." See 180f.
51. Ibid., 190f. Weiss also based his picture of the parousia on Daniel (Weiss, 118).
52. Schweitzer, 217. Also, *Kingdom of God and Primitive Christianity*, 109.

Jesus' Ministry and the Kingdom

In his later *Quest*, Schweitzer distinguishes his interpretation of Jesus and the kingdom from that of Weiss on the basis that Weiss only dealt with Jesus' teaching and failed to also consider his ministry from the vantage point of eschatology.[53] That assessment is not completely accurate, but it is certainly the case that Weiss was less interested in Jesus' life than his teachings.

Both Weiss and Schweitzer, however, note that Jesus related his ministry of the kingdom of God to John the Baptist's preaching.[54] Both authors agree that it was in connection with the Baptist that Jesus perceived his mission and understood his messiahship.[55] But their respective understandings of how Jesus related to John are different. Weiss says that Jesus' activity is no different than John's: "both men are moved by the overwhelming certainty that God is about to assert his rule."[56] "Indeed, one may say precisely from Jesus' own standpoint, his entire activity is not of messianic but of preparatory character."[57]

Schweitzer, however, distinguishes between Jesus and John both in their activity and their message. Jesus proclaimed a coming of the Messiah, while John proclaimed the Forerunner (ὁ ἐρχόμενος), whom he taught that Jesus might be—based on his deeds and signs (Mt 11:2–6).[58] Only Jesus knew that John was the Forerunner, because only Jesus knew himself to be the Messiah![59]

Again it is Schweitzer's theory of the messianic secret (taken from Mark) that creates the difference. Jesus' preaching is different from John's in that John preaches the Forerunner; Jesus, the coming kingdom. Jesus' work is also different from John in that Jesus heals and casts out demons, which John does not do. Thus Schweitzer insists that while only Jesus knows himself as Son of Man designate, he does think and act like the

---

53. See Schweitzer, *Quest*, 359–60. Also Lundström, 69f.: "The explanation of Jesus' activity from the dogmatic eschatological angle he calls 'the solution of consistent eschatology.'" Hiers and Holland give an informative review of the misunderstanding of this term in many interpreters of Schweitzer, and show that Schweitzer himself wishes to point out that his interpretation is more "thorough-going" than Weiss's. See Weiss, 31f.

54. Schweitzer, 202; Weiss, 85f., 115f.

55. Schweitzer, 127; Weiss, 115, 128. Neither explain *how* this understanding occurred at Jesus' baptism.

56. Weiss, 114.

57. Ibid., 82. Cf., 115, the difference was "in John's own opinion (Luke 3:16), as well as in Jesus' (Luke 7:28), John would have a place in the Kingdom of God like others. Jesus, on the other hand . . . himself would be the 'Messiah,' the King."

58. Schweitzer, 151. It is Jesus' exorcisms that make clear that he is the Messiah (p. 322). Weiss also acknowledges Jesus' exorcisms, but does not think that it is messianic work (Weiss, 42, 76f.). Again, we see that for Schweitzer Jesus is the Messiah in *deed* as well as word.

59. Schweitzer, 145–47.

Messiah during his earthly lifetime, although this will not be manifested to the people until his vindication by God.

A second event in Jesus' ministry, discussed both by Weiss and Schweitzer is the sending of the Twelve (Mt 10). For Weiss there is nothing exceptional about this incident. The Twelve, like Jesus and like John, go to preach the coming of the kingdom. They serve only to hasten the pace and broaden the range of the proclamation.[60] For Schweitzer, however, the sending of the Twelve is a decisive event for Jesus' ministry and teaching. For Schweitzer, the twelve disciples are the "men of violence" (Mt 11:12) whose preaching mission—from which they were not expected to return—was an act of violence that Jesus expected to provoke the messianic tribulation that would herald the arrival of the kingdom.[61] "They draw it (the kingdom) with power down to the earth."[62] It was when their mission failed to produce the "messianic woes" that Jesus first realized that he himself had to die to complete the requisite suffering.[63]

For Weiss on the contrary, the disciples are not the men of violence, and their mission is not connected to the tribulation of the messianic age. Indeed, he contends that the "men of violence" are rebuked by Jesus for their attempt to compel the kingdom. "They commit the greatest offense. They are irreligious."[64] This single incident reveals how differently Weiss and Schweitzer understand the ministry of Jesus for the kingdom. On the one hand, for Weiss one can only wait passively for God to grant the kingdom. The only acceptable activity is repentance, and it was the failure of the mission of the Twelve to produce repentance in Israel that made clear that the kingdom was not as close as Jesus had thought.[65] For Schweitzer, on the other hand, the mission failed to set off the persecution and suffering that it was designed to provoke.[66]

The difference in the interpretation of the mission of the Twelve points to an area of greater disparity between Weiss and Schweitzer concerning the ministry of Jesus, i.e., his death. Weiss contended that Jesus saw in his own death a way to atone for the failure of the nation to repent, a necessity if the kingdom of God were to come. Jesus was seized by "the audacious and paradoxical idea . . . that his death should be the ransom for the people otherwise destined to destruction" (Mk 10:45).[67] But Weiss

---

60. Weiss, 85.
61. Schweitzer, 88–89, 261.
62. Ibid., 112, cf. 116, 221.
63. Ibid., 234.
64. Weiss, 83, cf. 70.
65. Ibid., 83. One can only pray for its coming.
66. Schweitzer, 65, 261.
67. Weiss, 87f.; Schweitzer, 71; both accept the genuineness of Mk 10:45, since ἀντὶ πολλῶν ("for many") is indefinite, and does not specify the church.

does not explain how Jesus' death as a λύτρον is effective, other than as part of a series of events that precede the kingdom.

For Schweitzer, however, the major obstacle to the kingdom which Jesus' death overcomes is the final tribulations of the messianic age.[68] "The others are freed from the trial of suffering, Jesus suffers alone. . . . *He suffers in their stead, for he gives his life a ransom for many.*" Thus for Schweitzer, Jesus' death is not a passive act, but an active event on behalf of the kingdom. He gives his life in siding with the "men of violence."[69]

So, although the positions of Weiss and Schweitzer concerning Jesus and the kingdom may seem to be the same, they are really not. Simplified, their views are thus: for Schweitzer, Jesus expected the events around his death to proceed: death, arrival of the End, general resurrection, judgment, and establishment of the kingdom under the Son of Man. Weiss proposes: death, Jesus' own resurrection,[70] a short period in which the disciples continue to preach repentance while Jesus is at the side of God,[71] the End, general resurrection and judgment, and the establishment of the kingdom.

Evaluation

W. G. Kümmel has tried to show that there was a real turning point in NT studies about 1900 based upon the work of Weiss and Schweitzer.[72] The translators and editors of the English edition of Weiss' *Proclamation* describe that work as the turning point between nineteenth and twentieth-century NT research.[73] That Schweitzer's work became better known than that of Weiss for creating this shift, although Weiss wrote earlier than Schweitzer and received a better initial reception, was probably due to Schweitzer's masterful prose coupled with his ability to appear simply objective, driven by the evidence itself.[74] No doubt Schweitzer's sacrificial life in medical work in Africa also enhanced the impact of his theological writings.[75]

---

68. Schweitzer, 229. This is based upon Jesus' reading of Isa 40:66. Cf. 235, 265. In *Kingdom of God and Primitive Christianity*, 121–23, Schweitzer stresses the influence of Isa 53 on Jesus' decision to die to bring the kingdom of God.

69. Ibid., 232.

70. Weiss, 89, n. 50.

71. Ibid., 89, 91f. For Schweitzer, 245, the failure of the kingdom to come when Jesus died meant the failure of Jesus' eschatology.

72. Kümmel, "Jahrhundert," 81.

73. Weiss, 2. Hiers elsewhere, "Eschatology and Methodology," 171, says that NT scholarship since 1900 could be characterized as "the struggle against eschatology."

74. Werner, 13.

75. Glasson, 266.

As has been shown, the two writers shared many minor viewpoints as well as the major insight that Jesus was to be interpreted against the background of apocalyptic expectations and ideas in "late Judaism." Both made clear how greatly the historical Jesus differed from the theology of liberal Protestantism and the portraits of Jesus it offered. In so doing, both authors have been lauded for their objectivity and willingness to accept the "*majestas materiae*."[76]

Both these assessments, however, need reconsideration and modification. There is one major difference between the two books, which, in turn, accounts for several differences in details: Principally, Schweitzer wants to write a "Life of Jesus," despite the fact that he unmercifully criticized such works and that his theological monument, *Quest*, is widely regarded as the death blow to such projects![77]

That is why Schweitzer, often regarded as the father of radical theology, is surprisingly conservative in his assessment of the Gospels. He accepts as authentically from Jesus: the Sermon on the Mount, the commissioning of the Twelve, the feeding of the 5000 (although the story has been enhanced by legend into a full meal, instead of the sacramental one it really was), and Jesus' predictions of his passion, resurrection, and parousia.[78] As Martin Werner summarizes, "Schweitzer schätzt die geschichtliche Glaubwürdigkeit der ältern Evangelienberichte ungewöhnlich hoch ein."[79] Even Schweitzer's famous "messianic secret," which is decisive for his reconstruction of the ministry of Jesus, is really derived from Mark (which is why Schweitzer relies on Mark—supplemented from Mt 10 and 11 in his reconstruction). Weiss, though, is much less confident in the reliability of the Gospel sources. He explicitly rejects Mark's outline and tries to describe only Jesus' teaching, not his ministry.

The difference between Weiss's and Schweitzer's approach to writing a life of Jesus arises from the unique problem which each seeks to address. For Weiss, against Ritschl, the problem is Jesus' understanding of the kingdom. For Schweitzer, the problem is the radical skepticism of Wilhelm Wrede and Bruno Bauer, which would render it impossible to know historically about Jesus. This skepticism had been a concern of Schweitzer since his student days, and it is made evident in the writing of *Quest*, where most of that lengthy study deals with the skeptical lives of Jesus. It is difficult today to appreciate how strong this skepticism was in

76. Lundström, 41. Hiers, "Eschatology and Methodology," 174f.
77. Hiers, "Eschatology and Methodology," 174, n. 19. "Our common misreading (of the *Quest*) is that Schweitzer concluded that a life of Jesus could not be written." Cf. Lundström, 76f.
78. Schweitzer, 7f.
79. Werner, 14. "Schweitzer holds the historical trustworthiness of the oldest gospels uncommonly high."

Schweitzer's day, however. Werner reminds us that for the first decades of this century the question highly debated was "Did Jesus Live?"[80]

In the face of such skepticism about accurate knowledge about Jesus, Schweitzer defended the eschatological portrait of Jesus to rescue the picture in Mark (properly understood and rearranged). He insists, thus, that "either the Marcan text as it stands is historical and therefore to be retained, or it is not and thus it should be given up."[81]

The legacy of these two important works for NT studies is twofold. The first is the recovery of the significance of eschatology for understanding the Gospel's presentation of the kingdom and the life of Jesus. Scholarship's understanding of Jewish apocalypticism of the intertestamental period and the first Christian century has increased by quantum leaps since Weiss and Schweitzer wrote their pioneer studies. It appears, however, that the recent interest in symbolic and literary interpretation of the kingdom (late-Perrin and Crossan) may represent a paradigm shift away from historical and apocalyptic study.[82]

The second legacy is more far-reaching, namely, the decision to draw a line between the historical reconstruction of Jesus and the contemporary theological constructions.[83] As Schweitzer made clear, it was the lack of such a distinction that led the writers of the various "Lives" to find in Jesus a first-century reflection of their own ideology and interests. This distinction between the historical Jesus and contemporary theology is clearest in Weiss who acknowledged that Jesus' eschatological views of the kingdom could not be appropriated into contemporary theology. Holland says that his most unique contribution was that "Weiss did not need to have his own position seem to be identical with Jesus!"[84]

Yet one might argue that the reason both writers were willing to accept the "historical ditch" is that both also found a way to use it to theological advantage. By showing that the earliest disciples had modified Jesus' teaching, Weiss legitimizes a similar undertaking of recasting the kingdom for modern Christianity (so that Ritschl's theology is still viable).[85]

---

80. Ibid., 15f. Lundström, 88, quotes Loisy who said that it was necessary to follow Schweitzer to be able to defend Jesus' historical existence.

81. Schweitzer, Quest, 336. This challenge recurs frequently in Quest. See Werner, 16, and Reumann, 479, on the fallacy of Schweitzer's "Hobson's choice."

82. See Perrin's annotated bibliography in Jesus and Language, 209–15 for his tracing of this retreat from apocalyptic. See in this volume, E. Elmore, "Linguistic Approaches to the Kingdom: Amos Wilder and Norman Perrin."

83. This "hermeneutical gap" is the positive statement of Lessing's "ugly ditch."

84. Holland, 63. He concludes (p. 65) that it was thus Weiss's formal, rather than his material, insight which caught fire. See also Perrin, Jesus and Language, 68.

85. Weiss, 16–18. Weiss makes a positive connection between Jesus and contemporary theology based on a relationship with the exalted Lord; see p. 231. This is a view continued by his pupil, Rudolf Bultmann, in his kerygmatic theology. The exalted and living Lord meets us in the preaching. See also Holland, 58f.

Schweitzer is even more personally motivated in his eschatological picture of Jesus. In Jesus' attack upon his own culture with eschatological theology, Schweitzer found an ally for his own rejection of acculturated liberal Protestantism. He saw the culture of pre–World War I Germany as vacuous and on the brink of collapse—a collapse he not only anticipated, but affirmed.[86] With the same reliance on eschatology, Schweitzer was able to protect the historical Jesus from the threat of Wrede, while at the same stroke rescue Jesus from insipid liberal Protestantism. He thus makes of Jesus a heroic figure, whose valiant, if unsuccessful, struggle against the lack of understanding in his own society (even among his disciples!) was as noble as it was futile. It was a life worthy of imitation—and Schweitzer attempted to do so![87] In giving up Jesus to apocalyptic theology, Schweitzer lost nothing. For he could still relate to Jesus in the most important way—the will. Werner cites this revealing quotation, "Das wahre Verstehen Jesu ist das verstehen von Wille zu Wille."[88] As Walter Lowrie, translator of Schweitzer's *Mystery*, says, "In reality he (Jesus) is an authority for us, *not in the sphere of knowledge* (my italics), but only in the matter of the will."[89] This is why Schweitzer affirms the historical picture of Jesus the apocalyptic preacher so willingly. "In genuine historical knowledge there is liberating and helping power. Our faith is built upon the *personality* of Jesus."[90]

In conclusion, it is not really correct to portray Schweitzer as holding a position on Jesus and the kingdom of God that is equivalent to Weiss, much less derived from him. This misunderstanding has arisen from two causes. First, both Weiss and Schweitzer discovered the eschatological character of Jesus at about the same time and both used this eschatogical understanding to critique liberal theology. Both also presented the interpretation of Jesus' teaching of the kingdom on the basis of eschatology in

86. Well argued by D. L. Dungan, "Albert Schweitzer's Disillusionment with Historical Reconstructions of the Life of Jesus," *Perkins Journal* 29 (2, 1976) 35–38. This theme was always with Schweitzer and is definitively set forth in his last work, *The Decline and Restoration of Civilization.* So Schweitzer, 251, says "This (eschatological) Jesus is far greater than the one conceived in modern terms: he is really a super-human personality (here were should recall that Schweitzer was an admirer of Nietzsche in his philosophical outlook). With his death he destroyed the form of his *Weltanschaung.* . . . Thereby he gives to all people and to all times, the right to approach him in terms of their thoughts and conceptions." Similarly, see Lundström, 76. Grabs, *RGG* 3, 1607, points to Schweitzer's philosophical interest in Schopenhauer and Nietzsche.

87. Dungan, 34, quotes a letter from Schweitzer to a friend seeking to explain his decision to become a medical missionary in Africa, in which he refers to his criticism of colonialism, and said that he saw his mission as in some way an atonement for those sins of Christendom.

88. Werner, 14, 15. (Trans. "The true understanding of Jesus is the understanding of will to will.") He notes how well this follows the famous last paragraph of *Quest.*

89. Schweitzer, 50.

90. Schweitzer, *Quest,* 250–51. Italics added.

some similar ways, especially his passion and parousia predictions and his teaching on ethics.

Second, Schweitzer probably also contributed to this false equation because in his *Quest* he said that he was only extending Weiss's interpretation of Jesus' teaching to the entire ministry of Jesus.[91] It is also possible that even the title of the English translation of Schweitzer's initial eschatological interpretation may have contributed to the misunderstanding as well. It would have been much better if instead of *The Mystery of the Kingdom of God*, Lowrie had translated and used the subtitle of Schweitzer's work: *Eine Skizze des Lebens Jesu—An Outline of the Life of Jesus!*

91. Schweitzer, *Quest*, 350–51.

Pivotal Reactions to the Eschatological Interpretations: Rudolf Bultmann and C. H. Dodd

Richard H. Hiers, Jr.

Professor of Religion
University of Florida

BORN THE SAME YEAR (1884), Bultmann and Dodd were eight years old when Johannes Weiss published what Bultmann later was to call his "epoch-making" treatise,[1] *Jesus' Proclamation of the Kingdom of God*,[2] and seventeen when Schweitzer's *The Mystery of the Kingdom of God*[3] appeared. In the 1920s both began to address the troublesome issues bequeathed by Weiss and Schweitzer, and continued to do so throughout their long and prolific careers.[4] In quite different ways, each attempted both to present an accurate account of the substance of Jesus' activity and message in his own time, and to show how Jesus and his message could be affirmed as central and authoritative for faith and ethics in our time, notwithstanding his eschatological orientation. Dodd died in 1973, Bultmann in 1976.

Weiss's and Schweitzer's Problematic Legacy: A Historical, Eschatological Jesus

Weiss's and Schweitzer's independent research led each reluctantly to conclude that the Jesus of history believed and proclaimed that condi-

1. *Jesus Christ and Mythology* (New York: Scribner's, 1958) 12.
2. (1892); Chico: Scholars' Press, 1985.
3. (1901); Buffalo: Prometheus Books, 1985.
4. For fuller accounts of their work, see, Norman Perrin, *The Kingdom of God in the Teaching of Jesus* (Philadelphia: Westminster, 1963) chs 4 & 7; Charles W. Kegley, *The Theology of Rudolf Bultmann* (New York: Harper & Row 1966); Walter Schmithals, *An Introduction to the Theology of Rudolf Bultmann* (Minneapolis: Augsburg, 1968); R. H. Hiers, *Jesus and the Future* (Philadelphia: Westminster, 1968), chs 3 & 4; F. W. Dillistone, *C. H. Dodd, Interpreter of the New Testament* (London: Hodder & Stoughton, 1977); Norman Perrin, *The Promise of Bultmann* (Philadelphia: Fortress, 1979); E. C. Hobbs, ed., *Bultmann, Retrospect and Prospect* (Philadelphia: Fortress, 1985).

tions of life on earth would soon be radically transformed by the arrival of God's kingdom, possibly even within his own lifetime. The coming of the kingdom of God would be marked by the appearance of the supernatural Son of man (Jesus himself, transformed or transfigured), the resurrection of the dead of previous generations, and the time of judgment, when all would pass before the judgment seat of the Son of man—or of God himself. Those found fit for it would then enter into the kingdom of God, there to eat, drink, and otherwise enjoy together the blessings of eternal life, while the wicked and impenitent would be condemned to extinction or eternal torment in Gehenna or outer darkness. Jesus' teaching and preaching were not directed to us over the heads of his hearers and intervening generations, but were meant to call his own contemporaries to repentance and a life of responsive neighbor-love while there was still time. Jesus did not preach timeless truths, but rather, an "ethic" for his contemporaries to follow during the brief interval before the parousia events occurred.[5]

This historical, eschatological Jesus called into question the beliefs and claims of both liberal and traditional Christianity. Liberal Christianity viewed Jesus primarily as teacher and exemplar of a timeless ethic of love who had either proclaimed that the kingdom of God was present in the hearts of individuals through the experience of communion with God, or who had called people of all times to the task of bringing the kingdom of God (or extending its influence) on earth through moral action and social reform.[6] If Jesus had intended his message only for his contemporaries during a brief period of eschatological expectation, he would not have meant that message "for us," and its modern relevance would come into doubt. Moreover, if "kingdom of God" referred to the imminent eschatological establishment of God's rule rather than to individual religious experience or social reform, the basic theses of Protestant liberalism would be left without foundation. Further, if Jesus had expected the kingdom to come in the lifetime of his followers, he would have been mistaken; if mistaken about that, might he not also have been mistaken in his moral teachings? It is no wonder that liberal Christianity was moved to reject Weiss's and Schweitzer's findings.

Traditionalist Christianity paid little attention to these findings, since historical and critical research generally were not encouraged in such circles. Traditionalist Protestants generally relied on the Fourth Gospel's

5. Both Weiss and Schweitzer somewhat revised their positions over the years. See above, 1–14. Schweitzer's final study is *The Kingdom of God and Primitive Christianity* (New York: Seabury, 1968).

6. Wilhelm Herrmann and Adolf von Harnack construed the kingdom of God more in terms of religious experience; Julius Kaftan and Walter Rauschenbusch saw it more in terms of social-moral reform.

portrait of Jesus, while ignoring both the eschatological and ethical sayings ascribed to him in the Synoptics. Traditionalists would have had difficulty reconciling the idea that Jesus' parousia expectation had been mistaken with his purported divinity. From their standpoint, salvation was through faith in the crucified and risen Lord; Jesus' proclamation of the coming kingdom was unimportant, except, perhaps, as it might be read to sanctify the establishment of the church or to represent the idea that when they die, Christians go to heaven. When the Catholic scholar, Alfred Loisy, set out his conclusions as to Jesus' eschatological beliefs[7]—which closely resembled Weiss's and Schweitzer's—the Catholic Church responded with formal sanctions and personal vilification, and proceeded to put the lid on Catholic biblical scholarship for several decades. Traditionalist Protestants would find another aspect of the eschatological Jesus theologically troublesome: for them, the gift of salvation was received by faith; a Jesus who called on people to *do* things (other than "accept" or believe in him) would smack too much of Catholic "works-righteousness" or Jewish "legalism" to serve as a suitable founder for their kind of Christianity.

Both Dodd and Bultmann were influenced by Protestant liberalism. Bultmann, in addition, was a Lutheran minister with strong ties to traditional Protestantism. Though differing in both their strategies and their conclusions, Dodd and Bultmann each undertook to demonstrate that the historical Jesus was still *the* authoritative teacher and guide for the Christian life today. In addition, while Dodd wished to see Jesus as the founder of liberal theology, Bultmann was concerned to relate the historical Jesus to more traditional faith, but not in such a way as to prove the latter's validity. For both, the kingdom of God and, more inclusively, "eschatology" were the central issues.

C. H. Dodd and Realized Eschatology

Dodd's earliest work acknowledges that Jesus expected and proclaimed that the kingdom of God was near.[8] "Kingdom of God" meant "the Good Time Coming" for which "we" all hope. Yet Dodd denied that Jesus shared the "dreams" of contemporary apocalyptists. He "may have looked for some epoch-making event in the near future," but he did not say how much time might elapse in the meantime, and did not see the "Good Time

---

7. Alfred Loisy, *The Gospel and the Church* (1903; Philadelphia: Fortress, 1976). Ironically, Loisy meant to refute the position set out by that Protestant, Adolf von Harnack, in *What Is Christianity?* (1900; New York: Harper, 1957).

8. *The Gospel in the New Testament* (London: National Sunday School Union, 1926) 17–19, 33–34, 38–39.

Coming" as "some wholly unprecedented and supernatural intervention of God." From the outset, Dodd's reflections were strongly influenced by Harnack.[9] Harnack conceded that Jesus sometimes referred to the kingdom of God as a future cataclysmic event, but he insisted that for Jesus (and for Christians of all eras as well) the essential meaning was its presence in the hearts of men: "God and the soul, the soul and its God."[10] Dodd agreed: "The Kingdom of God means God reigning, reigning in the hearts of men. . . ." To enter the kingdom, wrote Dodd, meant "to make God King in one's own soul."[11]

Dodd initially held that Jesus regarded the kingdom of God both as the future era of salvation that was coming, and as somehow already present. He thus anticipated the majority of later Anglo-Saxon scholars who maintained that for Jesus the kingdom of God was both present and, in some (usually only unimportant) way, future.[12] Yet Dodd was not content with this position. If Jesus' seemingly apocalyptic statements were taken literally, it would mean that Jesus did expect the parousia in the near future. To grant this might validate the theory of "interim ethics," and that would "raise a difficulty" as to the authority and relevance of Jesus' teaching for later generations.[13] Dodd's solution was to urge that Jesus proclaimed "realized eschatology": the kingdom of God, the Son of man, judgment, and the ultimate blessings of life with God were already present in his own time.[14] Dodd believed that the kingdom really *was* present in Jesus' time; therefore Jesus was not mistaken as to when it would come. Moreover, Dodd claimed, the kingdom has remained present ever since. Jesus' ethical teachings were meant for all who experienced the presence of the kingdom; they are therefore valid for Christians of all times; and he *meant* them "for us," not just for his contemporaries.

Dodd did not undertake directly and systematically to refute Weiss and Schweitzer. His writings make no mention of Weiss, and contain only scattered references to Schweitzer.[15] Instead, Dodd's method was to see whether those synoptic texts that, in his view, referred to the kingdom as a present reality could be read as the key to interpreting the apparently

9. See Dillistone, *Dodd*, 54–57. Much of what Dodd wrote in *The Gospel* echoes Harnack's *What Is Christianity?*

10. Harnack, *What Is Christianity?* 56.

11. Dodd, *The Gospel*, 19, 23; see also pp. 32, 37–39.

12. See R. H. Hiers and D. L. Holland, "Introduction," to Weiss, *Jesus' Proclamation*, 34–48, and R. H. Hiers, *The Kingdom of God in the Synoptic Tradition* (Gainesville: Univ. of Florida, 1970) 10–21.

13. C. H. Dodd, *The Parables of the Kingdom*, rev. ed. (New York: Scribner's, 1961) 79.

14. See Ibid., 82.

15. These do not indicate that he entirely understood Schweitzer's position. See Dodd on "consequente Eschatologie," *Parables*, 34; cf. R. H. Hiers, *Jesus and the Future* (Atlanta: John Knox, 1981) 3–4.

futuristic references. Dodd set out his case for realized eschatology in his 1935 Shaffer Lectures, subsequently published as *The Parables of the Kingdom*.

The decisive text for Dodd was Mt 12:28=Lk 11:20: ἔφθασεν ἐφ᾽ ὑμᾶς ἡ βασιλεία τοῦ θεοῦ. Jesus' exorcisms mean that "the sovereign power of God has come into effective operation." Dodd then proceeds to read Mk 1:14–15 and Lk 10:9–11, in which ἤγγικεν appears rather than ἔφθασεν,[16] in the light of this text and concludes that these passages together show that Jesus declared the kingdom "a matter of present experience," not "something to come in the near future."[17] Such sayings, Dodd asserts, are "explicit and unequivocal." From such passages, Dodd derives "the fundamental principle" that "Jesus saw in His own ministry the coming of the Kingdom of God,"[18] and Dodd applies this principle to construe texts that otherwise seem to point to its future coming. The Gospels, Dodd says, contain no "unequivocal" statement that "'the Kingdom of God will come,' to balance the (unequivocal) statement, 'the Kingdom of God has come.'"[19] Dodd suggests that the meaning of Mk 9:1 is that "some of those who heard Jesus speak would before their death awake to the fact that the Kingdom of God had come."[20] According to Dodd, sayings about eating and drinking in the kingdom of God (Mt 8:11; Lk 13:28–29; Mk 14:25) do not refer to its future coming, but rather to future participation in the kingdom by those not yet there, or possibly to "the transcendent order beyond space and time."[21]

What about the other synoptic sayings that point to future eschatological occurrences? Dodd uses a number of different strategies to deal with them. One strategy is to characterize those sayings which, in his view, declare the kingdom present, as "characteristic and distinctive," in con-

---

16. Dodd, *Parables*, 28–30. Dodd ignores Mt 10:7 where the verb ἐγγίζειν ("to come near") also appears and Lk 10:12, which indicates the future context for Lk 10:9–11, and texts using the adverb ἐγγύς ("near"), such as Lk 21:31. He also overlooks many other passages that refer to future eschatological events. See infra paragraph preceding note 28. For a futuristic interpretation of Mt 12:28=Lk 11:20, see Hiers, *Synoptic Tradition*, 30–35. On the eschatological character of demon exorcism in the synoptics, see Hiers, *Jesus and Future*, 62–71.

17. Dodd, *Parables*, 29–31.

18. Ibid., 34, 87. See also C. H. Dodd, *The Founder of Christianity* (New York: Macmillan, 1970) 115: "Nothing in (the teaching of Jesus) is more clearly original or characteristic than his declaration that the kingdom of God is here." Here Dodd draws freely from the Fourth Gospel as a source of information about Jesus and his message.

19. Dodd, *Parables*, 37. See, however, infra paragraph preceding note 28.

20. Ibid., 37–38. This interpretation has been severely criticized, e.g., by R. H. Fuller, *The Mission and Achievement of Jesus* (SBT 1/12; London: SCM, 1954) 27–28.

21. Dodd, *Parables*, 38–40. As to the sayings about eating and drinking in the kingdom of God, cf. Hiers, *Jesus and Future*, 72–86.

trast to Jewish teachings and prayers of the time: "If . . . we are seeking the *differentia* of the teaching of Jesus upon the Kingdom of God, it is here that it must be found."[22] Here Dodd repeats Harnack's attempt to differentiate between Jesus' *distinctive* sayings about the presence of the kingdom and the *traditional* eschatological beliefs which he simply shared with his contemporaries. Christians, Harnack had urged, should take the distinctive aspect of Jesus' outlook as essential and treat his traditional, eschatological ideas as mere "husk" or background.[23] Unlike Harnack, Dodd, later followed by Norman Perrin and many others, used the "differentia" criterion as a way to set aside futuristic sayings as additions by the later Christian community or the evangelists. Like Harnack, Dodd and Perrin proposed that Jesus regarded the kingdom primarily as a matter of present religious experience.[24] All three asserted or implied that it was present not only to Jesus' contemporaries, but also is present, somehow, for "us" in the twentieth century as well.

Already in 1906, Schweitzer noted that interpreters who found Jesus' futuristic expectations theologically embarrassing tended to deal with the problem by excising the futuristic texts from the body of sayings attributed to Jesus. Schweitzer described this procedure as "the literary solution" to the problem of eschatology.[25] Dodd was not the first, then, to relegate futuristic traditions to the limbo of later Christian tradition. He found what he took to be redactional interpolations particularly in Matthew and Luke, and considered Mark 13 a secondary composition.[26] Dodd's ultimate position seems to have been that wherever futuristic eschatology appears in the Gospels, it should be attributed to the church, on the basis of his conclusion that "the earliest tradition" of Jesus' teaching is characterized by "realized eschatology."[27]

Dodd's commitment to this conclusion may account his use of another, albeit tacit, strategy: simply, to by-pass or ignore certain texts. Most notable among these is the first petition of the Lord's Prayer, Mt 6:10=Lk 11:2, which clearly indicates that Jesus looked for the future coming of the kingdom as the decisive event confronting his contemporaries. In his *Parables of the Kingdom*, Dodd makes no mention of several other texts that refer to the future coming of the kingdom of God, the Son of man, and the time of judgment, notably: Mt 10:7, 23; 16:28; 24:29–35; 26:29, 64; Lk

---

22. Dodd, *Parables*, 34. Italics in original.

23. Harnack, *What Is Christianity?* 53–56.

24. Norman Perrin, *Rediscovering the Teachings of Jesus* (New York: Harper & Row, 1967) e.g., 67, 74, 82, 89.

25. *The Quest of the Historical Jesus* (New York: Macmillan, 1968) ch 19.

26. Dodd, *Parables*, 36–37, 108, 110–11, 114–21, 138–39.

27. C. H. Dodd, *The Apostolic Preaching and Its Developments* (London: Hodder and Stoughton, 1936) 58–59.

10:12; 18:8; 19:11; 21:27–33; and 22:18. He does refer to the Great Judgment scene in Mt 25:31–46, but only to imply that it is secondary.[28]

Dodd's confidence in his conclusion that Jesus declared the kingdom present may also account for his willingness occasionally to amend the text so as to bring out that meaning more clearly. In rendering Mk 9:1, Dodd felt free to insert the adverb "already" and interpret "see" to mean recognize in retrospect: "The bystanders are . . . promised . . . that they shall come to see that the Kingdom of God *has already come*, at some point before they became aware of it."[29] The New English Bible likewise obligingly inserts an "already" here, as at Mt 12:28 and Lk 11:20, and also tilts various other futuristic texts towards realized eschatology: e.g., Mk 1:15; Mt 3:2; 4:17; 10:7; 21:31; Lk 10:9, 11; 17:21; 19:11. Dodd was Director of the NEB translation project.

Two other strategies appear in Dodd's treatment of problematic passages. One is to construe futuristic statements as references to *historical* crises of some sort. The other is to interpret future references as *symbolizing* more transcendent (but nontemporal) meanings.

What Dodd means by "crisis" often is uncertain. Commenting on the "parable of the Fig Tree" (Mk 13:28) he says, "Jesus was calling upon men to recognize the significance of the situation in which, at the moment, they stood." The original meaning of the parable of the Defendant (Mt 5:25–26, Lk 12:57–59), he suggests, is that Jesus' contemporaries, who were "faced by a tremendous crisis," should have seen "that they must act, now or never," in "the supreme crisis of all history."[30] What the crisis was, why they must act "now or never," or what they must do, Dodd does not say. Elsewhere Dodd indicates that "the crisis" was Jesus' own presence— which Dodd sometimes equates both with the presence of the kingdom or God himself and the time of judgments. Those who reject Jesus (or God) pronounce judgment upon themselves.[31] At other points, however, the crises are related to Jesus' predictions of future historical developments. Jesus, Dodd says, told the general public, "Be alert and prepared for any development in this critical situation," and, at Gesthemane, he urged his disciples to watch and pray, so as to be spared or ready for "the immediately impending attack upon Him and his followers."[32] Several of the

---

28. Dodd, *Parables*, 63–64. Dodd says little about these texts in his other writings, either.

29. Ibid., 37, note 1. Italics in original.

30. Ibid., 107, note 1, and 107–8.

31. Ibid., 56. Cf. Jn 3:18. Dodd adds, apparently also under the influence of the Fourth Gospel, "In rejecting Him, the Jewish nation rejected the Kingdom of God." Ibid. Cf. Jn 18:35–36. Presumably Dodd did not mean to encourage Christian anti-semitism; but like many Christians—especially those relying on the Fourth Gospel—he seems here to have forgotten that Jesus and *all* of the first Christians were Jews.

32. Ibid., 131–32.

crisis sayings, according to Dodd, should be seen as predictions of "historical" catastrophes "lying immediately in store—the persecution of Himself and His disciples, the destruction of the Temple and of the Jewish nation."[33] It was the church which then took such sayings and converted them into appeals to prepare for the parousia "which *it* believed to be approaching."[34]

At first, Dodd had conceded that Jesus might have used apocalyptic language, but indignantly dismissed the idea that he actually thought about the kingdom in terms of those apocalyptic "dreams."[35] In his later writings, Dodd characterizes apocalyptic imagery more positively, as a mode of expressing, symbolically, ultimate realities belonging to "the order beyond space and time." With this understanding of apocalyptic imagery, Dodd felt more comfortable in ascribing its usage to Jesus. Nevertheless, he continued to insist that Jesus *intended* such language to be understood symbolically, rather than literally.[36]

Critics have suggested that Dodd's Jesus resembles more nearly a Cambridge Platonist than a first-century Jew. Dodd's intent, certainly, was to preserve as authentic a core of Jesus' seemingly futuristic sayings, while construing them in accordance with his commitment to the conclusion that Jesus had declared the kingdom of God present.[37] His basic position was that the blessings of life in the kingdom of God, as well as the coming of the Son of man, judgment, and world transformation, can be experienced only in "the eternal order"; but in that eternal order, "there is no before and after"; rather, these ultimate realities are "timeless."[38] Thus, by definition, there could be no future coming of the kingdom of God, Son of man, judgment, or other eschatological events. (If the solution to the problem is by definition, one might ask why it is necessary to examine the NT evidence at all.)

Nevertheless, Dodd insists, the eternal order was actualized or realized in space and time, in Jesus' ministry, which exemplified and revealed "the reign of God, . . . the eternal God Himself, here present." This reign of God "gives an eternal dimension to the temporal present, and to each succeeding 'present.'"[39] Thus, even though Jesus himself is no longer present, the reign of God, somehow, continues to be so, or at least to give "an eternal dimension" to all subsequent "presents."[40] In these various

---

33. Ibid., 135; see also pp. 40 and 55.
34. Ibid., 139. Italics added.
35. Dodd, *The Gospel*, 19.
36. For an early criticism of Dodd's proposal, see C. C. McCown, "Symbolic Interpretation," *JBL* 63 (1944) 335–38.
37. Dodd, *Parables*, 79–84; Dodd, *Founder*, 113–18.
38. Dodd, *Parables*, 83. See infra, note 48.
39. Dodd, *Founder*, 115.
40. See also Dodd, *Parables*, 84: "Whether its subsequent span would be long or short,

ways, Dodd achieved the goal of his apologetic: to refute the idea that Jesus had mistakenly expected or proclaimed the imminence of the kingdom of God or any other eschatological events. Dodd's Jesus need be no stranger and enigma to modern religious sensibility.[41] There would be no occasion to deal with troublesome questions as to his relevance and authority "for us" that might arise if his message had been meant for those living during the brief interim before the expected arrival of the new age. Jesus could remain the great teacher and guide for the moral life of modern Christians.

Dodd devoted a considerable portion of his later work to setting out the nature and relevance of Jesus' ethical teaching.[42] Here Dodd repeatedly characterizes Jesus' teachings as precepts, principles or maxims illustrating the "quality and direction" of life appropriate for persons who have "received" or accepted the kingdom and now would live in accordance with the standard of divine love or charity Jesus taught.[43] Implicitly, Jesus meant this teaching "for us": "The several precepts, therefore, may be regarded as examples of the way in which divine charity may become effective in various relations and situations occurring in the course of our lives."[44] Dodd understood that the Christian life is based on the teachings of Jesus. Sometimes he characterized Jesus' moral discourse in terms of the demand for obedience.[45] More typically, however, Dodd described this discourse in terms of precepts, principles, and guideposts referring to the "quality and direction" of action, occasionally adding that the requisite quality and direction might be present even "at quite a lowly level of performance."[46]

C. H. Dodd was probably the most influential Anglo-Saxon NT scholar of the twentieth century. His work served to restore the authority and relevance of Jesus and his teaching for many, particularly Protestant liberals, who otherwise would have found an unbridgeable gap between the Jesus of history and the one they recognized as founder of their beliefs

men would *henceforth* be living in a new age, in which the Kingdom of God, His grace and His judgment, stood revealed." Italics added.

41. Similarly, Norman Perrin attributed to Jesus the intent to use open-ended (or "tensive") symbols, evidently in order to rescue him from the error of using literalistic or "steno-symbols": "If the Kingdom of God is a tensive symbol in the proclamation of Jesus then *the mythology of Jesus has not been discredited by the subsequent course of history.*" Norman Perrin, *Jesus and the Language of the Kingdom* (Philadelphia: Fortress, 1976) 78, italics added.

42. See esp., *The Gospel and the Law of Christ* (London: Longmans, Green & Co., 1947); *Gospel and Law* (New York: Columbia Univ., 1951); and "The Ethics of the New Testament," in Ruth N. Anshen, ed., *Moral Principles of Action* (New York: Harper, 1952) 543–58.

43. See also Dodd, *Parables*, 84.

44. Dodd, *Law of Christ*, 16.

45. Ibid., 17, 19.

46. Ibid., 17; Dodd, *Gospel and Law*, 73.

and values.[47] Nevertheless, few other scholars have subscribed to Dodd's proposal that Jesus regarded the kingdom as *entirely* present.[48] Instead, most have maintained that Jesus expected and proclaimed *both* that the kingdom of God was already present *and* that it (or its consummation) was yet to come, whether in the near or indeterminate future. How it might have been both present and future was another problem. In actuality, most proponents of both/and theories tend to emphasize the present kingdom and soft-pedal or forget the futuristic expectation.[49] Dodd's insistence on Jesus' declaration of the kingdom's presence seemed to justify their emphasis on the present dimension, while theological and ethical considerations served to diminish their interest in its futuristic aspects.[50]

Rudolf Bultmann, Demythologizing, the Kerygma, and Radical Obedience

---

Dodd had been influenced by Harnack; Bultmann, on the other hand, was impressed by his teacher, Johannes Weiss.

> Weiss showed that the kingdom of God is not immanent in the world and does not grow as part of the world's history, but is rather eschatological, i.e., the kingdom of God transcends the historical order. It will come into being not through the moral endeavour of man, but solely through the supernatural action of God. God will suddenly put an end to the world and to history, and He will bring in a new world, the world of eternal blessedness.[51]

47. Not all Anglo-Saxon interpreters were persuaded by Dodd's program. See, e.g., A. W. Argyle, "Does 'Realized Eschatology' Make Sense?" *Hibbert Journal* 60 (1953) 385–87. Millar Burrows, Morton S. Enslin, Robert M. Grant, William Manson, among others, gave greater weight to the futuristic sayings. A recent study persuasively argues that Jesus' expectations, which were entirely futuristic, prompted the early Christian community to see in his passion and resurrection the dawning of the new age: Dale C. Allison, Jr., *The End of the Ages Has Come* (Philadelphia: Fortress, 1985).

48. A few rather vague statements of Dodd's could be read to mean that even he sometimes allowed Jesus certain futuristic expectation. Discussing Mk 14:25, he wrote: "Are we to think of the Kingdom of God here as something yet to come? If so, it is not to come in this world, for the 'new wine' belongs to the 'new heaven and new earth' of apocalyptic thought, that is, to the transcendent order beyond space and time" (Dodd, *Parables* 40). See also Dodd, *Founder*, 115: "The kingdom of God, while it is present experience, remains also a hope, but a hope directed to a consummation beyond history." See also ibid., 117, on Jesus' reply to the high priest: ". . . Jesus also was pointing to the final victory of God's cause, or in other words the consummation of his kingdom beyond history. . . ." In all such instances, Dodd evidently meant that whatever might happen beyond time, space and history was not, by definition, something that could occur in the future.

49. See R. H. Hiers, "Eschatology and Methodology," *JBL* 85 (1966) 170–84.

50. See generally, Hiers, *Jesus and Future*.

51. *Jesus Christ and Mythology* (New York: Scribner's, 1958) 12.

Weiss, Bultmann concluded, was entirely correct; moreover, Bultmann believed that Weiss's position was generally accepted by modern scholars: "Today nobody doubts that Jesus' conception of the kingdom of God is an eschatological one—at least in European theology."[52] Bultmann's own study of the gospel sources confirmed Weiss's finding that Jesus had looked for the parousia events in the quite near future.[53] He dismissed Dodd's realized eschatology program as "escape reasoning": "On the contrary, Jesus clearly expected the irruption of God's Reign as a miraculous, world-transforming event. . . ."[54]

Rather than try to accommodate Jesus to modern thought by attributing to him the more theologically convenient theory of realized eschatology, Bultmann proposed to recognize Jesus' futuristic proclamation for what it was, but then interpret the basic "understanding of existence" embedded in his "mythological" (particularly his eschatological) concepts, and present that basic understanding to the modern world. Unlike Harnack—who had considered the eschatological "husk" or context of Jesus' beliefs entirely dispensable—Bultmann believed that the eschatological element was significant. Thus Bultmann undertook his famous "demythologizing" program in order to recover the essential understanding of existence contained in both Jesus' and the early church's eschatological outlook.[55]

Bultmann proposed that the understanding of existence that comes to expression in Jesus' eschatological proclamation is that each "now" or "crisis of decision" is always humanity's last time to decide against the world and for God.

> The one concern in this teaching was that man should conceive his immediate concrete situation as the decision to which he is constrained, and should decide in this moment for God and surrender his natural will. Just this is what we found to be *the final significance of the eschatological message*, that man *now* stands under the necessity of decision, *that his "Now" is always for him the last hour*, in which his decision against the world and for God is demanded, in which every claim of his own is to be silenced.[56]

52. Ibid., 13. Weiss's *Predigt* did not appear in English translation until 1971. This may partly account for its general neglect by Anglo-Saxon scholars. Interpreters generally did read Schweitzer, but usually not very carefully, and tended to reject some caricature of his position rather than take the trouble to understand and try to refute what he had to say. See Hiers, *Jesus and Future*, 3–4, 50–61.

53. Rudolf Bultmann, *History of the Synoptic Tradition* (1921; New York: Harper & Row, 1963).

54. Rudolf Bultmann, *Theology of the New Testament* (2 vols.; New York: Scribner's, 1954–55) 1:22. Realized eschatology, Bultmann stated, "cannot be substantiated by a single saying of Jesus" (ibid.).

55. His program was first set out in 1941 in the article, "New Testament and Mythology" reprinted in Hans Werner Bartsch, ed., *Kerygma and Myth* (New York: Harper, 1961) and, with later related essays, in Rudolf Bultmann, *New Testament and Mythology* (Philadelphia: Fortress, 1984). See also Bultmann, *Christ and Mythology*.

56. *Jesus and the Word* (New York: Scribner's, 1958) 131.

Bultmann's emphasis on renouncing the world as the corollary to deciding for God may reflect Weiss's characterization of Jesus' message as a negative and ascetic turning from the old world in preparation for the new.[57] It may also reflect a Kierkegaardian existentialist "Either/Or." We shall see, however, that Bultmann also found a positive ethic of radical neighbor-love in Jesus' demand for radical obedience. First, it might be asked whether Bultmann's proposed equation of Jesus' eschatological message with a recurrent crisis of decision can be justified. How, it may be asked, does it follow that Jesus' eschatological message means that every "Now" is always, "the *last* hour"? Why, and in what sense is it "the last"? Bultmann implies that Jesus *first* understood human existence to consist of a series of crises of decision, in each of which the individual is confronted by the necessity of choosing between God and "the world" (or pursuit of his or her own worldly interests). Then, *because* Jesus so understood human existence, it was only natural that he should have expressed this understanding "in the garments of a passing cosmology."[58] In other words, Bultmann suggests, Jesus used the categories of apocalyptic Judaism only incidentally; his *real* understanding, prior to and independent of these categories, can readily be extracted and made central to our understanding. Such a Jesus is no stranger and enigma to modern, at any rate, early twentieth-century existentialist thought after all; he could have occupied an office next to Martin Heidegger's with no questions asked. Perhaps Bultmann was prompted by an apologetic desire to make Jesus and Christianity respectable in the twentieth-century academic world by showing that these need not forever be bound to the prescientific, mythological outlook of the first century.

Bultmann was also a Lutheran theologian who was concerned lest faith be "proven" or "legitimated" by being grounded on historically verifiable "facts" rather than on divine grace.[59] He regularly insisted that Christian faith was not based on Jesus' own self-understanding, preaching, or understanding of existence; instead, it was founded on the church's preaching (or kerygma) about him—notably about his death and resurrection—which, in turn, was grounded only on the "thatness" of the "Christ

57. See Weiss, *Jesus' Proclamation*, 105–14.

58. Rudolf Bultmann, "Jesus and Paul," in *Existence and Faith* (New York: Meridian, 1960) 186. See also Bultmann, *Jesus*, 52, 55. Strangely, Bultmann sometimes forgets that he had conceded that Jesus borrowed existing Jewish beliefs as the medium for his message, and states that Jesus himself devised these expectations as a vehicle for his own underlying convictions. See, e.g., Rudolf Bultmann, *Primitive Christianity* (New York: Meridian, 1957) 92; *Christ and Mythology*, 26; *Jesus*, 52. See also Rudolf Bultmann, "The Study of the Synoptic Gospels," in F. C. Grant, ed., *Form Criticism* (New York: Harper & Row, 1962) 73.

59. *The Primitive Christian Kerygma and the Historical Jesus*, in Carl E. Braaten and Roy A. Harrisville, *The Historical Jesus and the Kerygmatic Christ* (Nashville: Abingdon, 1964) 25.

event." Bultmann was, therefore, content to leave open the question whether Jesus had identified himself with the coming Son of man, or whether he looked for someone else to appear in that role. (He considered the latter likely.) He at least claimed to be indifferent as to whether the earliest layer of synoptic tradition or any particular saying attributed to Jesus derived from his actual preaching or from later tradition or redaction. Because of his theological stance, it was not so theologically difficult for Bultmann as it had been for liberal Protestantism to acknowledge the eschatological character of Jesus' proclamation. If Jesus had mistakenly expected the eschatological kingdom to come in the near future, there was no occasion for alarm, for Christianity was founded on the kerygma, not on the preaching or outlook of the historical Jesus. Bultmann even suggested that the kerygma replaces the historical Jesus as the authoritative message addressing later generations. Liberal Protestantism, represented by Harnack and Dodd, wanted a historical Jesus whose beliefs and preaching about the kingdom of God could be seen as the basis for modern Christian faith and life. For Bultmann, a gap between the Jesus of history and the preaching of the later church was not only harmless, it was to be preferred. Nevertheless, Bultmann insisted that it was important *that* Jesus had existed, and even suggested that "Jesus is really present in the kerygma."[60] "Kerygma" seems to mean several different things in Bultmann's usage: the preaching of the early Christian community, the faith-understanding of Paul (or of the Fourth Evangelist), or the preaching that goes on in modern churches. It is often unclear whether the term refers to the act of preaching, or to its content. When Bultmann says that Jesus is present in the kerygma, he may mean that Jesus is made present to modern believers in either the content or the act of preaching. But is this Jesus the same as the historical Jesus?[61]

If the substance of Jesus' preaching is as of little consequence, theologically, as Bultmann claims, one might ask why he goes to the trouble of "demythologizing" Jesus' message. Bultmann makes clear that the purpose of demythologizing was to remove false or unnecessary stumbling blocks to the faith of modern people, e.g., belief in the three-storied universe and in demons.[62] He insists that because Jesus' "understanding of human life" was anterior to his expectation of the imminent end of the world, it "clearly does not stand or fall" with that expectation.[63] Evidently Bultmann meant to say that Jesus' understanding of the meaning of exis-

60. Ibid., 40–42.
61. See Schubert M. Ogden, "Rudolf Bultmann and the Future of Revisionary Christology," in Hooks, ed., *Bultmann Retrospect*, 37–58.
62. Bultmann, *Christ and Mythology*, 14–23.
63. Bultmann, *Primitive Christianity*, 92; see also *Jesus*, 55–56, and *Christ and Mythology*, 25–26.

tence "stands," i.e., is valid for modern belief as well. But why, on Bultmann's terms, would that matter? Bultmann's position remains ambiguous at this point. Yet if it is unclear whether Bultmann considered Jesus' message (or understanding of existence) relevant for contemporary faith, there is no doubt that he understood Jesus' message or "word" to be of the essence for ethics or the moral life of modern Christians.

Commentators have strangely neglected Bultmann's strong interest in ethics, specifically, the fact that he presents the historical Jesus' demand for radical obedience as the basis for the Christian life. Bultmann insists that Jesus' demands were "absolute," by which he means that they were and are fully valid and relevant today, and were "by no means influenced in their formulation by the thought that the end of the world is near at hand."[64] Bultmann refuses to categorize Jesus' ethical teaching as interim ethics for another reason, namely, that to do so would be to attribute to him a kind of legalism, as if he had required the performance of "prudent" or "practical rules" or some "arbitrarily set task."[65] All through *Jesus and the Word*, Bultmann describes not only what Jesus demanded of his first-century hearers, but also what he demands of people generally, namely, radical obedience.[66]

By radical obedience, Bultmann meant *both* that Jesus taught individuals to decide "Either-Or," between God's reign and "the world," or between "God's will" and their "own will,"[67] *and* that the obedience called for must be a willing and understanding obedience, not merely obedience to law or external authority.[68] The content of radical obedience—that which is to be willed and understood—is love of neighbor. "I can love my neighbor only when I surrender my will completely to God's will, so I can love God only while I will what He wills, while I really love my neighbor."[69] To be sure, Bultmann sometimes writes as if the substance of radical obedience consists in renunciation of one's own claim; but his fuller meaning is that renunciation (or surrender) of one's own

64. Bultmann, "Study of the Synoptics," 73; See also Bultmann, *Jesus,* 127–28. Dodd, too, understood Jesus' ethic to be "absolute," i.e., no interim ethic, but an ethic binding on all who have experienced the coming of the kingdom of God—including, therefore, twentieth-century Christians. C. H. Dodd, *History and the Gospel* (London: Nisbet & Co., 1938) 125–28.

65. Bultmann, *Jesus,* 127, 129; *Theology* 1:20. Like Dodd and most other interpreters, Bultmann misconstrued what Schweitzer had meant by "interim ethics." See Hiers, *Jesus and Future,* 50–61.

66. Bultmann characterizes Christian ethics in precisely the same way that he describes the substance of Jesus' demand: "Das christliche Gebot der Nächstenliebe," (1930) in *Glauben und Verstehen* (Tübingen: J. C. B. Mohr, 1933) 1:229–44.

67. Bultmann, *Primitive Christianity,* 90; *Jesus,* 78, 83–84.

68. See Bultmann, *Jesus,* 72–98; *Theology* 1:12; and "Reply," in Kegley, ed., *Theology of Bultmann,* 283.

69. Bultmann, *Jesus,* 115.

claim frees one to serve the neighbor: "Love means the surrender of one's own will for the good of the other man, in obedience to God."[70] In the concrete situation, Bultmann insisted, a person will know what to do in order to effectuate love of neighbor. Evidently he wished to avoid identifying more specific norms in Jesus' teaching lest they become a new legalism.[71]

Bultmann seems to understand that each encounter with one's neighbor is an occasion for radical obedience. In Bultmann's view, as we have seen, Jesus' understanding of human existence is that persons are continually confronting a "crisis of decision" for God and his will, or for the world and their own wills. This recurrent "now" or "crisis of decision" is the "real" or essential meaning of Jesus' eschatological preaching, and thus the demythologized essence of Jesus' proclamation of the kingdom of God. So far as Christian *ethics* is concerned, then, Jesus' message of the coming kingdom has its meaning in his summons to radical obedience in the form of radical love in every encounter people have with their neighbors.[72] There was a further problem, however.

Did Jesus require radical obedience as a requisite to entering the kingdom of God? If so, people might have been motivated by the desire to be *rewarded* for what they did. But then "the radical character of obedience would be lost."[73] Bultmann was troubled by the idea that Jesus sometimes seemed to promise rewards, even "to those who are obedient without thought of reward."[74] His solution was to suggest that Jesus was thinking in existentialist (if individualistic) terms: "The motive of reward is only a primitive expression for the idea that in what a man does his own real being is at stake—that self which . . . he is to become. To achieve that self is the legitimate motive of his ethical dealing and of his true obedience. . . ."[75] Here—as in Heidegger's formulations[76] and modern secular bourgeois thought generally[77]—ethics is conceptualized entirely in terms of self-centered self-actualization; the neighbor drops out of sight. One might ask here again whether Bultmann really understood that Jesus had expected and proclaimed that the time of judgment was near, and that

70. Ibid., 117–18; see also pp. 112, 114.

71. Ibid., 84–98.

72. Despite the apparent individualism of Bultmann's usual exposition inherent in his use of existentialist philosophy, he does sometimes suggest that Jesus' love command may have important social implications. *This World and Beyond, Marburg Sermons* (New York: Scribner's, 1960) 148–49; *Primitive Christianity*, 25; "The Sermon on the Mount and the Justice of the State" (1936), in *Existence and Faith*, 202–5.

73. Bultmann, *Jesus*, 121.

74. Ibid., 79.

75. Bultmann, *Theology* 1:15.

76. See Martin Buber, *Between Man and Man* (New York: Macmillan, 1965) 163–81.

77. See generally, Robert Bellah, et al., *Habits of the Heart* (New York: Harper & Row, 1986).

only those who repented and turned in radical obedience to God and neighbor would enter into the coming kingdom. Had Jesus so believed, he would not have been concerned with "rewards" at all, but rather with the urgent need for his contemporaries to repent and respond in radical obedience, so that they might share the blessed life of the coming age *which was coming in any event.* Here, as in the case of Bultmann's suggestion that Jesus' eschatology was only the "mythology" or "garments" in which his "real meaning" finds its outward expression,[78] it appears that Bultmann considered Jesus an existentialist preacher of radical obedience who only incidentally proclaimed the coming of the eschatological kingdom of God. The question here is whether Bultmann demythologized the substance of Jesus' eschatological proclamation or whether he read into Jesus' message and intent the beliefs of a twentieth-century Christian existentialist moralist.

Bultmann is certainly the giant of twentieth-century NT scholarship. He did it all: he was a leading figure in literary and historical criticism, particularly with his *History of the Synoptic Tradition* and his work on the Fourth Gospel; he was a pioneer of form criticism and redaction history; he launched his famous demythologizing program; and he wrote what is still the classic *Theology of the New Testament.* Not all European scholars concurred with his stance that Jesus viewed the kingdom of God as an entirely future, world-transforming event, but those who wished to claim that Jesus thought the kingdom somehow present have had to reckon with Bultmann, as well as with Weiss and Schweitzer. Several of his pupils, particularly the presumptuously self-styled "post-Bultmannians," have wished to combine Bultmann's futuristic interpretation with one or another version of "realized eschatology," perhaps in order to avoid some of the theological difficulties inherent in maintaining that Jesus had been mistaken about the coming of the kingdom. Some of these seized upon statements by Bultmann to the effect that the kingdom of God was "dawning," "beginning," or "breaking in," to try to show that the master shared their mediating views. Whenever Bultmann (or his translators) used such expressions, however, it is clear from the context that he was not referring to the presence of the kingdom, but to Jesus' expectation that it would come soon.[79] The post-Bultmannians especially wanted to bridge the gap between Jesus' own self-understanding and that expressed in or called forth by the kerygma of the early church, evidently so as to be in a better position to claim him as founder of the kind of Christology they believed meaningful. Such concern prompted the "new quest of the historical Jesus" that flourished in the 1950s and 1960s. Invariably, the

78. Bultmann, *Jesus,* 55–56; idem, "Jesus and Paul," 58.
79. See, e.g, Bultmann, *Jesus,* 29, 38; Bultmann, *Christ and Mythology,* 12–13.

"new questers" proposed that Jesus had, somehow, affirmed the presence of the kingdom of God.

Dodd and Bultmann: Comparative and Concluding Comments

Dodd and Bultmann wished to make Jesus both intelligible to modern culture and relevant to contemporary Christian faith and life. The central problem was that Jesus had apparently expected the kingdom of God to come in the near future. If he had been mistaken about that, how could he and his first-century message be relied on in the twentieth? Moreover, what could the kingdom of God mean to people today who do not share the eschatological world-view? Dodd programmatically undertook to re-examine the synoptic evidence in order to show that Jesus had *not* subscribed to the apocalyptic beliefs of his Jewish contemporaries; instead, Dodd argued, Jesus had declared the kingdom present in his own person and ministry; furthermore, Dodd urged, the kingdom *has* remained present ever since. Jesus was not mistaken; the kingdom had come. Modern Christians can claim him as founder of Christianity as they know it, and find in his teachings the principles needed for ethics today. Bultmann considered the synoptic account of Jesus' futuristic beliefs basically accurate, but then undertook programmatically to reinterpret the *meaning* of those beliefs. He concluded that Jesus had understood the human situation as a series of crises of decision in which each person must choose between God and his will, and worldly self-interest. Such was the real meaning of Jesus' eschatological message, once the mythological garments—which he had either borrowed from Judaism or created himself—in which he had clothed that understanding were demythologized or reconstrued.

Both Dodd and Bultmann concluded that Jesus' message of the kingdom of God was essentially *timeless*. Dodd's Jesus did not expect or proclaim any future eschatological events; Bultmann's Jesus was a proponent of an understanding of existence that focussed entirely on the present "now" or crisis of decision; the only future matter of interest was how decision now would affect achievement of one's future self. Both paid tribute to Jesus' continuing authority by ascribing to him the fruit of their labors: as if Jesus himself had conceived and validated their interpretations of his understanding and message. Dodd's and Bultmann's "presentist" focus was challenged in the 1960s and 1970s by proponents of the "new theology" or "theology of hope."[80] The latter were impressed

80. See esp., the work of Carl E. Braaten, Jürgen Moltmann, and Wolfhart Pannenberg.

both by the importance of the future for Jesus and early Christianity, and with the importance of hope for the future for people confronting the world-and-life-threatening crises of the late twentieth century. For the "new theologians," both ethics and eschatology were matters of urgent existential consequence.

Dodd's work served to rehabilitate Jesus particularly for Protestant liberals, for whom his authority as teacher was especially important. Bultmann's work was received with special appreciation by more traditional Protestants for whom the idea that Jesus (whom the Fourth Evangelist already had represented as divine and omniscient) might have been mistaken was anathema. Dodd drew on the Fourth Gospel to corroborate his conclusion that Jesus had espoused realized eschatology; Bultmann cited John's reinterpretation of Jesus' eschatological outlook as validation for his own demythologizing program, for the process had already begun within the NT canon itself. Both Dodd and Bultmann saw Hellenism as the primary milieu for Jesus and early Christianity; neither was especially familiar with intertestamental Judaism, and both viewed Judaism largely as something to be contrasted unfavorably with Jesus' originality and more profound beliefs and ethics.

Both Dodd and Bultmann found Jesus' message authoritative and relevant for the Christian life, indeed, its basis. Each related Jesus' ethics to the kingdom of God which, in different ways, they considered present in the experience of both Jesus' original hearers, and of twentieth-century believers. Both described Jesus' ethics as his demand for obedience. Bultmann saw the demand more radically, requiring devotion of the whole person to God and neighbor, while Dodd suggested that the "quality and direction" of life Jesus called for might be fulfilled at lower levels of performance. Both emphasized love as the central substance of Jesus' demand; but Dodd urged that Jesus' teaching provided a number of principles and guideposts. Bultmann insisted that one who loves will know *what* to do in the situation, and avoided specifying further particular norms, lest such give rise to a new legalism. In Dodd's view, the kingdom of God continues to be present, and Jesus' ethic is an ethic for those who have received the kingdom or experienced its presence. For Bultmann, the kingdom is present in the recurrent now of decision which people can experience in the demand for radical obedience as they continue to encounter their neighbors. Neither Dodd nor Bultmann saw any problem in characterizing Jesus' demand or message as authoritative and relevant "for us."[81] Whether either succeeded in showing how Jesus' message can be so readily extricated from his eschatological beliefs and

---

81. E.g., Dodd, *History,* 127–28; "Ethics," 555, *Gospel and Law,* 62–64; Bultmann, *This World,* 24–33, 122, 145; *Primitive Christianity,* 45, 77; *Jesus,* 8, 11.

expectations is another question. Amos Wilder would take up this question.[82]

Dodd and Bultmann both realized that the eschatological picture of Jesus was highly problematic for contemporary faith and ethics. Neither had the last word, either as to what Jesus believed, or as to how his beliefs should be understood today. But their work has provided the basic reference points for all subsequent study of the historical Jesus, his eschatological beliefs, and his proclamation of the kingdom of God.

82. See E. Elmore, "Linguistic Approaches to the Kingdom: Amos Wilder and Norman Perrin," this volume, pp. 53–65.

3 Mediating Approaches to the Kingdom: Werner Georg Kümmel and George Eldon Ladd

Eldon Jay Epp

Harkness Professor of Biblical Literature
Case Western Reserve University

Introduction

THE LIMITED NEW TESTAMENT SCHOLARSHIP that could be carried on during World War II was largely parochial, with little international interchange of ideas and only sparse use of published materials from other countries. W. G. Kümmel wrote his *Verheissung und Erfüllung*[1] during the last year of the war, but even in Switzerland, as he says in his preface, he had no access to relevant English and American publications. He corrected this deficiency in his comprehensive revision of 1953, and the resulting volume was among the very first post-war European works of NT scholarship not only to recognize English-language contributions, but to utilize them extensively. In fact, Kümmel's bibliography contains 25 British and American titles out of the 77 monographs listed, a most unusual circumstance if one compares it with almost any other German NT work of the early post–World War II period (or before, for that matter).

Whether it was this unusual openness to English-language works, or for other reasons, *Verheissung und Erfüllung* not only was quickly translated into English (under the title, *Promise and Fulfilment*[2]) in 1957, but quickly took its place in the American, as it had in the European, discussion of

---

1. *Verheissung und Erfüllung: Untersuchungen zur eschatologischen Verkündigung Jesu* (ATANT 6; Basel, 1945; 2d ed., Zürich: Zwingli-Verlag, 1953; 3d ed., 1956).
2. *Promise and Fulfilment: The Eschatological Message of Jesus* (tr. D. M. Barton; SBT 23; London: SCM, 1957). Tr. from the 3d German ed. of 1956.

Jesus' view of the kingdom of God. Soon, along with contributions by
C. H. Dodd, Oscar Cullmann, and Rudolf Bultmann, Kümmel's work became a major factor in that international discussion.[3] Already in 1950—
before its translation into English—Amos N. Wilder referred to *Verheissung und Erfüllung* as "the best recent canvas of the whole question
from the point of view of historical-critical exegesis."[4]

The direction of the discussion in the earliest post-war period was
toward the generally recognized synthesis or "consensus on the kingdom
of God," that is, that Jesus viewed the kingdom both as in some sense
present and as in some sense future. This consensus or compromise
followed a well-known fifty-year period of vigorous debate. On the one
hand, scholars from Johannes Weiss and Albert Schweitzer (1892–1910) to
Martin Werner (1941)[5] had emphasized the futurity of the kingdom in
Jesus' view. On the other hand, a variety of differing views had emphasized the beginning or the presence of the kingdom in Jesus' ministry.
These included the Old Liberal scholars like Adolf von Harnack, for
whom the kingdom of God was a present, inner, spiritual reality which
Jesus had initiated on its social, evolutionary development;[6] but particularly prominent was the arresting view of Rudolf Otto (1934),[7] who—
contrary to the then dominant futurist eschatology—showed that a number of central, genuine sayings of Jesus announced that the kingdom was
present and active there and then, as he was teaching (e.g. Mt 11:12/Lk
16:16 and Mt 12:28/Lk 11:20). C. H. Dodd (1936)[8] then capitalized on these
"present" sayings and built on them his audacious "realized eschatology,"
which affirmed that Jesus viewed the kingdom as entirely present and
fulfilled in his own time.

As these and other scholars pushed the pendulum of the kingdom of
God from one extreme to the other,[9] the period during and just after

3. Witness, e.g., Oscar Cullmann's *Christus und die Zeit: Die urchristliche Zeit- und
Geschichtsauffassung* (Zollikon-Zürich: Evangelischer Verlag, 1946) and its very heavy
reliance on Kümmel (e.g., 62; 72; 76; 130–32; cf. *Christ and Time: The Primitive Christian
Conception of Time and History* [Philadelphia: Westminster, 1950] 71–72, where he
speaks of "this unusually important work"; 83–84; 88; 148–49; same pages in the rev. ed.,
1964).

4. Amos N. Wilder, *Eschatology and Ethics in the Teaching of Jesus* (rev. ed.; New
York: Harper & Row, 1950; original, 1939) 47–48.

5. Martin Werner, *Die Entstehung des christlichen Dogmas* (Bern: Paul Haupt, 1941);
The Formation of Christian Dogma: An Historical Study of Its Problem (rewritten in
shortened form by the author and tr. by S. G. F. Brandon; London: A. & C. Black, 1957).

6. E.g., *What Is Christianity?* (Harper Torchbook; New York: Harper & Row, 1957;
original, 1900) 49–62.

7. Rudolf Otto, *The Kingdom of God and the Son of Man: A Study in the History of
Religion* (new ed.; London: Lutterworth Press, 1943; original, 1934) esp. 69–155.

8. Notably in his *The Parables of the Kingdom* (London: Nisbet, 1935; rev. ed., New
York: Scribner's, 1961).

9. See the excellent, brief summary in Wilder, *Eschatology and Ethics*, 37–52; for more
extended treatments, see Gösta Lundström, *The Kingdom of God in the Teaching of*

World War II saw the emergence of the "consensus" position: the kingdom for Jesus was both present and future. Oscar Cullmann's timely and picturesque model employed World War II terminology: Jesus, in casting out demons and in other activities of his ministry, represented the decisive defeat of the powers of evil by the powers of the kingdom ("I saw Satan fall like lightning from heaven"—Lk 10:18; "If I by the Spirit of God drive out demons, then the kingdom of God has already come to you"—Mt 12:28/Lk 11:20), and this is D-Day (as was June 6, 1944). There remains, however, the "mop-up" operation, a period of continuing struggle until the final consummation of the sovereignty of God, and this is V-Day—Victory Day (the Allies did not "wrap up" the European war until May 8, 1945). Thus, Cullmann affirmed that "the hope of the final victory is so much the more vivid because of the unshakably firm conviction that the battle that decides the victory has already taken place."[10]

Whether Rudolf Bultmann's image of the future but imminent kingdom as already casting its light in the present fits this consensus may be a matter of judgment or interpretation, for he held a "consistent" eschatological view, essentially—though certainly not identically—the Weiss/Schweitzer position on the futurist nature of the kingdom in Jesus' view: conceived in apocalyptic terms, "the kingdom is imminent."[11] Yet, Bultmann could affirm that for Jesus, at the same time, "the Kingdom of God is beginning, is beginning now!"[12] Indeed, for Jesus "even now the turning point of the times is at hand, and the powers of the imminent Kingdom can already be discerned."[13] Thus, this image that the kingdom, "which, although it is entirely future, wholly determines the present,"[14] does fit the post-war consensus view, though one must be careful not to oversimplify Bultmann's highly complex and sophisticated conceptions of Jesus' understanding of the kingdom of God.[15]

Jesus: A History of Interpretation from the Last Decades of the Nineteenth Century to the Present Day (tr. J. Bulman; Edinburgh/London: Oliver and Boyd, 1963); Norman Perrin, *The Kingdom of God in the Teaching of Jesus* (Philadelphia: Westminster, 1963); George E. Ladd, *The Presence of the Future: The Eschatology of Biblical Realism* (Grand Rapids: Eerdmans, 1974) 3–42; Richard H. Hiers, *The Kingdom of God in the Synoptic Tradition* (Gainesville: University of Florida Press, 1970) 6–21.

10. *Christ and Time* (rev. ed.,), 87; see 71–72; 82–88.

11. On Jesus' expectation of the near-end, see Rudolf Bultmann, *Theology of the New Testament* (2 vols.; tr. K. Grobel; New York: Scribner's, 1951–55) 1:22–23. But that it is "not something which is to come in the course of time," see his *Jesus and the Word* (tr. L. P. Smith and E. H. Lantero; New York: Charles Scribner's Sons, 1958; original 1926) 51; cf. Perrin, *Kingdom of God*, 114–18.

12. *Jesus and the Word*, 30, though this is originally a 1926 work.

13. Ibid., 156; cf. Bultmann, *History and Eschatology* (Gifford Lectures, 1955; Edinburgh: University Press, 1957) 30: "The reign of God was immediately imminent, indeed already dawning in his exorcisms."

14. *Jesus and the Word*, 51.

15. See ibid., 27–56; 120–32; *Theology*, 1:4–11; 19–23; on Bultmann's entire view, see

Reginald H. Fuller, in his *The Mission and Achievement of Jesus* (1954), represents a third and similar "consensus" model, with his "proleptic" understanding of the kingdom in Jesus. For Fuller (like Bultmann), the kingdom is future though so very near that it is "operative in advance" in Jesus' ministry. The signs of the impending kingdom, such as the exorcisms, are so vivid that Jesus "speaks of it as though it had arrived already."[16]

The fullest statement of the "consensus" from this early period, however, is found in W. G. Kümmel. Prior to that discussion, it should be observed that German-language scholarship still dominated the early post-war period in this field (and in NT studies generally), under such prominent names as Bultmann, Cullmann, Jeremias, Bornkamm, Conzelmann, and, of course, Kümmel. British and American scholarship, if not slower in redeveloping after the war, was at least lagging in both creativity and influence.[17] Then in 1963 and 1964 three large-scale works on the kingdom of God appeared in English—two with the same title and the same publication date: *The Kingdom of God in the Teaching of Jesus* by Gösta Lundström and (under the same title) by Norman Perrin in 1963, and George E. Ladd's *Jesus and the Kingdom* in 1964.[18] Perrin followed this survey with his influential *Rediscovering the Teaching of Jesus* in 1967, which is devoted almost entirely to Jesus' view of the kingdom as present and future, and with *Jesus and the Language of the Kingdom*,[19] though Perrin's untimely death in 1976 precluded further contributions in

---

Perrin, *Kingdom of God*, 112–18; cf. Lundström, *Kingdom of God*, 150; also his critique (155) that "the Kingdom of God is never really represented as present in Jesus" by Bultmann.

16. *The Mission and Achievement of Jesus: An Examination of the Presuppositions of New Testament Theology* (SBT 1/12; London: SCM, 1954) 26.

17. C. H. Dodd, of course, continued his work, and R. H. Fuller has been mentioned above; in addition, Amos N. Wilder, C. J. Cadoux, A. M. Hunter, and Vincent Taylor, among others, stated in various ways the consensus position; and G. R. Beasley-Murray, T. F. Glasson, and J. A. T. Robinson, again in various ways, treated the parousia expectation of Jesus. See the summary and assessment in Perrin, *Kingdom of God*, 79–89; 130–47; 155–57.

18. Lundström's work appeared earlier in Swedish (1947); the English translation was published in Edinburgh by Oliver and Boyd (1963); Perrin's was published in Philadelphia by Westminster; and Ladd's in New York by Harper & Row. On all three volumes, see E. J. Epp, "Norman Perrin on the Kingdom of God," *Christology and a Modern Pilgrimage: A Discussion with Norman Perrin* (ed. H. D. Betz; Claremont, Calif.: New Testament Colloquium, 1971) 113–22; revised ed., Missoula: SBL and Scholars, 1974, 75–80.

19. *Rediscovering the Teaching of Jesus* (New York: Harper & Row, 1967; the preface indicates that the work was intended as an expansion of the conclusion to his *Kingdom of God*); *Jesus and the Language of the Kingdom: Symbol and Metaphor in New Testament Interpretation* (Philadelphia: Fortress, 1976); portions are reprinted in *The Kingdom of God* (ed. Bruce Chilton; Issues in Religion and Theology, 5; Philadelphia: Fortress; London: SPCK, 1984) 92–106.

this area from his unusually creative mind. Ladd followed his volume with a revised version in 1974 under the title, *The Presence of the Future*, and with his broader, full-scale work, *A Theology of the New Testament*, also in 1974,[20] as well as other studies. The works of Perrin, who studied under T. W. Manson and Joachim Jeremias, and of Ladd, whose doctoral studies at Harvard were carried out during and just after World War II, are in an interesting way representative of the post-war American scene in NT scholarship. Perrin, an Englishman teaching in the United States, represents the European-trained scholar writing in English who moved— rather dramatically—from the traditional views of his particular British-Germanic training toward the Bultmannian school, while Ladd, trained in the liberal traditions of a great American university, represents an enlightened evangelical conservatism that has compelled increasing consideration across this country, both in theological seminaries like Fuller (where Ladd taught) and in biblical scholarship more generally. Both have been influential, though largely within their respective circles— Perrin for his more radical reading of the NT texts and through his doctoral students at the University of Chicago, and Ladd for a solid exegetical scholarship with a traditional stamp, though one well-informed by the wider international scholarship of his day. We shall return to Ladd's work at a later point.

Werner Georg Kümmel

Though Cullmann—with his vivid D-Day/V-Day imagery—often receives first mention in the post-war "consensus" on the kingdom of God (witness our own discussion above!), it is Kümmel who rightly deserves first place in any post–World War II assessment. The methodical, meticulous, and comprehensive argumentation carried through his *Promise and Fulfilment* is a veritable *tour de force*—especially for its time. Kümmel begins his three-part argument by establishing the fact that Jesus held to "The Imminent Future of the Kingdom of God" (19–87). Surprisingly—at least from our present perspective—this is by far the longest portion of the volume, for Kümmel felt that Jesus' "announcement of the imminent end of the world as the central theme of his message" had been seriously eroded during the 1930s and 1940s, especially by Dodd's views, but also by other interpretations. He felt it necessary, therefore, to examine anew "the complete record of Jesus' preaching" (15–16). This is not really necessary in our time, so we may quickly summarize the crucial points in Kümmel's argument.

20. Both Grand Rapids: Eerdmans.

The entire section on the imminent expectation—indeed, the entire book—takes an exegetical approach, dealing with the relevant material text by text. In the course of the analysis, however, Kümmel interacts with virtually every relevant view, either in the body of the text or in the extensive footnotes. Kümmel begins with the meaning of ἐγγύς ("near") and ἐγγίζειν, ("to be at hand") for which the parable of the fig tree (Mk 13:28–29) is a key passage for his analysis (20–22). He concludes that "New Testament usage is therefore completely uniform as regards the temporal use of ἐγγύς: it denotes that an event will happen soon, by which it is meant or presumed that there will not be a long time to wait before it happens" (20). He then strengthens his point by showing that Jesus employed a number of "statements which presume or expressly mention not the nearness but the futurity of the kingdom of God" (25), such as "Thy kingdom come" (Mt 6:10/Lk 11:12); "There are some standing here who will not taste death before they see the kingdom of God come with power" (Mk 9:1—another key passage for Kümmel and against Dodd, who understands it as "until they have seen that the kingdom of God has come with power"); "I shall not drink again of the fruit of the vine until that day when I drink it new in the kingdom of God" (Mk 14:25); and "the kingdom of God is present in your midst" (Lk 17:21).

Kümmel continues his analysis of the synoptic material by examining Jesus' statements about the eschatological "day," as in the expressions "the day of judgment," "that day," or "the day of the Son of Man." He concludes that in these sayings about the eschatological day "the Kingdom of God is expected as a future reality in Jesus' message and that this is attested with such certainty that there are no possible grounds for denial" (43). The same point appears through analysis of passages that concern the "coming judgment," such as Mk 8:38—"that a man's attitude to Jesus in the present time is decisive for the sentence he will receive at the final judgment" (45; cf. 46–47)—as well as other passages. This interplay of present and future—of fulfillment and promise—emerges increasingly as Kümmel proceeds. For example, after treating additional texts stressing the future kingdom, he says: "In Jesus' thought the expectation in the future of the kingdom of God and of the salvation given with it is closely connected with the certainty that the promise has already in some way been fulfilled, although the futurity of the promised gift is not affected" (54). Finally, in this connection, Kümmel treats the *imminence* of the end-expectation in Jesus, employing an array of texts on watchfulness, alertness, and preparedness, but also those indicating that "this generation will not pass away before all these things take place" (54–64; Mk 13:30; cf. Mt 10:23). He claims now to have dealt with "all the relevant texts which show that Jesus proclaimed the proximity of the *eschaton* (within a limited time) or at least its coming *in the future*" (64).

It remains only for Kümmel to argue that Jesus expected an interval between his death and parousia, and here he takes on an array of scholars, including A. Schweitzer, O. Cullmann, J. Jeremias, E. Lohmeyer, and C. H. Dodd. His argument is complicated—with a number of perils—for Kümmel must claim that Jesus expected his (violent) death and his subsequent resurrection (see esp. 71–72) and then show that he envisioned an interval between them and the soon-coming parousia. For the latter, he employs the saying about fasting when the bridegroom is taken away (Mk 2:19–20 and parallels), the saying on not drinking wine until he drinks it new in the kingdom of God (Mk 14:25), and others, concluding that such an interval "is proved so conclusively . . . that it is impossible from any point of view to accept the idea recently advocated in various forms that Jesus expected his resurrection and parousia to be closely connected in time" (83). His overall conclusion, then, is that "all these texts confirm that Jesus did indeed count on a shorter or longer period between his death and the parousia, but that he equally certainly proclaimed the threatening approach of the Kingdom of God within his generation" (87).

Kümmel reinforces this temporally near expectation of the kingdom of God by Jesus in his 1964 article in the Bultmann *Festschrift* on "Eschatological Expectation in the Proclamation of Jesus."[21] His goal here is to defend and to buttress Bultmann's undocumented position that Jesus proclaims the "immediately impending irruption" of the reign of God. Kümmel carefully assesses the relevant texts and concludes that they show "unequivocally that Jesus counted on the nearness of the future reign of God, a future confined to his own generation" and that "it is also beyond dispute . . . that Jesus was mistaken in this expectation."[22]

Returning to *Promise and Fulfilment*, a brief section on "Eschatological Promise, Not Apocalyptic Instruction" (88–104) analyzes the "little apocalypse" of Mk 13 and parallels—which, for Kümmel, "cannot belong to the oldest Jesus tradition"—and makes the point that Jesus' eschatological message is not merely a piece of Jewish apocalyptic instruction: "Accordingly not apocalyptic instruction, but a mysterious yet unmistakable message from God who would operate in Jesus at the end of time would be the real meaning of Jesus' eschatological preaching" (108).

The critical second half of the "consensus" is presented concisely and decisively in the third chapter, "The Presence of the Kingdom of God" (105–40). Here Kümmel brings together Jesus' conviction of the imminent

21. W. G. Kümmel, "Die Naherwartung in der Verkündigung Jesu," *Zeit und Geschichte: Dankesgabe an Rudolf Bultmann zum 80. Geburtstag* (ed. Erich Dinkler; Tübingen: Mohr [Siebeck], 1964) 31–46; tr. as "Eschatological Expectation in the Proclamation of Jesus," in Chilton, *Kingdom of God*, 36–51.
22. Ibid., 44 (Eng. tr.).

coming of the kingdom and his insistence that his future eschatological consummation is "effective already in the present in that the *eschaton* showed itself effective in his own person"—"Jesus was the determining factor" (105). How is this relationship to be understood? First, Jesus is victorious over the demons and in this action "the kingdom of God has come upon you" (Mt 12:28/Lk 11:20)—that is, "Jesus' conviction shows itself clearly that the future Kingdom of God has already begun in his activity" and that "it is the person of Jesus whose activities provoke the presence of the eschatological consummation and who therefore stands at the center of the eschatological message" (107–8). When Jesus announces the *approach* of the kingdom of God, he makes this future "at the same time already now a present reality" (109), thus tying together the two convictions so firmly held by him: the future but imminent appearance of the kingdom and its presence here and now in his ministry. Other acts of Jesus (which Kümmel calls "Messianic acts") affirm the kingdom's presence, such as his entry into Jerusalem, the clearing of the temple, and the Last Supper; these "symbolic actions" show that Jesus viewed the coming consummation as already "breaking in on the present in his works" (121).

The presence of the kingdom is confirmed also by the famous passage, "From the days of John the Baptist until now the kingdom of heaven is being violently assaulted and violent men wish to rob it" (Mt 11:12, as Kümmel translates it, and Lk 16:16), a clear indication that the kingdom, since already it can be attacked, is something present. Another of Kümmel's forceful conclusions appears at this point:

> The fact that for Jesus the Kingdom of God is a present reality is thereby proved with as much certainty as the proclamation of its imminent entry. . . . Therefore the full meaning of the eschatological message of Jesus can be grasped only by understanding that the preaching both of the imminent future and of the presence of the Kingdom of God must be taken seriously. (124)

Not only has Kümmel established these two convictions of Jesus as historical realities (notwithstanding the inevitable questions that one might raise here and there), but he has succeeded in showing their logical and necessary connection in and for the message of Jesus. To appreciate this accomplishment fully, one must remember the bifurcation—the polarity—of views in pre–World War II times on this matter; on the one hand, the "consistent" eschatology position of Weiss and Schweitzer, and later of Martin Werner; and, on the other hand, the "realized" eschatology position of C. H. Dodd. Each of these schools sought to eliminate as authentic to Jesus the body of synoptic evidence that suggested the opposite position. Kümmel, like others in the "consensus"—though more thoroughly and consistently—sought ways not only to accredit both streams of early tradition, but also to show their necessity to, their inner connection with, and their consistency within the message of Jesus. This is Kümmel's significant achievement in his rich and compact study, *Promise and Fulfilment.*

It is precisely this relationship of the imminent and the present that occupies the concluding chapter on "The Meaning of Jesus' Eschatological Message." Kümmel's first concern is to show that these two conceptions existed side by side in Jesus' view, and not one before the other—as though there were some kind of inner, progressive development in Jesus' thought. A second concern is to reinforce his earlier demonstration that Jesus thought in temporal terms—a real "futurist" understanding of the imminent kingdom as opposed to views that attempt "to eliminate the concept of time itself from Jesus' eschatological message" (as in Dodd) or to reinterpret Jesus' contemporary language as a timeless message that in reality is concerned only with the present—again Dodd, but also Bultmann and Wilder (142–48). Not all will readily agree that the interpretation of Jesus' message can or should be thus restricted, but again Kümmel's conviction is strongly stated:

> Since the New Testament announces as its central message an act of God at a definite moment in history to be a final redemptive act, the mythological form of the conception cannot simply be detached from this central message: for it would mean that the New Testament message itself is abrogated if a timeless message concerning the present as the time of decision or concerning the spiritual nearness of God replaces the preaching of the eschatological future and the determination of the present by that future. . . . Therefore it is impossible to eliminate the concept of time and with it the "futurist" eschatology from the eschatological message of Jesus. (148; cf. 152–53)

Moreover, "it is perfectly clear," says Kümmel, "that this prediction of Jesus was not realized and it is therefore impossible to assert that Jesus was not mistaken about this"—for his message in this respect was "conditioned by time" (149). Yet, the essential meaning of Jesus' message does not depend on the end of the world as such, "but in the fact that the approaching eschatological consummation will allow the Kingdom of *that* God to become a reality who has already in the present allowed his redemptive purpose to be realized in Jesus" (154). "Promise and fulfilment are therefore inseparably united for Jesus and depend on each other; for the promise is made sure by the fulfilment that has already taken place in Jesus, and the fulfilment, being provisional and concealed, loses its quality as a σκάνδαλον ("offense") only through the knowledge of the promise yet to come" (155). That, for Kümmel, is the sum of it: "the reality of the Jesus in whom God brought his salvation to fulfilment in history and through whom God authoritatively promised his approaching consummation of history" (155).

Lundström, in his comprehensive survey of interpretations of the kingdom of God, quite correctly characterizes Kümmel as one "who keeps closely to the text and does not try to remove by critical procedure sayings which do not fit in with his ideas as a whole."[23] The same certainly could not be said of Schweitzer or Dodd in the pursuit of their radically different interpretations of Jesus and the kingdom, and if only for this reason Kümmel's thoughtful analysis in *Promise and Fulfilment* will commend itself to many for continued study.

The pervasive significance of the kingdom of God for understanding Jesus' *entire* proclamation and ministry comes out more fully, however, in Kümmel's *The Theology of the New Testament*.[24] Chapter 1 treats "The Proclamation of Jesus," beginning with "The Kingdom of God" in general, first in John the Baptist, then in Jesus (27–39); Kümmel next shows how Jesus' view of the kingdom shapes his understanding of God (39–46), of God's demand (46–58), and finally how it shapes Jesus' personal claim (58–85) and his suffering and death (85–95). This is followed by the second major portion of the work, "The Faith of the Primitive Community." Throughout all of his explication of Jesus' proclamation, it is the near and present kingdom of God that is constitutive for Jesus as Kümmel understands him.

This arrangement of material (proclamation of the kingdom, Jesus' view of God, of God's demand, and Jesus' personal claims, followed by the *kerygma* of the earliest church) is by no means original with Kümmel, for in more than general ways it is reminiscent not only of Bultmann's *Jesus and the Word* (original 1926) and the brief section on Jesus in his *Theology of the New Testament*, but also of G. Bornkamm's *Jesus of Nazareth* and H. Conzelmann's *An Outline of the Theology of the New Testament*.[25] But in works such as these, the constitutive character of the kingdom of God is by no means as obvious or as consistently maintained as it is in Kümmel. For example, though "eschatology" (conceived existentially, however) is crucial for Bultmann's understanding of Jesus and of the NT as a whole, Jesus' views of God and ethics are not directly connected with eschatology by Bultmann.[26] Nor does Conzelmann see an eschatological link between Jesus' view of the kingdom and his understanding of God or ethics: "In the context of the idea of God there is no thought of an imminent end to the world" or "the content of the demand— loving one's enemy, etc, is not derived from the nearness of the kingdom

23. Lundström, *The Kingdom of God*, 212; cf. Hiers, *Kingdom of God in the Synoptic Tradition*, 18–19.

24. *The Theology of the New Testament according to Its Major Witnesses: Jesus– Paul–John* (Nashville/New York: Abingdon, 1973; original 1969) 22–95.

25. Bornkamm (New York: Harper & Row, 1960; original 1956); Conzelmann (New York: Harper & Row, 1969; original 1967).

26. See the analysis in H. Conzelmann, *An Outline of the Theology of the New Testament* (tr. J. Bowden; New York/Evanston: Harper & Row, 1969; original, 1967) 125–26.

of God." Rather, for Conzelmann, "all parts of Jesus' teaching are stamped with an indirect christology."[27] In Bornkamm, to continue the examples identified above, there is a much closer relationship with the proclamation of the near and present kingdom. For example, in the context of showing Jesus' meaning of the "Render to Caesar . . . render to God" saying, Bornkamm can say that this "is to be considered, like all Jesus' teaching, in the light of the coming kingdom of God, which is already present in Jesus' words and deeds and has begun to realize itself."[28] Or, in discussing the idea of reward, he says that it "has now been completely absorbed into the message of the coming kingdom of God which is dawning now."[29] This connection is less obvious in Bornkamm's consideration of "Law" and "Love," yet to some degree the kingdom of God informs his entire analysis.

This is also the approach of Kümmel in his *Theology of the New Testament*, but carried farther (even if not entirely in the same direction), for Jesus' proclamation of the near and present kingdom affects his understanding of everything he proclaimed, including law and love. As far as Torah was concerned, "to those Jews who, believing, saw in Jesus the soon-to-come kingdom of God as having already dawned, *Jesus'* demand appeared as an 'ethic of the time of salvation,' in which God's will was finally and authoritatively proclaimed" (53). As to love, "the response to the encounter with God in Jesus and to the promise of the kingdom of God can only be love for God which is actualized in love for one's neighbor" (55). And in this manner Kümmel's analysis of Jesus' proclamation proceeds, but with a more direct relationship between the kingdom and the various areas of Jesus' teaching than the other representative scholars of the time reveal. This is exemplified in his discussions of Jesus' view of God as judge, of God as Father and God acting in the present, of repentance, of ethics generally, of reward and punishment, as well as in Jesus' personal claim and his suffering and death (see ch. 1, 22–95). This consistency will come as no surprise, however, to any who have bothered to read Kümmel's preface to *Promise and Fulfilment*, where he states his conviction that

> It is only against the background of Jesus' preaching concerning the Kingdom of God correctly understood that the right answers can be given to the questions about the significance of the person of Jesus in the formation of primitive Christian thought . . . , and without a clear insight into the *historical* reality of Jesus' eschatological message no reliable results can be obtained. (16)

27. Ibid., 124–27.
28. Günther Bornkamm, *Jesus of Nazareth* (tr. I. and F. McLuskey with J. M. Robinson; New York: Harper & Row, 1960; original, 1956) 123.
29. Ibid., 141.

Most—though not all—will agree with this statement of method, and many—though certainly not all—will agree with the general lines of Kümmel's analysis of Jesus' eschatological message as presented both in *Promise and Fulfilment* and in his *Theology of the New Testament*. Regardless of the degree of agreement, NT scholarship owes a large debt to Kümmel for his impressive effort and its important and lasting result.

George Eldon Ladd

Ladd represents a similarly moderating interpretation of Jesus' understanding of the kingdom of God. It is of interest that Lundström placed Kümmel in the category of "Bible Realism" (along with J. Jeremias, O. Cullmann, and others); if Ladd's work had appeared prior to Lundström's, certainly he would have been placed in the same category.[30] Indeed, Ladd's *Jesus and the Kingdom* (1964) carried the subtitle, *The Eschatology of Biblical Realism*, and, when it was revised and updated in 1974 as *The Presence of the Future*, this same subtitle was retained. This work and his large 1974 work, *A Theology of the New Testament* (which draws a great deal of its material on the kingdom from *The Presence of the Future*), constitute Ladd's final, mature statements on the issue, though the topic appeared often in his other writings, especially in his first book, *Crucial Questions about the Kingdom of God* (1952).[31] This first publication, which set the stage for the career-long attention to and involvement with the theme of the "kingdom of God," was actually prompted by and targeted at a parochial dispute about the kingdom in various premillennial views in ultra-conservative Christianity. In a rare autobiographical reference later, Ladd alluded to this controversial and formative era to which he attributed his life-long interest in this "central theme in the Synoptic Gospels," the kingdom of God. It originated, he said, during his theological study as an undergraduate when "no available interpretation of the Kingdom of God seemed to square with the

30. Lundström, *The Kingdom of God*, x; 201–31; Lundström's book first appeared in Swedish in 1947, and the English translation, with a lengthy "Postscript," appeared in 1963, the year before Ladd's *Jesus and the Kingdom* was first published.

31. G. E. Ladd, *Jesus and the Kingdom: The Eschatology of Biblical Realsim* (New York: Harper & Row, 1964); *The Presence of the Future: The Eschatology of Biblical Realism* (Grand Rapids: Eerdmans, 1974); *A Theology of the New Testament* (Grand Rapids: Eerdmans, 1974); *Crucial Questions about the Kingdom of God* (Grand Rapids: Eerdmans, 1952). See the bibliography of Ladd's work up through 1978 in *Unity and Diversity in New Testament Theology: Essays in Honor of George E. Ladd* (ed. R. A. Guelich; Grand Rapids: Eerdmans, 1978) 214–17. Since several chapters in *Theology* and *Presence* are similar if not identical, our references will be primarily to the latter, since that is Ladd's more detailed treatment of the subject.

biblical data."[32] Those, like the present author, who studied with Ladd in the earliest years of his career, felt both the centrality that he gave to the kingdom of God in his explication of NT biblical theology, and also the infectious enthusiasm and deep conviction with which he pursued the issue. The interaction no longer, however, was only with "premillennial dispensationalists," but with writers in the mainstream of international scholarship, primarily (in the early 1950s) with Dodd, Cullmann, Bultmann, and Wilder—scholars who figured so largely, as we have seen, in Kümmel's *Promise and Fulfilment*. Ladd was determined that he and his students would move in that same mainstream and would somehow affect the course of modern scholarly discussion on this and similar topics. His determination has not gone unfulfilled, though it is fair to say, I think, that Ladd's work did not itself achieve the place or have the impact that he had hoped,[33] for its greatest influence was and continues to be within the circles of what should be called enlightened, evangelical Christian scholarship, though certainly his impact in those circles has been worldwide, particularly in Great Britain and on the Continent.

Where does Ladd begin in his view of the kingdom of God? With a definition of the kingdom and with the OT promise. For Ladd—as modern scholarship discovered in the days of Gustaf Dalman and Johannes Weiss—"The Kingdom is God's kingly rule which [as Ladd puts it] has two moments: a fulfillment of the Old Testament promises in the historical mission of Jesus and a consummation at the end of the age, inaugurating the Age to Come" (*Theology*, 60).

> The Day of the Lord for the prophets was *both* the immediate act of God expected in history and the ultimate eschatological visitation. The prophets did not usually distinguish between these two aspects of the Day of the Lord, for it is the same God who would act. . . . God *did* act. The Day of the Lord *did* come; and yet, the Day of the Lord continued to be an eschatological event in the future. This tension between the immediate and the ultimate future, between history and eschatology, stands at the heart of the ethical concern of the prophetic perspective. For the important thing is not what is going to happen and when it will happen, but the will of God, who is Lord of both the far and the near future, for his people in the present. (*Presence*, 74–75).

For Ladd, apocalyptic eschatology plays little role in this background of promise, for at least three reasons. First, apocalyptic has replaced "the living word of the Lord" in the prophets with mere "revelations and visions" (*Presence*, 80); second, it has "lost this tension between history and eschatology," for in apocalyptic "God is no longer redemptively

---

32. G. E. Ladd, *The Pattern of New Testament Truth* (Grand Rapids: Eerdmans, 1968) 47. For a summary of the "dispensationalist" controversy, see his *Theology*, 60.

33. Notice, e.g., one of the latest summaries of work on our topic, Chilton, *Kingdom of God*, where Chilton, in his introduction, refers to the 1963 volumes by Perrin and Lundström (see nn. 9 and 18, above) but does not even mention Ladd's 1964 volume on the same subject.

active in the present" (93–94); and third, apocalyptic became ethically passive, with eschatology merely "a guarantee of ultimate salvation, not an ethical message to bring God's people face to face with the will of God" (99; 101).

John the Baptist forms the final segment of Jesus' background, for in him "the prophetic Spirit was once more active in Israel," with a message that God was about to act—the kingdom of God was at hand (106–7). When Jesus appears with his message, there is a difference: "He asserted that this visitation was in actual progress, that God was already visiting his people. The hope of the prophets was being fulfilled" (111).

With this as background, Ladd is ready to describe Jesus' view of the kingdom of God, and he does so with comprehensiveness and care. The main lines of interpretation, however, are not unexpected. His central thesis is that

> The Kingdom of God is the redemptive reign of God dynamically active to establish his rule among men, and that this Kingdom, which will appear as an apocalyptic act at the end of the age, has already come into human history in the person and mission of Jesus to overcome evil, to deliver men from its power, and to bring them into the blessings of God's reign. The Kingdom of God involves two great moments: fulfillment within history, and consummation at the end of history. (*Presence*, 218)

This reign of God is "not merely in the human heart but dynamically active in the person of Jesus and in human history," and this, says Ladd, makes it possible to understand "how the Kingdom of God can be present and future, inward and outward, spiritual and apocalyptic" (42)—a tall order!

Ladd focuses first on the fulfillment of prophetic hopes in the message and action of Jesus, a theme that occurs "again and again" in the Gospels and sets Jesus apart from Judaism. He briefly discusses texts like Lk 4:18–19; 4:21; Mk 2:19; Lk 10:23–24/Mt 13:16–17; and Mt 11:4–5. At the same time, he stresses the dualism of the two ages, whose terminology appears "in every stratum of the Gospel tradition except Q" (*Presence*, 115), and highlights some of the evidence indicating that for Jesus there was a future "age to come." This—in juxtaposition with the fulfillment passages—poses the question, "How can the Kingdom of God be both future and present?" Ladd believes that the solution lies in the "dynamic meaning" of the kingdom of God (121), that is, understanding it as the "reign" or "rule" of God (as opposed to "realm"). He pursues this matter in three chapters. In "The Kingdom: Reign or Realm?" he tackles the problem in general and concludes that the kingdom is not an "eschatological realm" (as seems to be Kümmel's view; *Presence*, 127–30), nor "merely an abstract concept that God is the eternal King and rules over all"—though it is that—but it is the dynamic presence of his reign, for "it means that God is no longer waiting for men to submit to his reign but has taken the initiative and has invaded history in a new and unexpected way." The kingdom is "a dynamic concept of the acting God" (144).

The focus of the chapter on "The Kingdom Present as Dynamic Power" is Mt 12:28: "If it is by the Spirit of God that I cast out demons, then the kingdom of God has come upon you." Ladd exegetes this passage to show that God's dynamic reign invades the present age "without transforming it into the age to come" (149), and supports this result with other sayings from Jesus' ministry. Among these are Lk 10:18, about Jesus seeing Satan falling like lightning from heaven (a vision Ladd interprets as figurative, 156); and Mt 11:12, about the kingdom that "exercises its force/makes it way powerfully" since the days of John the Baptist—which reflects a dynamic understanding of kingdom (159–64). The next chapter, "The Kingdom Present as Divine Activity," is designed to support further the dynamic concept of the kingdom, now from what Jesus affirms about God. The assumption is that "if the Kingdom is the rule of God, then every aspect of the Kingdom must be derived from the character and action of God," and the thesis is that "the presence of the Kingdom is to be understood from the nature of God's present activity; and the future of the Kingdom is the redemptive manifestation of his kingly rule at the end of the age" (171). The main point is that Jesus proclaims "the reality of God as *seeking* love"—not waiting for the lost, but seeking out and also inviting the sinner (174). The parables of Lk 15 are employed to document the point, as well as other texts. God is seen also as Father (the kingdom of God and the fatherhood of God are inseparable, 178) and as Judge (the meaning of the kingdom is both salvation and judgment, 185). This leads to the conclusion that "the Kingdom is altogether God's deed and not man's work"; it is neither the ideal good, nor inevitable progress, nor history, nor merely God working in history, but it is "God's supernatural breaking into history in the person of Jesus. The coming of the kingdom into history as well as its eschatological consummation is miracle—God's deed" (188–89). That is Ladd's concept of the "dynamic" kingdom.

At this point, however, Ladd's exposition of the kingdom in Jesus' teaching takes a surprising turn, for under "The Kingdom Present as the New Age of Salvation" he argues that, while the dynamic meaning of "Kingdom" is "the truly distinctive element in Jesus' teaching," a number of uses of "Kingdom" portray "an eschatological realm into which men enter" and also "a realm of salvation which is present" (195–96). Here Mt 11:11–13 is again crucial, and the reference to those "in the kingdom of heaven" (v 11) shows that, for Jesus, a new era has begun since the days of John the Baptist. What Ladd means by this is that the dynamic kingly rule of God, by its action in history, has created "a new realm of blessing into which men may [now] enter. This too is called the Kingdom of God" (201–2). He spells out the content of this present realm in terms of the benefits of "messianic salvation," including God's gifts to his people (as in the Beatitudes), salvation proper (resurrection life, restoration of communion with God), physical healing, forgiveness, and righteousness: "Jesus did not promise the forgiveness of sins; he bestowed it. . . . He did not merely promise vindication in the day of judgment; he bestowed upon them a present righteousness" (205–17). So it is "both/and" for Ladd: "God's Kingdom is first of all his kingly rule, his sovereign redeeming activity, and secondarily the realm of blessing inaugurated by the divine act."[34] But it is also—as a third point—a real, eschatological/apocalyptic event to come in the temporal future, for which Ladd prefers the term, "eschatological consummation," though he used the terms "apocalyptic" and "age to come" as well.

Both the manner and the time of the occurrence of this eschatological consummation pose problems for Ladd, particularly the passages on imminence and specifically Mk 13:30: "This generation will not pass away before all these things take place." He does not shrink, however, from dealing with the problem in its most acute form, the Olivet Discourse (= the "little apocalypse" of Mk 13 and parallels—though Ladd does not wish to call it "apocalyptic," 316), and the other relevant texts. Appealing—as he has throughout his work—to the claim that Jesus stands closer to the prophets than to the apocalypticists (e.g., *Presence*, 146–47; 173; 315–20; 324–26), he argues (as did Kümmel) that Jesus was not interested in apocalyptic instruction and, therefore, that "Jesus described the consummation in semipoetical language and parabolic pictures which are not meant to be taken literally, but which represent eschatological events and an order of existence that transcend present historical experience" (317). "We call it 'semipoetical,'" Ladd says, "for while the language is poetical, it designates real future events of cosmic proportions, indescribable though they be."[35]

The question of imminence—indeed, of the expectation of the appearance of the final event in Jesus' own time—is Ladd's final major topic in *The Presence of the Future*. Mark 9:1 ("There are some standing here who will not taste death before they see the kingdom of God come with power") is explained by saying that God did act in Jesus and this was an anticipation of the eschatological consummation, but that the kingdom "did not come without remainder; the consummation still lay in the indeterminate future. The substance of Jesus' saying cannot be reduced to a simple calendric statement" (323). Ladd acknowledges that it is widely believed—since Schweitzer—that Jesus was in error about the time of the

34. Ladd, *Pattern of New Testament Truth*, 53.
35. Ibid.

eschatological consummation, but such an admission is not acceptable to Ladd. Strong, defensive statements appear:

> If, as is widely held today, Jesus was in error in the *main emphasis* of his message, if he was mistaken as to the *central purposes* of his mission—to proclaim and to prepare men for an imminent end of the world—it is difficult to understand how the other elements in his religious message remain trustworthy . . . [or] how the present signs and powers of the future Kingdom can retain any validity or worth. They would be signs produced by a delusion and therefore must themselves be illusory. To imagine that one sees on the horizon the rosy blush of the breaking dawn and in its faint light sets out upon a journey only to wander in the darkness of midnight is utter deception. (*Presence*, 125)

So the Olivet Discourse and other texts, according to Ladd, show that Jesus interweaved the historical and the eschatological in a way that makes it difficult to say where one leaves off and the other begins. "The historical is described in terms of the eschatological and the eschatological in terms of the historical"—something perhaps insoluble for the modern exegete, "but it can be understood and appreciated even if the texts cannot be dissected into neat chronological patterns" (323–24). History and eschatology are held together in Jesus by the dynamic prophetic tension in which "the very coming of the apocalyptic Kingdom is made dependent upon what God is doing in history through the mission and death of Jesus" (325). This, says Ladd, is where the Gospels leave us: "anticipating an imminent end and yet unable to date its coming. Logically this may appear contradictory, but it is a tension with an ethical purpose—to make date-setting impossible and therefore to demand constant readiness" (328).

Much more could be said of Ladd's attempt to encompass a great portion of biblical theology and, indeed, of Christian theology under the rubric, kingdom of God, as seen, for instance, in his chapters on the church and ethics (both in *Presence* and in *Theology*). This tendency toward comprehensiveness and wide application of the kingdom of God concept perhaps is both Ladd's strength and his weakness, for it shows how important "kingdom of God" is in Jesus and the Synoptic Gospels, but it also raises questions as to whether exegesis on occasion has too easily been pressed into the service of theology or of a specific ideology.[36]

The reader of *The Presence of the Future* will be struck both by its thoroughness and by a measure of repetitiousness. The latter reinforces Ladd's points, and no one will miss them, even should the volume be opened at several random places. One may find at the beginning of two chapters, for example, a statement of the thesis of the book (218; 307) and innumerable summaries of the dynamic concept of the kingdom through-

---

36. See the review of *Presence* by Norman Perrin, "Against the Stream," *Int* 19 (1965) 228–31; but also the lengthy reply by Ladd in his *Pattern of New Testament Truth* 57–63.

out the volume. This is all to the good and never are Ladd's points unclear or his meaning obscure, though one misses, I suspect, the compactness of Kümmel's analysis. What one also misses in some portions of Ladd's exposition is the critical stance, for there is, overall, an easy acceptance of the synoptic material pretty much at face value. Of course, Ladd—as described earlier—interacts with the leading scholars, past and contemporary, who are relevant to the subject, and battles with them over the interpretation of synoptic passages, but basic questions of the historicity or tradition-history or redaction of the gospel material (though not entirely absent) are infrequent. Then too, on occasion views are rejected "because they do not square with the biblical data,"[37] which would seem to be a form of begging the question. Yet, notwithstanding these and other criticisms, Ladd's work is a significant achievement, and one that has been overlooked by many, and that is their loss.

Conclusion

We conclude with a significant and interesting point of comparison between Kümmel and Ladd. Whereas Kümmel saw Jesus' teaching on the kingdom of God as encompassing *Promise* and *Fulfillment*, Ladd ends with a threefold statement of the matter: *Promise, Fulfillment*, and *Consummation*: "The Old Testament *promise* of the coming of the Kingdom, *fulfillment* of the promise of the Kingdom in history in the person, words, and deeds of Jesus, *consummation* of the promise at the end of history—this is the basic structure of the theology of the Synoptic Gospels."[38] Space does not allow us nor is this the place to pass judgment on these—or other—options, but certainly the analyses of the kingdom of God in the teaching of Jesus by both Kümmel and Ladd will and must be consulted in the continuing study of this important concept.

37. *Pattern of New Testament Truth*, 60.
38. Ibid., 54.

4 Linguistic Approaches to the Kingdom: Amos Wilder and Norman Perrin

W. Emory Elmore

Associate Professor of Philosophy/Religion
The School of the Ozarks

TWO SCHOLARS HAVE LED THE WAY to a new appreciation of linguistics for understanding the kingdom of God: Amos N. Wilder and Norman R. Perrin—Wilder through his book, *Early Christian Rhetoric: The Language of the Gospel*, and Perrin through his book, *Jesus and the Language of the Kingdom*. This chapter will review these works, focusing on the thoughts in the two books being reviewed—not comparing extensively with other scholars or presenting their reviews of other scholars' works. Wilder's book will be reviewed first; and then moving into Perrin's book, focusing on chapter 2, sections A and B, one can see the importance of Wilder for Perrin's work as well as the significant contribution of each author to the modern study of the kingdom of God.

Scholarship which preceded Amos Wilder and Norman Perrin,[1] beginning with Johannes Weiss,[2] who initiated the discussion in 1892, had essentially understood the kingdom of God as a concept. Weiss and Albert Schweitzer,[3] whose writings appeared only a few years later, saw Jesus proclaiming the kingdom of God as an apocalyptic concept in which the kingdom was imminent. Rudolph Bultmann,[4] following his teacher, Weiss, also saw the kingdom of God conceptually and in apocalyptic terms but attempted to bridge the gulf between the NT and subsequent

---

1. This approach included Norman Perrin himself as late as 1974. *The New Testament: An Introduction* (New York: Harcourt, Brace Jovanovich, 1974) 67.

2. Johannes Weiss, *Jesus' Proclamation of the Kingdom of God* (Philadelphia: Fortress, 1971).

3. Albert Schweitzer, *The Quest of the Historical Jesus* (London: Black, 1911).

4. Rudolph Bultmann, *Jesus and the Word* (trans. by L. P. Smith and E. H. Landers; New York: Charles Scribner's Sons, 1934).

generations by recasting the mythological language of the kingdom (but not demonstrating any real concern for the literary form) in order to get at the text's understanding and claims on human existence. Significant, however, in arguing against the view of a future kingdom was C. H. Dodd,[5] who proposed that Jesus proclaimed a kingdom that was present (had already come) in his ministry, a "realized eschatology." After Dodd, scholars generally agreed that in Jesus' teaching concerning the kingdom of God there was both a present and a future aspect. W. G. Kümmel[6] and G. E. Ladd[7] came to the forefront among many making an important contribution here.

From this heritage Amos Wilder and Norman Perrin have opened a new door to the study of the kingdom of God by treating gospel (Wilder) and kingdom (Perrin) from a wholly different perspective: language—and in particular, symbol. Wilder, as a NT scholar, literary critic, and poet, has greatly influenced American scholars. Indeed, Norman Perrin expressed his indebtedness to Wilder, particularly for "insights from the world of literary creativity and of literary criticism."[8] In *Early Christian Rhetoric: The Language of the Gospel*,[9] Wilder's varied background is apparent as he convincingly demonstrates how inseparable are the form and substance of the gospel. In his review of that book Holt Graham says concerning creative power in the use of language, "It is to the examination of this evidence that Amos Wilder brings a rare capacity for analysis and summary, wide-ranging scholarship and profound understanding of literature."[10] Wilder's examination of various NT modes and genres (dialogue, story, parable, poem, and finally image, symbol, and myth) has enabled students in the wide range of NT studies to discover, as they never have before, that the form of communicating the gospel is absolutely indispensable to understanding the message being communicated.

It is important to emphasize Wilder's penetrating insights into the overall language of the gospel because of how significantly they opened the way specifically to new vistas in the study of the kingdom of God whose content can be understood fully only within its literary mode. Norman Perrin, in particular, while attempting to revise his work on the kingdom,

5. C. H. Dodd, *The Parables of the Kingdom* (New York: Charles Scribner's Sons, 1935).

6. W. G. Kümmel, *Promise and Fulfilment* (Naperville, Ill.: Allenson, 1957).

7. G. E. Ladd, *The Presence of the Future*, rev. ed. of *Jesus and the Kingdom* (Grand Rapids: Eerdmans, 1974).

8. Norman Perrin, *Jesus and the Language of the Kingdom* (Philadelphia: Fortress, 1976) 128.

9. Amos Wilder, *Early Christian Rhetoric: The Language of the Gospel* (Cambridge, Mass.: Harvard University, 1971).

10. Holt H. Graham, review of *Early Christian Rhetoric: The Language of the Gospel* by Amos Wilder, *ATR* 48 (Jan., 1966) 90.

became aware that his thinking had developed so rapidly under the influence of Amos Wilder that he could not simply revise; he had to rewrite. The result is *Jesus and the Language of the Kingdom.*[11]

Amos N. Wilder

As background for his study, Wilder reviews earlier approaches which have left a gulf between studying the Bible strictly either as literature or religion. However, new contributors, especially William Beardslee,[12] have expressed concern for linking form and content in literary works. Wilder sees important contributions here from existentialism—that "'Meaning' is related not to the literary work as object, even when taken as a whole, but to that ultimate Real or Being itself which discloses itself in the work, in the language event . . . that unites text and reader, past and present."[13] Wilder accepts this view of language but with reservations, because he sees in it an attempt "to resolve all complexities by some too easy formula for ultimacy" at the expense of short-changing rich and varied structures of religious symbolic elements.[14] Indeed, the symbol is the key to the hermeneutics of the gospel (and thereby, of course, the kingdom).

In discussing the novelty of early Christian utterance Wilder begins with the oral stage. It was promised "that in the day of salvation God's people would speak with new tongues and sing a new song, and that the mouth of the dumb would be opened."[15] This resultant creativity also brought new literary forms, such as the "gospel." The rhetoric of the NT is distinctive, not because it is "holy language," as reviewer Thomas Olbricht[16] emphasizes, but because the message and the task of the communicator are different. One outstanding feature of the earliest Christian speech is that it was extemporaneous, dynamic, and directed to the occasion, not developed for a future time. Seen in the context of kingdom studies, this observation challenges an apocalyptic and conceptual approach to understanding the kingdom of God.

Wilder notes four distinct literary types in the NT that were different from existing Greek literary forms, which were written for a wide audience with a definite artistic purpose in mind. These four are gospel, acts,

11. Perrin, *Jesus*, xi.
12. William Beardslee, *Literary Criticism of the New Testament* (Philadelphia: Fortress, 1970).
13. Wilder, *Early*, xxvii-ix.
14. Ibid., xxix. Wilder elaborates further in his final chapter, 118–28.
15. Ibid., 5.
16. Thomas Olbricht, review of *Early Christian Rhetoric: The Language of the Gospel* by Amos Wilder, *Quarterly Journal of Speech*, 51 (Oct., 1965) 348.

letters, and apocalypse. He ventures into a highly debated area and asserts "Gospel" to be "the only wholly new genre"; it is good news of a "total and ultimate kind, and not only recited but effectively and dynamically demonstrated."[17] Applied to good news of the kingdom, one can see a clear impact which imagery itself produced upon Jesus' audience.

Wilder moves on to discover older Christian speech behind the NT writings. One genre is story. Here Wilder helpfully declares, "The life of a Christian is not like a dream shot through with visions and illuminations, but a pilgrimage, a race, in short, a history. The new Christian speech inevitably took the form of story."[18] When Wilder significantly observes that the narrative mode in Scripture is such that the hearer or reader finds himself in the middle of the action, one easily notes the impact of the language of the kingdom. There are two story types: Jesus' *own* parables, which the author discusses later, and anecdotes *about* Jesus. An anecdote, like the cure of Bartimaeus, an example of the gospel in miniature, is called a paradigm because it goes beyond physical healing to the heart of the gospel—deliverance for all people whether blind or not. In this expected messianic activity itself one, therefore, sees an unmistakable symbol of the kingdom.

From anecdotes *about* Jesus, Wilder turns to the parables *of* Jesus, emphasizing that they were told not merely to hold attention but were evoked by the nature of the gospel itself, making them essential to a message being communicated, like the message of the kingdom. There are varieties of story parables; one type is the example story, a straight narrative, such as the parable of the Rich Fool, ending with an application. Another type, such as the parable of the Lost Sheep, is the extended image, a narrative which reveals. This is a point which is particularly important for Perrin.[19] Enlisting the support of Günther Bornkamm, Wilder urges that "It is this revelatory character of Jesus' parables which is to be stressed. 'The parables are the preaching itself.'"[20] This quality is apparent particularly in parables of the kingdom in which Jesus communicates his own vision and faith. Wilder sees this kind of parable as a metaphor in which "we have an image with a certain shock to the imagination which directly conveys vision of what is signified."[21]

Another literary aspect of concern to Wilder is that these parables are "so human and realistic," even "secular," in that the person, scenes, and actions are not usually "religious."[22] Parables reveal something very

17. Wilder, *Early*, 28–29.
18. Ibid., 56–57.
19. Perrin, *Jesus*, 128.
20. As cited in Wilder, *Early*, 72 and n. 1; G. Bornkamm, *Jesus of Nazareth* (tr. I. and F. McLuskey, with J. M. Robinson; New York: Harper & Row, 1960) 69.
21. Ibid.
22. Ibid., 73.

important about Jesus and the gospel: they challenge people to face life by calling forth memories of everyday experiences. There is no "other-worldly" approach here. Also, Jesus' parables are very different from the stories of other societies and religions which are told for their lessons. The rabbis, for example, can use a parable to illustrate a variety of subjects. The uniqueness of Jesus' parables is related to the urgency of the kingdom.

Wilder gives special attention to the parables of the kingdom found in Mk 4 and Mt 13. First, he discusses his criteria for determining a parable's authenticity. One criterion is the tight form of organic unity and coherence which helps guarantee them against change. Another criterion is the characteristics which the parables share with other forms of Jesus' speech. In this connection Wilder makes a statement that is important both in connection with understanding the parable and in the link with the symbol of the kingdom of God found in other forms of speech. He says that in the parables we have action-images, extended metaphors. He adds that a true metaphor is a "bearer of the reality to which it refers," and the hearer participates in it. Jesus' speech had "the character not of instruction but of compelling imagination, of spell, of mythical shock and transformation."[23] It is in these statements that one can see the profound effect of Wilder upon Perrin: "These words are the essential clue to understanding both the symbolic language of the Kingdom sayings and the metaphorical language of the parables on the lips of Jesus."[24]

Wilder returns to the Markan parables of the Sower, the Seed Growing by Itself and the Mustard Seed. First, Wilder contends that in the parable of the Sower Jesus was not simply using the farmer as an example to guide his followers to trust God for a good outcome, even though they were experiencing losses and disappointments in proclaiming the kingdom. This illustration does not always succeed, because the farmer sometimes has a poor harvest. Consequently, the disciples would not thereby have the assurances they needed. Wilder, likewise, dismisses as banal similar interpretations of the other two parables. Wilder is saying that these parables do not encourage by offering a sermonic illustration from nature. Their effectiveness is in imparting to the disciples Jesus' own situation, "his own vision by the power of metaphor."[25] Likewise, citing the Matthean twin parables of the Hidden Treasure and the Pearl of Great Price, Wilder follows Joachim Jeremias[26] and moves away from interpreting as significant either the treasure's value or the sacrifice made

23. Ibid., 84.
24. Perrin, Jesus, 130.
25. Wilder, Early, 85.
26. Joachim Jeremias, The Parables of Jesus, 2d ed. rev. (New York: Charles Scribner's Sons, 1972) 200–201.

for the pearl; instead he underscores the note of joy in the discovery, "the sense of the power and grace of God at work and the wonder and promise of the outcome."[27] Therefore, it is the combination of the power of metaphor and the power of Jesus' own faith that give the parables such a dynamic impact.

What place does poetry have in this early Christian rhetoric? The biblical poetry has its special character of being "ordered about the story of the Lord's deliverances, and these are always at least in the background of the recitations and songs of the New Testament."[28] The full symbolism of poetry, exclaiming God's activity as king, provides convincing evidence against understanding the kingdom of God as a concept. Wilder observes an interesting feature of NT poetry on its Jewish side: its ultimate origins in Canaanite and Mesopotamian prototypes, even hymns to their gods. Thus, he sees in Christian songs an implied harmony with ancient humanity. Wilder may not be convincing enough here, but out of his observation has come an additional reason to approach the language of the kingdom from a broad perspective. "The idiom of Christian poetry and song should not be that of the peculiar language of Zion. . . . Faith grows bright because it is fed by the fuel of generic mortal experience."[29]

In his final chapter, "Image, Symbol, Myth," Wilder considers more fully an aspect of speech which he has only indirectly recognized—its metaphorical and symbolic character. In the NT there is an abundance of pictorial imagery telling the good news about the kingdom. These include spiritual beings presented figuratively, mythological statements given to events and divine acts, and numerous dramatizations concerning Christ. If we rightly appreciate the mythological character of much of the NT, we will not be tempted to literalize it. Wilder appreciates Bultmann for his efforts to retain the impact of the myth by translating it into other categories. "Faith should not be confused with acceptance of pictures of God's dealings taken as blueprints for beliefs, let alone credulity."[30] However, Harvey McArthur notes, "Wilder protests against the reduction of the Christian message which he feels is characteristic of the Bultmann position."[31] Wilder is convinced that demythologizing falls short, failing to do justice to the message within the medium, the imagery. He asks, "Should we not recognize that the symbol for all its imaginative and ancient character, yet tells us something Christian not only about our-

27. Wilder, Early, 86.
28. Ibid., 90–91.
29. Ibid., 97.
30. Ibid., 125.
31. Harvey K. McArthur, review of Early Christian Rhetoric: The Language of The Gospel by Amos Wilder, Int 18 (Oct., 1964) 480. A similar observation is made by Jules L. Moreau, review of Early Christian Rhetoric: The Language of the Gospel by Amos Wilder, JBL 84 (1965) 88.

selves but also about the visible world of time and space and about the work of God in a real world process?"[32] Wilder concludes that those who confine all meaning to an existentialist dimension simply misunderstand the "truth-aspect of Christian imagery and myth."[33] It is this kind of creative reassessment that has been so significant in turning the attention of scholars, like Perrin, to the language of the gospel generally and to the language of the kingdom specifically. Wilder closes his book with final reflections on the gospel as representing a "new outburst" in all aspects of language, leaving us with a metaphor which underscores his contribution to NT hermeneutics.

Norman R. Perrin

Norman Perrin described his career as an "academic pilgrimage." In 1974 he wrote,

> I began with Life of Jesus research and that led me to the Son of Man and New Testament Christology. The Son of Man is most prominent in the Gospel of Mark and that fact led me to Markan and redaction criticism. In its turn redaction criticism led me to literary criticism and hermeneutics, the most recent phases of my interest and concerns.[34]

Welton Seal, Jr., in his response to this pilgrimage, appropriately commented, "Perrin repeatedly challenged his peers with bold positions on methodology and interpretation."[35] Similarly Eldon Epp concluded, "Both the rapid progression in his development and his 'openness for the future' in scholarship constitute a challenge and an inspiration to every working scholar."[36]

In *Jesus and the Language of the Kingdom* written in the final phase of his pilgrimage, with acknowledged thanks to the seminal work of Amos Wilder, especially in regard to symbols and myths, Norman Perrin breaks new ground. First, he understands the kingdom not as a concept but as a *symbol* which evokes a *myth*[37] of God's kingship; and second, he views

32. Wilder, *Early*, 125.
33. Ibid., 126.
34. Norman Perrin, *A Modern Pilgrimage in New Testament Christology* (Philadelphia: Fortress, 1974) 1.
35. Welton O. Seal, Jr., "Norman Perrin and His 'School': Retracing a Pilgrimage," *JSNT* (Feb., 1984) 87.
36. Hans Dieter Betz., ed., *Christology and a Modern Pilgrimage: A Discussion with Norman Perrin*, rev. ed. (Missoula: SBL and Scholars, 1974) 78.
37. Perrin likes the definition of Alan Watts: "Myth is to be defined as a complex of stories—some no doubt fact, and some fantasy—which, for various reasons, human beings regard as demonstrations of the inner meaning of the universe and of human life." (As quoted in *Jesus*, 22.)

the parables as metaphors—interpreting the gospel as it is woven into the fabric of language.

The author organizes his work into two major divisions: "The Interpretations of the Kingdom of God in the Message of Jesus" and "Modern Interpretation of the Parables of Jesus." In introducing his study Perrin notes that the kingdom of God is "the ultimate referent of the parables of Jesus."[38] Once the text to be interpreted has been established, Perrin's concern is "to go beyond historical criticism to a *literary criticism*."[39] Perrin continues his argument, declaring that literary criticism is essential furthermore "because it opens up new possibilities for a valid understanding of the text in a context different from its original historical context."[40] Seal, responds insightfully, "Perrin is not actually going 'beyond historical criticism,' but is in fact developing and emphasizing the natural role of literary criticism in establishing a 'historical understanding' of the text."[41]

Perrin begins his first major division with a background section on "The Kingdom of God in Ancient Jewish Literature." The roots of the symbol, "kingdom of God," lie in the ancient Near Eastern myth of the kingship of God, common to all the peoples of that time and place. Israel inherited two traditions, which they brought together and interpreted in light of each other: one, the common ancient myth of the activity of God as king in creation and renewal, and the other, the myth of the *Heilsgeschichte* ("Salvation History") out of its own past. The symbol "kingdom" (or reign), therefore, combined the features of the history of God's saving acts with the idea of God as powerful Re-creator to form one myth by which they came to understand themselves as people of God, the beneficiaries of his kingly activity, delivering them time and again. During the Roman rule, this symbolic language of the kingdom grew more metaphorical.[42]

Another important use of this symbol was in the Kaddish prayer, which was close in its use to the prayer Jesus taught his disciples. The similar phrase is, "May he establish his kingdom."[43] The significance of its use in this way is that it, like other symbols in prayer, was plurisignificant; it varied from individual to individual in the meaning of the myth of God active as king which it evoked. Here Perrin employs Philip Wheel-

38. Perrin, *Jesus*, 1.
39. Ibid., 5.
40. Ibid., 9.
41. Seal, 101.
42. Perrin illustrates from the apocalyptic work, *The Assumption of Moses* 10, which was written shortly before the time of Jesus: "Satan shall be no more, and sorrow shall depart with him. . . ." "the Heavenly One will arise from his royal throne . . . with indignation and wrath on account of his sons" (*Jesus*, 26–27).
43. As quoted in Perrin, *Jesus*, 28.

wright's[44] terminology, and explains that a symbol can be either one of two kinds. (1) It can be a "steno-symbol," like the mathematical symbol π, having a "one-to-one relationship to that which it represents."[45] It then refers to only one concrete event expected, such as the dramatic interruption of God into history. No doubt for many Jews the symbol of the kingdom of God was exhausted in that one apprehension of meaning. Consequently, such a myth evoked by a steno-symbol can be invalidated by the failure of the event to take place. But there is, also, a second kind of symbol: (2) a "tensive symbol," having a "set of meanings which can neither be exhausted nor adequately expressed by any one referent."[46] Perrin sees most apocalyptic symbols generally as steno-symbols, but he also sees other major apocalyptic symbols as tensive symbols. In light of the Kaddish prayer, he considers the kingdom of God in ancient Judaism as fundamentally a tensive symbol.

Having established this essential background, Perrin proceeds into the nucleus of his perspective on "The Kingdom of God in the Message of Jesus." He begins by rejecting the labeling of the kingdom of God as a "concept"; such language is imprecise and misleading. Perrin declares the kingdom of God to be a tensive symbol: "as a symbol it can *represent* or *evoke* a whole range or series of conceptions, but it only becomes a conception or idea if it constantly represents or evokes that one conception or idea."[47]

The author then reviews "The Scholarly Discussion of Kingdom of God in the Message of Jesus," discussing briefly the contributions of Weiss, Schweitzer, Bultmann, and especially Dodd, upon whom Perrin primarily focuses here because of his influential treatment of the parables of Jesus in the discussion of the kingdom of God. Concerning Dodd's conclusions he states, "If we agree to discuss the Kingdom in terms of 'present' and 'future,' then Dodd was correct: the parables of Jesus imply the presence of the Kingdom."[48] But as late as 1974[49] Perrin also saw a future aspect to the message of Jesus. Now in *this* book he is challenging this whole "temporal" approach by offering what he hopes will be a "new perspective on the discussion by approaching Kingdom of God as a

44. Phillip Wheelwright, *Metaphor and Reality* (Bloomington, Ind.: Indiana University, 1962).
45. Ibid., 93–96.
46. Perrin, *Jesus*, 30. The italics in the quotation are the emphasis of this reviewer. Wheelwright's distinction between "steno-symbol" and "tensive symbol" is similar to Paul Ricoeur's distinction between "sign" and "symbol" (*The Symbolism of Evil* [Boston: Beacon Press, 1969] 15).
47. Perrin, *Jesus*, 33.
48. Ibid., 39.
49. Norman Perrin, *The New Testament: An Introduction*, 289.

symbol and by approaching the message of Jesus concerning the Kingdom of God in terms of Jesus' use of the symbol."[50]

So Perrin turns to "The Use of Kingdom of God in the Message of Jesus," selecting the minimum of what he has proposed and believes "competent scholarly opinion would recognize as authentic"[51] for interpretation: three kingdom sayings, the Lord's Prayer, and fourteen proverbial sayings. He also mentions eighteen parables but does not interpret them.

Kingdom sayings

(1) *Luke 11:20:* "But if it is by the finger of God that I cast out demons, then the kingdom of God has come upon you." Perrin sees here an unmistakable link with the Kaddish prayer, because "the use of the symbol in connection with so immediate and personal a thing as the healing of an individual must be understood as a reinforcement of the trend from the cosmic to the personally experienced reality."[52] This saying establishes the kingdom of God as a tensive symbol on the lips of Jesus, because his exorcisms clearly do not exhaust the possibilities with regard to the activity of God on behalf of his people.

(2) *Luke 17:20–21:* "The Kingdom of God is not coming with signs to be observed; nor will they say, 'Lo, here it is!' or 'There!' for behold, the kingdom of God is in the midst of you." Here Jesus categorically rejected all apocalyptic seeking after "signs to be observed" and in doing so equally categorically rejected the treatment of myth as allegory and its symbols as steno-symbols. Consequently, "the kingdom of God in the midst of you" means that "the symbol of the kingly activity of God on behalf of his people confronts the hearers of Jesus as a true tensive symbol with its evocation of a whole set of meanings . . ." with "power to mediate the experience of existential reality."[53] Seal suggests an important conclusion here: "Jesus' use of the Kingdom of God as a tensive symbol means . . . that he did not mistakenly predict its coming in his day."[54]

(3) *Matthew 11:12:* "From the days of John the Baptist till now, the kingdom of heaven has suffered violence and men of violence plunder it." This saying envisages the *present* activity of God as king in conflict with evil—in relation to the fate of John the Baptist and to the potential fate of Jesus and his disciples.

50. Perrin, *Jesus*, 40.
51. Norman, Perrin, *Rediscovering the Teaching of Jesus* (New York: Harper & Row; London: SCM, 1967) 39–47.
52. Perrin, *Jesus*, 43.
53. Ibid., 45.
54. Seal, 102.

The Lord's Prayer

Recalling the earlier discussion of the parallel use of the kingdom petition in the Kaddish prayer and the varied expectations it evoked, the Lord's Prayer is further evidence for Jesus' use of kingdom of God as a tensive symbol. Because of the nature of symbol in prayer, which expresses *personal* concerns of *individuals*, "kingdom" in the Kaddish prayer and in the Lord's Prayer, therefore, cannot be limited to only one apprehension of meaning. Once "kingdom" in the Lord's Prayer is recognized as a tensive symbol, then other petitions "represent realistic possibilities for the personal or communal experience of God as king. God is to be experienced as king in the provision of 'daily bread,' in the experienced reality of the forgiveness of sins, and in support in the face of 'temptation.'" These petitions are "explorations of fundamental possibilities for the experience of God as king in human life; they are neither mutually exclusive nor exhaustive."[55]

Proverbial Sayings

(1) The most radical sayings: Lk 9:60a, leaving the dead to bury the dead; Mt 5:39b–41, turning the other cheek. These sayings "challenge the hearer, not to radical obedience but to radical questioning. . . . They jolt the hearer out of the effort to make a continuous whole of his or her existence and into a judgment about that existence."[56]

(2) The Eschatological Reversal Sayings: Mk 8:35, saving one's life; Mk 10:23b, 25, how hard it will be for the rich; Mk 10:31, the first and the last; Lk 4:11, humbling and exalting oneself. Perrin interprets these as proclaiming a reversal of the present and so demands judgment upon that present.

(3) The Conflict Sayings: Mk 3:27, entering a strong man's house; Mk 3:24–26, the kingdom divided against itself. Perrin's interpretation here is the same as for Mt 11:12, a kingdom saying which envisages God's present activity as king in conflict with evil.

(4) The Parenetical Sayings: Lk 9:62, putting the hand to the plough; Mt 7:13–14, entering by the narrow gate; Mk 7:15, the things which defile; Mk 10:15, receiving the kingdom as a child; Mt 5:44–48, loving your enemies. The other three groups of proverbial sayings appear to link with the kingdom sayings, "not in terms of the end of *the* world but in terms of the end of *world itself*."[57] But this last group seems to link with the "as we

---

55. Perrin, *Jesus*, 47–48.
56. Ibid., 52.
57. Ibid., 54. Perrin is indebted to Dominic Crossan for this phrase. A fuller explanation by Perrin, however, would have helped remove the gnostic overtones here.

forgive . . ." of the Lord's Prayer—being understood as metaphors of response on the part of the hearer.

Parables

The final group of material is the parables. Perrin does not interpret here but follows the lead of Wilder and concludes that parables are "bearers of the reality with which they were concerned," that is, "extended metaphors."[58] The parables of Jesus, therefore, mediate to the hearer an experience of the kingdom of God. They are like Jesus' use of the symbol of the kingdom of God in other forms of his proclamation.

Perrin then concludes this particular study with a brief survey of the "Kingdom of God in Christian Literature" from the theology of the NT evangelists through Augustine, Ritschl, Weiss, and Rauschenbush to Bultmann.

In his final section Perrin focuses on "The Modern Interpretation of the Parables of Jesus." He does not give his own exegesis but concentrates on hermeneutics of major contributors to the discussion: Jülicher, Dodd, Jeremias, Fuchs, Linnemann, Jüngel, Wilder, Funk, Via, and Crossan. Where possible, Perrin gives each scholar's interpretation of "The Good Samaritan." The review concludes with a summary of the work of the SBL Parables Seminar.

As Perrin brings his book to a close, he further comments that he regards some parables as having a paranetic function. Relying on Dominic Crossan's designation, "parables of action," Perrin defines these parables as inviting and demanding "commitment to God's Kingdom." So, Perrin concludes with an appeal for a hermeneutic which, as reviewer, Malcolm Peel, has noted,[59] emphasizes the metaphoric and tensive symbolic character of both parables and kingdom of God, that we might be more effective in allowing the text itself to speak to the hearer, and thereby, as the precursor Wilder poignantly expresses it, "compelling imagination . . . and transformation."

58. Perrin, actually understood "parable" more broadly. In his final chapter he says that a parable can be either a simile or a metaphor. For him a simile is essentially illustrative; and, therefore, the parable as simile "teases the mind into recognition of new aspects of the reality mediated by the myth of God active as king." As metaphor, the parable "contrasts two fundamentally different categories of reality and hence produces a shock to the imagination . . . which induces a new vision of world and new possibilities . . . for the experiencing of that existential reality" which the myth of God active as king mediates. (202)

59. Malcolm L. Peel, review of *Jesus and the Language of the Kingdom* by Norman Perrin, *Christian Century* 22 (Sept., 1976) 795.

Conclusion

Amos Wilder opened the door to a wholly new approach to understanding the gospel in general and the kingdom of God in particular as a message to be understood within the language itself, especially symbol and metaphor. Norman Perrin in his academic pilgrimage, profoundly influenced by Wilder, opened the door more widely, challenging NT scholarship no longer to think of the kingdom of God as a concept (or steno-symbol) understood temporally but as a tensive symbol, evoking varied meanings of the myth of God's activity as king without reference to a "present" or a "future." What is essential about the symbolic language of the gospel (Wilder) or kingdom (Perrin), especially in the metaphorical language of parables, is that it proclaims God as king for the existential realities of human life, jolts the hearer with the challenge of this experience, and compels commitment.

5   The Kingdom of God in the Old Testament

Dale Patrick

Professor of Religion
Drake University

T HE THEOLOGUMENON, "KINGDOM OF GOD," until fairly recently was taken by critical scholars to be an apt and well-grounded summation of OT theology, but in recent decades it has been dispensed with or rejected outright. At the outset of this study we need to consider the reasons for its eclipse in current scholarship. Perhaps we can fashion a model of synthetic concepts which will allow us to reconsider it.

Old Testament scholars have been reluctant to take up the topic of "kingdom of God" because there is the conviction that it is imposed upon the text from outside. Two hermeneutical rules seem to inform this judgment: (1) Exegesis should restrict itself to the explicit meaning of the text. Since few passages in the OT actually contain the expression, the only way to introduce it into the exposition of most is to argue that it is implied. Arguments from implication are definitely suspect.

(2) Comprehensive, systematic schemes for synthesizing the variegated body of literature and thought that makes up the OT violate the essential pluralism of the book. The theologumenon, kingdom of God, like "covenant" and "saving history," was attractive precisely because of its synthetic potential, and becomes rather uninteresting when synthesis is categorically renounced.

The generation of our mentors had less qualms about tracing the kingdom of God through the OT. They believed that the authors of the OT shared a common conception of God and his relationship to Israel and the world, with diversity being a matter of divergent articulations of the common faith. Accordingly, they debated which theologumenon could best encompass the common theology.[1]

1. W. Eichrodt, *Theology of the Old Testament* (2 vols.; London: SCM, 1961–67) is the

Those scholars who supported the kingdom of God as a comprehensive theologumenon were somewhat embarrassed by the infrequency of the actual expression, but insisted that it was not the verbal formulation that matters, but the idea denoted by it. John Bright's *The Kingdom of God* is the epitome of this approach. At the outset he states:

> It is at once apparent that the idea is broader than the term, and we must look for the idea where the term is not present. . . . it is by no means confined to the New Testament. . . . it had a long history and is, in one form or another, ubiquitous in both Old Testament and New. It involves the whole notion of the rule of God over his people and particularly the vindication of that rule and people in glory at the end of history.[2]

He then proceeds to rehearse the story of YHWH's dealings with Israel as the unfolding of the conception of the kingdom of God.

Bible dictionaries tend to proceed on the same set of principles. After discussing the occurrence and meaning of the expressions, the entry proceeds to set forth the substance of the idea according to a scheme of development.[3]

As one would expect, the subject of the kingdom of God is a staple of OT theologies.[4] Some give it more weight than others. On the one hand, Walther Eichrodt comes close to identifying his comprehensive theologumenon, "covenant," as the OT equivalent of kingdom of God.[5] Gerhard von Rad, on the other hand, is reluctant to use the expression frequently or comprehensively.[6] In this he was a precursor of the pluralistic principles of the present generation.

Were these earlier scholars justified in assuming the existence of a common theology underlying the diverse material of the OT and taking recourse to the idea denoted by the expression even when the expression was absent? An affirmative case can be made. (1) The very idea of canon

---

epitome of the search for an OT theology unified around one comprehensive theologumenon. His position is well articulated in his argument against G. von Rad, which concludes: "The one task which OT theology can never abandon (is) . . . of pressing on from the OT evidence to a system of faith which shall, by virtue of its unified structure and consistent fundamental attitude, present a character unique in the history of religions . . ." (1:520).

2. John Bright, *The Kingdom of God* (Nashville: Abingdon, 1953) 18.

3. For example, O. E. Evans, "Kingdom of God, of Heaven," *IDB* (Nashville: Abingdon, 1962) 3:17–26.

4. One finds the expression in the subject indices of such standard theologies as Th. C. Vriezen, *An Outline of Old Testament Theology* (Newton, Mass.: C.T. Branford, 1958); E. Jacob, *Theology of The Old Testament* (New York: Harper & Row, 1958); L. Kohler, *Old Testament Theology* (Philadelphia: Westminster, 1957) and W. Zimmerli, *Old Testament Theology in Outline* (Atlanta: John Knox, 1978); also in G.E. Wright, *The Old Testament and Theology* (New York: Harper & Row, 1978).

5. Eichrodt, 1:40, 67, 176, 386, 428, 501.

6. The subject index of his *Old Testament Theology* (2 vols.; New York: Harper & Row, 1962–65) lists only "kingly predicates" (one reference) and "rule of God" (one reference).

bespeaks an intention of providing a unified theological message. Before canonization, the works which were passed on as legitimate Yahwistic tradition would have met the test of expressing the common faith of YHWH.[7] Thus, it should be deemed a valid inquiry to seek to work out that common faith.

(2) It should be possible to identify the idea denoted by an expression without the expression being present. A narrative in which YHWH performs some action surely embodies the general proposition that God acts in human affairs even if the text does not make a general statement to that effect. Likewise, a narrative in which YHWH commands a human to perform some action embodies the idea of divine sovereignty, with or without the expression "kingdom of God."[8]

However, we do need to reconceptualize the status of comprehensive, synthetic schemes. (1) Let us admit that a conception like kingdom of God is a heuristic scheme devised by the interpreter to synthesize the manifold texts before us. In other words, we should not argue that the scheme was in the mind of the author, but rather that what was in the mind of the author (as articulated in the text itself) fits within the scheme. When we say that the "substance of the idea" is in the text, we are saying that the communication in the text conforms to the abstract idea denoted by the expression under consideration.

(2) Let us renounce any claim that a particular comprehensive, synthetic scheme is valid to the exclusion of others. Any given text may be congruent with a plurality of such schemes. It would be quite possible for a narrative to conform to the idea that God is sovereign and at the same time that he acts in history and that the patterns of human affairs exemplify divine wisdom. Each may account for different features of the same story. One surely can argue that a given scheme is comprehensive and synthetic without maintaining that it is the one and only such scheme or that all other schemes can be subsumed under it.

Having defended inquiry into the kingdom of God in the OT, the way should be clear to determine whether it constitutes a scheme fitting to a significant portion of the OT text and provides a unifying conception or common underlying theology for that portion.

The place to begin is with uses of the expression which clearly aspire to

---

7. See my *The Rendering of God in the Old Testament* (Philadelphia: Fortress, 1981) 137–40.

8. If one follows the recent movement in theology to recognize story or narrative as a viable mode of theological discourse in its own right, any endeavor to subsume biblical texts under a general concept will have to redefine the status of the general concept. It seems to me that it continues to be legitimate to abstract conceptual components of stories if we recognize that a narrative text can yield a plurality of concepts or fit a plurality of conceptual schemes. As some are fond of saying, narratives are multivalent.

be comprehensive and synthetic. Since it is uncertain whether the usage of the OT can be so described, it is advisable first to examine the synoptic Jesus' usage. If it can be determined that the expression aspires to comprehensiveness and synthesis in Jesus' proclamation, we can trace its OT antecedents to ascertain whether Jesus' usage is exegetically justified.

The Kingdom of God in the Message of the Synoptic Jesus

The interpreter's interest in studying the expression, kingdom of God, and the conception it denotes, is aroused chiefly by its use by the Jesus of the Synoptic Gospels. If the expression were not on his lips on frequent and strategically important occasions, one might treat it as simply one among a variety of metaphors employed to portray the relationship of God to his people or to the entire human race. Jesus seems to raise it to the level of a heuristic scheme for understanding God's purposes in human affairs. In what follows, I will endeavor to show (1) *that* the expression constitutes a heuristic scheme and (2) *what* the expression denotes.

(1) Jesus employs the expression βασιλεία τοῦ θεοῦ ("kingdom of God") to arouse in his listeners a complex of ideas, associations, and metaphors.[9] They already have some idea of what he is talking about. Whatever particular twist he wishes to give to this idea, he relates it to the various conceptions his hearers have in their minds. To the degree that their conceptions clash with his, he is endeavoring to get them to reconceptualize, to understand something in a new way.

This is evident in Mark's summary of Jesus' proclamation in 1:15. When Jesus says, "The time is fulfilled, the kingdom of God is at hand; repent and believe the good news," the hearers must make a number of connections to understand what he has said. They must know that the kingdom comes at the end of time as the culmination of everything that has happened from creation until now. They must know that the kingdom requires them to exemplify a certain type of character if they are to enter, if they are to receive his message as "good news." And so forth.

The expression "the time is fulfilled" has specific consequences for the reading of the Hebrew Scripture. All that God has said and done in Israel's history is brought to completion in the kingdom of God. All that the audience knew of God's redemptive plans is to be synthesized in one image. In other words, in the proclamation of Jesus "kingdom of God" has become a heuristic scheme for interpreting Scripture and tradition.

---

9. Two other essays in this volume—Ron Farmer's "Kingdom of God in Matthew" and Emory Elmore's "Amos Wilder and Norman Perrin"—underline the point that the expression βασιλεία τοῦ θεοῦ refers to a complex of ideas and associations.

The same conclusions could be drawn from other uses of the expression in the synoptics, but one more example will suffice. When Jesus introduces a parable, "the kingdom of God is like . . ." (Mk 4:31, etc.), the parable is made to interact with the audience's prior conceptions of the kingdom.[10] The story taken from nature or social life gains its significance by the comparison. Jesus challenges and alters the conceptions and expectations of his auditors, but there must be something there already to be challenged or altered.

(2) The expression chosen to evoke the auditors' conceptions of God's intervention is itself important in shaping their perception. All their images and associations are given a political context. The βασιλεία τοῦ θεοῦ is a political state ruled by God, a theocratic state if you will. Since it is an eschatological reality, it is not exactly like any other state, but it is nevertheless a political reality and stands in opposition to actual political states. Jesus, therefore, may be said to "politicize" the Scripture and tradition.

At the same time, the expression is legal. It defines the state of salvation in terms of sovereignty. God exercises the authority of a sovereign in his kingdom. What is this authority? To command and enforce his commands over subjects who are duty-bound to obey.[11]

That the synoptic tradition understands the kingdom of God as the establishment of God's sovereignty over the human race can be shown from the Lord's Prayer. The Matthean version reads: "Thy Kingdom come, thy will be done on earth as it is in heaven" (6:10). The Lukan version lacks "thy will be done" (see 11:2). It is probable that the Matthean phrase is an addition meant to explicate the petition for the coming of the kingdom.[12] The explication virtually states the definition of sovereignty just offered.

To sum up, Jesus uses kingdom of God to call to mind all that his auditors knew about the coming intervention of God to redeem his people and pacify the world. It gathers and concentrates the Scriptures and received tradition around a specific conception of God's plans and purposes in history. The expression itself gives a particular coloring to the denouement of history, namely, a political and legal coloring. The whole of the Scripture and tradition prepare for and are completed in a political state in which God alone exercises sovereignty.

10. R. Funk, *Jesus as Precursor* (Semeia Supl.; Missoula: Scholars) 19–26, argues that Jesus overturns the expectations of his auditors in the parable of the Mustard Bush. This requires, I am arguing, that the auditors knew enough whereof he spoke to have their ideas challenged and changed.

11. This is the definition of sovereignty offered by D. Lloyd in his primer, *The Idea of Law* (Baltimore: Penguin, 1964) 38–48.

12. R. Hamerton-Kelly, *God the Father* (Philadelphia: Fortress, 1979) 73–74.

Antecedents and Precedents

Jesus did not coin the expression kingdom of God, it was already in circulation during his time.[13] Whether or not it had attained the status of a heuristic scheme is outside the scope of this paper. I want to put Jesus' heuristic scheme on trial regarding its validity as an interpretation of Scripture. While the judgment is a matter of faith as well as reason, we can examine certain lines of evidence relevant to it. I propose the following: (1) Does Jesus have antecedents of the expression in the OT, and do they constitute sufficient precedent to justify his use of the expression as a comprehensive, synthetic characterization of the manifold traditions of Hebrew Scripture? (2) Do the OT expressions denote the same range of ideas as "kingdom of God" does in the NT?

The OT does contain ample antecedents of the Greek expression. If one assumes YHWH to be a semantic equivalent of Elohim, we have a number of exact equivalents in Hebrew and Aramaic to the Greek βασιλεία τοῦ θεοῦ. First Chronicles 28:5 reads malkût YHWH, and Pss 103:19; 145:11, 12, 13, and 1 Chr 17:14 have malkût with a pronoun. Psalm 22:28, Ob 21, and 1 Chr 29:11 have a slightly different nominal formation of mlk, and Dan 4:3, 34; 7:27 (cf 2:44) contain the Aramaic form of the expression. In addition to these equivalents in Hebrew and Aramaic, there are a number of references to Israel as YHWH's kingdom: e.g., mamleket cōhenîm (Ex 19:6), yisrāēl mamselôtāu (Ps 114:2), etc.[14]

Another class of expressions also flows in the Greek βασιλεία τοῦ θεοῦ, namely, the appellation, melek ("king"), for YHWH. These occur both in verbal and nominal formations. The verbal formation yimlōk, etc., is found in Ex 14:18; 1 Sam 8:7; Isa 24:32; 52:7; Ezk 20:33; Mic 4:7; Pss 47:9; 93:1; 96:10 (=1 Chr 16:31); 97:1; 99:1, cf. Jdg 8:23 (rt. mšl). The nominal melek appears in Num 23:21 (?); Dt 33:5; 1 Sam 12:12; Isa 6:5; 41:21; 43:15; 44:6; Jer 10:7, 10 (cf. 46:18); 48:15; 51:57; Zep 3:15; Zec 14:9, 16, 17; Mal 1:14; Pss 5:3; 10:16; 29:10; 45:5; 47:3, 7, 8; 48:3; 68:25; 74:12; 84:4; 145:1; 149:2.

These numerous occurrences come from all segments of the canon and from all eras of Israel's history. The image of YHWH as a sovereign over his people and all peoples came so naturally to the biblical authors that one can justifiably say that it was a common possession.

It may have been noticed that I have described YHWH's sovereignty rather awkwardly as "over Israel and over all peoples (or, the world)." It

---

13. See the essays in this volume by John J. Collins and Ben Viviano.

14. These last two cases, in particular can be dated relatively early, perhaps as early as the ninth century: on the source and dating of Ex 19:3b–8, see my "The Covenant Code Source," VT 27 (1977) 145–57.

so happens that these examples tend to fall into two categories: universal sovereignty and sovereignty over Israel.[15] The word "kingdom" includes all humans or nations, and even the natural environment, in Pss 22:28; 103:19; 1 Chr 29:11, and the examples from Daniel.[16] YHWH's "kingship" is over the entire world in the enthronement psalms,[17] Isa 6:5, and the examples from Jeremiah. Some of these passages speak of YHWH's sovereignty as beginning with creation, while others are clearly eschatological.[18]

The word "kingdom" refers to Israel in 1 Chr 28:5, 17:14. Probably Ob 21, Ex 19:6, and Ps 114:2 designate Israel as YHWH's sphere of sovereignty. YHWH's "kingship" is over Israel in Ex 15:18, Dt 33:5, 1 Sam 8:7, 12:12, and the examples in Ezekiel and Second Isaiah; Jdg 8:23 belongs here too, though another word (mšl) is used. All of these refer to a present historical reality.

These are, from all appearances, independent traditions. The universal sovereignty of YHWH derives from being the Creator and the ruler of creation, and from the intrinsic quality of being God. Perhaps myth and cultic celebration stand in the background. YHWH's sovereignty over Israel derives from the actual history of this people and its theocratic constitution. The two traditions undoubtedly tended to interact and qualify each other throughout Israelite history and were ripe for synthesis, but it is worth noting that they had not been fully synthesized at the close of the OT canon.

Obviously at a purely statistical level, the expression "kingdom of God" has sufficient antecedents in the OT to justify Jesus' use of it. In other words, the antecedents are sufficiently frequent, widely distributed, and prominent to constitute precedents for the use of this expression as a comprehensive, synthetic theologumenon. If YHWH's saving deeds in Israel's history, his covenant with Israel, the political arrangements of the pre-monarchical and monarchical eras, and the acts of judgment and redemption of his people, along with his control of the history of humanity and his banishment of all opposition in the future could all be subsumed under this one image or idea, it has good credentials for being a comprehensive designation of God's relationship with his creatures.

15. This division is so commonplace that F. Brown, S. R. Driver and C. A. Briggs, *Hebrew and English Lexicon of the Old Testament* (London: Oxford, 1907, corrected ed. 1959) use it in their entry for *melek*.

16. Probably Ps 145:11–13 as well.

17. That is, Pss 47:3, 7–9; 93:1; 95:3; 96:10; 97:1; 98:6; 99:1.

18. Isa 6:4; Ps 103–19; 145:11–13; 1 Chr 19:11 are present tense, while the passages in Daniel have in mind an eschatological order. The enthronement psalms are ambiguous. S. Mowinckel, *The Psalms in Israel's Worship* (Nashville: Abingdon, 1962) 106–92, construes them as depicting a present, cultic reality, while C. Westermann, *The Praise of God in the Psalms* (Richmond: John Knox, 1965) 145–57, concludes that they are eschatological.

Now the question is: Do these OT uses of the antecedent expressions mean the same thing as the synoptic βασιλεία τοῦ θεοῦ? In particular, let us consider the idea of divine sovereignty itself: Does YHWH's kingship involve the exercise of the authority to command and enforce his commands?

Divine Kingship in the Old Testament

Not all OT uses of equivalents of "kingdom of God" are equally productive for determining the meaning of divine sovereignty. The liturgical uses give little content to the expression, though one can assume that they called forth political and legal associations. A few texts do yield a great deal, and we will do well to concentrate on them.

One of these is the account of the negotiation between Samuel/YHWH and the elders of Israel over the establishment of the monarchy (1 Sam 8). When the people of Israel describe the king's role, they say they want him to "govern us and go out before us and fight our battles" (1 Sam 8:20). The authority to make and enforce law is encapsulated in the word translated "govern." The Hebrew word behind this translation is špt, normally translated to "judge." I take its usage here to be an extension of the idea of judging, namely, establishing and maintaining a just order.

Up until now, YHWH has exercised that authority. The law has been commanded by him and the judicial authorities have acted as his representatives. Hence he was the "king" (1 Sam 8:7). The people, by asking for a human king, are rebelling against YHWH. The strict theocracy that began with Moses and endured through the period of the judges was being repudiated.

However, the king did not actually usurp the sovereignty of YHWH. According to 1 Sam 12, YHWH pardons the people and accepts a constitutional arrangement involving a human king. He does not yield his exclusive claim to law-making authority to the king (cf. 1 Sam 12:20–21, 24–25). The king's authority to "govern" was limited to the enforcement of the law and administration of the kingdom.

Actually, the restricted view of monarchical authority was not unique to Israel. There was a rather general understanding in the ancient Near East that the authority of a ruler was circumscribed by divine and natural law.[19] There were legal codes issued in the names of rulers, but note that

19. By divine law, I mean a set of laws or legal principles instituted by a deity; those ANE lawbooks which appeal to divine revelation would fall handily under that description. By natural law, I mean an order built into the world governing both physical process and moral actions. This metaphysic was widely distributed in the ANE, evidenced in the Egyptian term ma'at and equivalents in other languages. On ma'at see

the Code of Hammurabi is portrayed as a revelation of Shamash. The royal law-giver is an agent of the gods and depends upon the "higher law" as the foundation of his own. Israel seems to have pushed this idea one step further, until the human king is dispensed with; the king must set beside the commoner as a student of the law (Dt 14:14–20).[20]

The upshot of our analysis is that the ancient Near Eastern kings, and especially Israelite kings, were not fully sovereign. There is no question but the authority to command and enforce one's commands inhered in the idea of sovereignty, but it was only deity that possessed this authority fully; human rulers derived their sovereignty from deity.[21]

One of the covenant texts depicts the origin and nature of YHWH's sovereignty. This is Ex 19:3b–8. Israel is designated "a kingdom of priests and a holy nation" (v 6). That is to say, the people constituted a national political entity with YHWH as their king. The people are offered this constitutional arrangement on the condition that they agree to obey YHWH (v 5a), which they do in their response to the offer (v 8, also 24:3–8).[22] The offer and its acceptance put in force a structure of authority in which YHWH has the sole authority to command, and the people of Israel are bound by pledge to obey him.

This covenant text constitutes the initial negotiation of the covenant. Before the covenant is ratified (Ex 24:3–8), YHWH exercises his authority by declaring his law. God's will or command is concretely articulated in legal corpora; a legal community is founded, an order of justice instituted.

We have, thus, arrived at the conclusion that these two prominent passages involve precisely the idea of divine kingship that we found in Jesus' proclamation. On the conception of divine sovereignty, Jesus' synthetic expression "kingdom of God" represents the OT covenant accurately.

Of course, the evidence presented does not show that the idea of divine sovereignty over Israel pervades the covenant traditions. The language of kingship is relatively rare in these texts, and it would be rather tendentious to argue that it is nevertheless on every author's mind. However, all the texts portray a relationship between YHWH and his people which fits

H. Frankfort, *Ancient Egyptian Religion* (New York: Harper & Brothers, 1948) 53–58.

20. There may have been royal lawbooks that were not accepted into the Yahwistic tradition; e.g., Mic 6:16 refers to the "statutes of Omri," possibly an actual legal document. It is not correct to classify the Deuteronomic law as a royal enactment, for it is in no way dependent upon royal authority. It does not even depend upon Josiah's adoption to be put in force, but rather on a formal covenant binding king and people (2 Kgs 23:1–3).

21. D. Lloyd, 170–1 draws this conclusion. Since he does not recognize the idea of divine sovereignty as a concept of sovereignty, he denies the idea of sovereignty to antiquity.

22. On the constitutional theory, see the chapter entitled "Law and Covenant" in my *Old Testament Law*, (Atlanta: John Knox, 1984) 223–39.

the definition of sovereignty; that is, YHWH assumes the authority of law-giver and enforcer of his law and the people assume the duty of obeying him. This suffices to validate the heuristic scheme as a comprehensive synthesis of this large and prominent OT tradition.

History and Eschatology

While it has been shown that there is ample precedent for construing the relationship between God and his people and all the peoples of the earth as that of a sovereign to his subjects, Jesus' conception of the kingdom of God diverges in significant respects from the OT conception of divine sovereignty. For simplicity's sake, we can categorize the divergences under two headings, time and space. (1) Both the universalistic and particularistic linguistic antecedents of the expression, kingdom of God, speak of God's exercise of dominion over the historical present, whereas Jesus announces an eschatological kingdom breaking into history in the present. (2) Both the OT and Jesus have universalistic and particularistic strains in their conceptions of the sovereignty of God, but the boundary is drawn nationally in the OT, volitionally in the message of Jesus. Let me flesh out in turn these two differences.

(1) The majority of the antecedents designating YHWH sovereign over the nations and the non-human world locate it in the temporal present. The Creator has exercised control of the created order since the beginning and will continue to do so forever. All the particularistic antecedents depict YHWH as exercising sovereignty throughout Israel's history. If a particular beginning is identified, it is the act of covenanting at Sinai.

The OT does have an important eschatological dimension. At least as early as the classical prophets, a new, transformed historical order is promised. Israel's penchant for rebellion against its sovereign God will be purged and it will become loyal, just, and merciful, while peace and justice will prevail on the international scene. The basis for this hope is the past actions and promises of YHWH. Eschatology is the denouement and resolution of history. Although there are a few antecedents of the expression, kingdom of God, that look forward to its establishment for the first time, they do not break the dominant temporal structure of OT theology.[23]

23. I would like to take issue with Gerhard von Rad on his characterization of prophecy as determined by the eschatological event: "The prophetic message differs from all previous Israelite theology, which was based on the past saving history, in that the prophets looked for the decisive factor in Israel's whole existence—her life or her death—in some future event" (2:117). The classical prophets of judgment were more

Jesus' message of the kingdom of God appears to follow and modify the marginal, apocalyptic antecedents of the OT. The kingdom has not been present since creation and the election of Israel; it is breaking in only now. Until now God's sovereignty has been contested, and therefore cannot really be said to have been "established." But in these latter days it has come near, so near that one can enter it by submitting to God's will.[24]

For Jesus, the kingdom is so overwhelming in its importance and decisive for the meaning of life that it has become the hermeneutical key for interpreting Scripture. The kingdom is the known, sacred history the unknown. The historical revelation of God in Scripture must be "deciphered" in the light of the end, for it was given to prepare people for the time when salvation would be accomplished. The past has been reduced to the status of prefigurement which requires the figure, the fulfillment, to be understood.[25]

(2) The OT does not synthesize the universalistic and particularistic strains in its depictions of YHWH's sovereignty. They are simply complementary aspects of YHWH's exercise of power. If he did not control the history of the nations and processes of nature, he could not be counted on; if he did not exercise royal sovereignty over Israel, YHWH's control of the world would have no purpose or denouement.

Jesus does not preserve the OT dialectic between national and universal divine sovereignty. He is conscious of the uniqueness of his people, accepts their Scripture as authoritative, and apparently restricts his ministry to them. However, none of his utterances about the kingdom differentiates between the destiny of the Jews and that of the Gentiles.[26]

However, a particularistic strain remains; Jesus does divide the human race. In Luke's version of the Beatitudes (6:20–26) the division is between the haves and the have-nots; In the parable of the Great Banquet (Lk 14:15–24), it is between those who decline the invitation and those brought in in their place. The parable of the Sower (Mk 4:3–9) divides between those who yield and do not yield. Perhaps we could generalize

---

conservative than that; von Rad's description fits Second Isaiah and early apocalyptic better.

24. This is my attempt to summarize the already-not yet ambiguity in Jesus' message. See, e.g., the much more thorough analysis of this issue in Eldon J. Epp's essay in this volume.

25. The NT virtually equates the kingdom of God with the Messiah Jesus, so the strictly apocalyptic quality of Jesus' conception is synthesized with Christology. Within the NT as a whole, it is not so much the impending future event which functions as the hermeneutical key to the OT, but the historical-eschatological Christ (that is, an historical figure with eschatological significance).

26. Although I have doubts about its simple scheme, J. Jeremias' *Jesus' Promise to the Nations* (London: SCM, 1958) introduces one to the relevant logia and issues.

to say that the promise of the kingdom has been transferred from Israel to those who have been excluded from power and reward in this world and those who have renounced them.[27]

There are numerous attempts by scholars and theologians either to harmonize the historical orientation of the OT and eschatological orientation of the NT or to show that Jesus' message is the culmination of a development leading from the history of election through the prophecy of judgment. In the latter vein, one might argue that the experiences under the election and covenent led to prophecy, then apocalyptic, and finally to Jesus.[28] Even if such a line can be traced, however, the interpreter must be careful. There are other ways of construing the OT story which have equal claim to validity. The Rabbinic tradition, in particular, has much to support its view that the original election and covenant remain in force, and the prophets and apocalypticists are to be treated as subordinate to the Torah. The historical critic can only trace the possible lines of inheritance, not decide the competing claims of Jews and Christians. The biblical theologian should likewise respect the claims of both traditions.

Summation

At the outset of this study I argued that it is legitimate to inquire into comprehensive syntheses of OT theology if we recognize that they are heuristic schemes devised by the interpreter and none can claim exclusive validity. It was on this basis that I proceeded. We began with Jesus' use of the expression kingdom of God, for it is in his proclamation that we meet this term as a comprehensive, synthetic scheme for interpreting Scripture and tradition. His choice of this expression to designate the coming intervention of God gave the event a particular coloring, namely, a political and legal coloring.

The OT evidence was examined with the purpose of judging the validity of Jesus' heuristic scheme. We found sufficient terminological antecedents to conclude that Jesus had precedent for subsuming the theology of the OT under this expression. An examination of two prominent,

27. According to Paul Hanson, *The Dawn of Apocalyptic* (Philadelphia: Fortress, 1975) 147–55 and elsewhere, a hallmark of apocalypticism from its beginnings onward, is the division of the people of Israel into the saved and damned. No longer is the whole nation elect, but only a loyal, righteous remnant within it. Jesus seems to be operating with this apocalyptic type of particularism.

28. This sequence approximates the progress of the kingdom set forth by J. Bright (*Kingdom of God*); note his chapter titles: "The People of God and the Kingdom of Israel," "A Kingdom Under Judgment," "A Remnant Shall Repent," "The Broken Covenant and the New Covenant," "Captivity and the New Exodus," and "Holy Commonwealth and Apocalyptic Kingdom."

conceptually rich passages yielded a definition of divine sovereignty: the exclusive authority of YHWH to command and enforce his commands and the duty of the people of Israel to obey. This definition was congruent with Jesus' understanding of the kingdom of God. On the other hand, Jesus' kingdom is eschatological and universal, whereas the kingdom language of the OT is historical and contains an irreducibly national strain.

6 The Kingdom of God in the Apocrypha and Pseudepigrapha

John J. Collins

Professor of Theology
University of Notre Dame

K INGDOM OF GOD DOES NOT APPEAR as a standard, fixed expression in the Apocrypha and Pseudepigrapha as it does in the Gospels. There are however various motifs associated with "kingdom" which are important for establishing the possible range of meaning of the phrase.

Daniel

We begin our review with the canonical Book of Daniel, which is in fact a pseudepigraph in chs 7–12, and belongs chronologically with the Apocrypha. The tales in chs 1–6 are somewhat older than the apocalyptic visions of the Maccabean era, and, at least in some cases, are traditional stories which developed over a long period of time.[1] The theme of world kingdoms runs throughout these stories as they trace the career of Daniel under Babylonian, Median, and finally Persian rule. The inclusion of Darius the Mede in this sequence is a notorious problem, since Babylon was never ruled by Media, and Darius was the name of a later, Persian king. The solution of the problem lies in the discovery that Daniel was adapting a scheme which was conventional in Near Eastern political propaganda. According to this schema there would be a sequence of four world kingdoms followed by a fifth, final one.[2] The schema is known from

1. J. J. Collins, *The Apocalyptic Vision of the Book of Daniel* (Harvard Semitic Monographs 16; Missoula: Scholars, 1977) 8–11. The tradition-historical background has been most vividly illustrated in the case of Dan 4 by the discovery of the Prayer of Nabonidus at Qumran.
2. The existence of this schema was pointed out by J. W. Swain, "The Theory of the

a Roman chronicler, Aemilius Sura, who wrote about 175 B.C.E.. Aemilius lists the kingdoms as Assyria, Media, Persia, and Macedonia, followed by Rome. The same kingdoms are listed in the Fourth Sibylline Oracle, a Jewish work from the late first century C.E., which may, however, incorporate an older source.[3] Because of the inclusion of Media, the schema is thought to have originated in Persia. Originally, the schema served as propaganda against the Greek empire of Alexander. The implication was that history had run its course and that the fourth, Greek, kingdom would soon be overthrown.

The schema of the four kingdoms is found explicitly in Dan 2 in the interpretation of Nebuchadnezzar's dream, and again in ch 7. It also informs the structure of the book as a whole. Chapters 1–6 mention Babylonian, Median, and Persian kings. Chapters 7–12 repeat this sequence and anticipate the coming of "the prince of Greece" (10:20). It is apparent then that Daniel identifies the kingdoms as Babylon, Media, Persia, and Greece—Babylon is substituted for Assyria because of its role in the destruction of Jerusalem.

In Nebuchadnezzar's dream in Dan 2 the four world kingdoms are symbolized as a statue, made of metals of declining value, which is destroyed by a stone that then becomes a great mountain.[4] Daniel explains that "in the days of those kings the God of heaven will set up a kingdom which shall never be destroyed, nor shall its sovereignty be left to another people. It shall break in pieces all these kingdoms and bring them to an end, and it shall stand forever" (2:44). This kingdom set up by God is not further described. From the context we should suppose that it is a Jewish kingdom which will rise to replace, and destroy, the previous gentile kingdoms. It differs from other kingdoms insofar as it will not pass away, but it is presumably a political, earthly kingdom like them.[5]

The kingdom set up by God must, however, be distinguished from the kingdom, or kingship, of God. In Dan 3:33 Nebuchadnezzar praises God: "His kingdom is an everlasting kingdom, and his dominion is from generation to generation." Here again there is a contrast between the transience of human kingdoms, even that of the mighty Nebuchadnezzar, and the permanence of God's reign. The kingdom of God here is not an

Four Monarchies: Opposition History Under the Roman Empire," Classical Philology 35 (1940) 1–21. The most complete discussion is by David Flusser, "The Four Empires in the Fourth Sibyl and in the Book of Daniel," Israel Oriental Studies 2 (1972) 148–75.

3. J. J. Collins, "The Sibylline Oracles," The Old Testament Pesudepigrapha, 2 vols. (ed. J. H. Charlesworth; Garden City: Doubleday, 1983) 1:381–89.

4. On the symbolism of the dream see Collins, The Apocalyptic Vision of the Book of Daniel, 34–46.

5. It is possible that Daniel was adapting a Babylonian prophecy which predicted a lasting Babylonian kingdom. See Collins, The Apocalyptic Imagination, (New York: Crossroad, 1984) 76–77 and compare the Babylonian Uruk prophecy.

earthly kingdom set up by God, but the power by which "the Most High rules the kingdom of men and gives it to whom he will" (Dan 4:29). In these hymnic passages Daniel draws on the biblical tradition where Yahweh is proclaimed king in the Psalms.

The four-kingdom schema is taken up again in Dan 7 in the context of an apocalyptic vision from the time of the persecution of Antiochus Epiphanes. In this case the four kingdoms are represented as beasts rising from the sea. The dominant imagery of the passage is drawn from the myth of combat between a god and a sea monster or dragon, which Israel had adapted from the more ancient Near Eastern cultures.[6] God, the ancient of days, is depicted as a royal judge who confers "dominion and glory and kingdom" on "one like a son of man" (7:13–14). Subsequently we are told that "the holy ones of the Most High shall receive the kingdom, and possess the kingdom for ever" (7:18) and finally that "the kingdom and the dominion and the greatness of the kingdoms under the whole heaven shall be given to the people of the holy ones of the Most High: their kingdom shall be an everlasting kingdom, and all dominions shall serve and obey them" (7:27).

The interpretation of this chapter, which has had such profound influence on the Gospels, remains very controversial. There is evidently a contrast between the everlasting kingdom conferred by God and the transient human kingdoms which precede it, as in Dan 2. Further, it is clear that an earthly Jewish kingdom is envisaged, which will be world-wide and everlasting (7:27). The controversy concerns the interpretation of the "one like a son of man" and the "holy ones of the Most High." Some scholars take these expressions simply as ways of referring to the Jewish people.[7] Against this, however, is the fact that every undisputed mention of "holy ones" in Daniel refers to angels,[8] and that figures who appear in human likeness are also angels.[9]

If Dan 7 is read in the context of chs 10–12, it is clear that Daniel envisaged two dimensions in history. The conflict on earth between Jews and Greeks is only the reflection of the battle between their angelic patrons. The victory of the Jews corresponds to, and depends on the

6. Collins, *The Apocalyptic Vision of the Book of Daniel*, 95–101; *The Apocalyptic Imagination*, 79–80. For the background myth see John Day, *God's Conflict with the Dragon and the Sea* (Cambridge: Cambridge University, 1985) and Adela Yarbro Collins, *The Combat Myth in the Book of Revelation* (Harvard Dissertations in Religion 9; Missoula: Scholars, 1976) 57–100.

7. So, recently, L. F. Hartman and A. A. DiLella, *The Book of Daniel* (AB 23; Garden City: Doubleday, 1978) 85–102; M. Casey, *Son of Man: The Interpretation and Influence of Daniel 7* (London: SPCK, 1979) 7–50; W. S. Towner, *Daniel* (Interpretation; Atlanta: John Knox, 1984) 105–6.

8. Dan 4:10, 14, 20; 8:13. Cf. the angelic "holy ones" in 1 Enoch 14:22–23.

9. Dan 8:15–16; 9:21; 10:5, 16, 18; 12:6–7. Cf. the Animal Apocalypse in 1 Enoch 83–90 where men represent angels, or humans transformed to an angelic state.

victory of the archangel Michael. Accordingly it seems most probable that the "one like a son of man" is Michael, who represents Israel on the heavenly level. The "holy ones" are the angelic host and "the people of the holy ones" are the Jews.[10] The kingdom then is realized on two levels and involves simultaneously an angelic kingdom and the earthly domin- ion of the Jewish people. A precise parallel to this idea is found in the Qumran War Scroll, where God is said to "raise up the rule of Michael in the midst of the gods and the realm of Israel in the midst of all flesh" (1QM 17:7).[11]

The apocalyptic kingdom of Dan 7 is not simply identical with that envisaged in Dan 2 but involves an otherworldly dimension. Dan 12 promises that the faithful Jews can share in this dimension by resurrec- tion, and that the wise teachers will shine like the stars forever and ever, which in apocalyptic idiom, means to join the fellowship of the angels.[12] The everlasting kingdom thus becomes accessible not only to future generations but also to the righteous after death.

On the basis of our examination of Daniel, then, we can distinguish three aspects of the kingdom motif. First, there is the hymnic use for the sovereignty of God, by which he disposes of all kingdoms. Second, there is the earthly dominion of the Jewish people, which is a kingdom set up by God. Finally, there is the apocalyptic kingdom of the angels, which involves the exaltation of righteous human beings after death. These three ideas are not mutually exclusive. All three are implied in the apocalyptic vision in Dan 7.

The Sibylline Tradition

The theme of world kingdoms plays a major role in the Sibylline Oracles from the Jewish Diaspora. The main body of Sib Or 3 was composed in Egypt around the middle of the second century B.C.E..[13] Sib Or 3:97–161 introduces the theme of kingship and shows that it was a cause of strife from the beginning. The section concludes with a list of world kingdoms in 3:156–61. The other main sections of the original corpus follow a pattern of sin, followed by tribulation, followed by the advent of a king or

10. Collins, *The Apocalyptic Vision of the Book of Daniel*, 123–47; *The Apocalyptic Imagination*, 78–85. Cf. A. Lacocque: *The Book of Daniel* (Atlanta: Knox, 1979) 131–34; C. Rowland, *The Open Heaven* (New York: Crossroad, 1983) 178–83; Day, *God's Conflict with the Dragon and the Sea*, 167–78.

11. U. B. Müller, *Messias and Menschensohn in jüdischen Apokalypsen und in der Offenbarung Johannes* (Gütersloh: Mohn, 1972) 28.

12. Cf. 1 Enoch 102:2, 6.

13. J. J. Collins, *The Sibylline Oracles of Egyptian Judaism* (SBLDS 13; Missoula: Scholars, 1974) 24–37; "Sibylline Oracles," OTP 1:354–61.

kingdom. In Sib Or 3:196-294 this pattern is demonstrated from Jewish history at the time of the Babylonian exile. The exile comes to an end when God sends a king (286), who must be identified in this context as Cyrus of Persia.[14] In other passages the focus of the sibyl is on Hellenistic Egypt. In Sib Or 3:192-93 the time of deliverance will come in "the seventh reign, when a king of Egypt, who will be of the Greeks by race, will rule." The king in question is either Ptolemy VI Philometor (if Alexander is counted as the first) or his anticipated successor. Similar references to the seventh king are found in Sib Or 3:318 and 608. In Sib Or 3:652 "God will send a king from the sun, who will stop the entire earth from evil war." The reference again is to a Ptolemaic king.[15] The sibyl looked for a king from the Ptolemaic line who would mediate deliverance for the Jews as Cyrus of Persia had done at the end of the Babylonian exile.

In the final section of the book the sibyl speaks of a kingdom which will be raised up by God (767-795). The temple will be a center of pilgrimage for all nations; wolves and lambs will feed together, as envisaged in Isa 11. This eschatological kingdom is apparently distinct from the reign of the seventh, Ptolemaic king, but it is also an earthly kingdom, which will bring to an end the sequence of world kingdoms. Throughout Sib Or 3 God is "the great King" (499, 560, 616, 784, 808) who must be worshipped by all. As in Dan 1-6 the kingship of God is his sovereignty by which he disposes of all kingdoms.

The Sibylline tradition is continued in additions which were made to Sib Or 3 in the first century B.C.E.. One of these oracles (3:46-62) anticipates that after the Roman conquest of Egypt (31 B.C.E.) "the most great kingdom of the immortal king will become manifest over men" (Sib Or 3:47-48). This will be a universal kingdom ruled by a "holy prince." This figure is not identified as a Roman or Egyptian leader and may be a Jewish messiah. The advent of the "kingdom of God" here is understood primarily as the occasion for "the judgment of the great king, immortal God" (3:56), executed by means of a fiery cataract from heaven.

A similar expectation of destructive judgment pervades the fifth book of Sibylline Oracles, composed in Egypt on the eve of the great Diaspora revolt of 115 C.E..[16] In v 108 the judgment is brought about by "a certain

---

14. Contra J. Nolland, "Sib Or 111. 265-94. An Early Maccabean Messianic Oracle," *JTS* 30 (1979) 158-67, who finds a typological allusion to a Davidic messiah here.

15. Collins, *The Sibylline Oracles of Egyptian Judaism*, 40-44. The Egyptian background of the phrase "king from the sun" is shown by its occurrence in the Potter's Oracle, col. 3.

16. Collins, *The Sibylline Oracles of Egyptian Judaism*, 73-95; "Sibylline Oracles," 1:390-2. On the historical setting see also M. Hengel, "Messianische Hoffnung und politischer 'Radikalismus' in der jüdisch-hellenistischen Diaspora," in *Apocalyptyicism in the Mediterranean World and the Near East* (Tübingen: Mohr, 1983) 653-84.

king sent from God," about whom we are told no more. Elsewhere in Sib Or 5 the savior figure is said to come from heaven. The most explicit passage is found in vv 414–28:

> For a blessed man came from the expanses of heaven with a scepter in his hands which God gave him and he gained sway over all things well, and gave back the wealth to all the good, which previous men had taken.

He is also said to refashion "the city which God desired" by building a tower which touches the clouds. (cf. Sib Or 5:252, where the wall of Jerusalem is said to extend as far as Joppa). Despite the heavenly origin of the savior king, Sib Or 5 remains true to the Sibylline tradition. God himself is the king (5:499) who must be worshipped by all. His kingdom on earth is an eschatological kingdom centered in Jerusalem but universal in scope. The Egyptian Sibylline tradition is remarkable for its lack of the otherworldly dimension so characteristic of the apocalyptic literature. There is no talk of angels and no expectation of resurrection. The hope is the traditional Israelite hope for the transformation of the earth.

The fourth book of Sibylline Oracles, which, in its present form comes from Syria or the Jordan valley (ca. 80 C.E.), shows more affinity with apocalyptic eschatology.[17] Here again the sequence of world kingdoms provides the context for the eschatological expectation. The sibyl, like Daniel, speaks of a sequence of four kingdoms, over ten generations, ruled in turn by Assyria (six generations), Media (two generations), Persia and Macedonia (one each). The rise of Rome follows. Since Rome is not integrated into the numerical sequence, it appears to have been added to update an older oracle. The final demise of the world kingdoms does not lead to a final "kingdom of God" in Sib Or 4. Instead, God will "burn the whole earth and destroy the whole race of men" (Sib Or 4:176). This universal destruction is then followed by a resurrection and final judgment. The resurrection is a restoration on earth: those who are pious "will live on earth again" (187). This final state is not called a kingdom in Sib Or 4, but it takes the place of the world kingdoms.

Other Diaspora Usage

The Sibylline Oracles, with their focus on the succession of world empires, are an important, but somewhat atypical, strand of Diaspora Judaism.[18] The idea of the sovereignty of God is the common denominator

17. Collins, "Sibylline Oracles," *OTP* 1:381–83.
18. For a survey of Jewish Hellenistic literature apart from Philo see J. J. Collins, *Between Athens and Jerusalem, Jewish Identity in the Hellenistic Diaspora* (New York: Crossroad, 1983).

of all references to the kingdom, including those of the Sibyllines. This idea did not necessarily entail the expectation of an eschatological kingdom.[19] For 2 Macc, God is the "King of Kings" who controls the course of history (13:4). The revolt of Jason, the Hellenizer, is a revolt against "the holy land and the kingdom" (1:7). Kingdom here can only mean the sovereignty of God, perhaps as expressed through the law.[20] The second letter pre-fixed to 2 Macc declares that God "has saved all his people, and has returned the inheritance to all, and the kingship and priesthood and consecration" (2:17). Whether the "kingship" here refers to the Hasmonean dynasty[21] or whether it is meant as equivalent to consecration in a spiritual sense, it is certainly conceived as present after the re-consecration of the temple.

In the philosophical circles of Diaspora Judaism the "kingdom" took on a more spiritual, or ethical sense. The Wisdom of Solomon declares that "there is no dominion ($\beta\alpha\sigma\iota\lambda\epsilon\iota\omicron\nu$) of Hades on earth, for righteousness is immortal" (1:14–15). Even though the righteous "seemed to have died" (3:2), they will judge nations and rule over peoples and the Lord will reign over them forever (3:8). Here the kingdom is something that the righteous enjoy after death: "But the righteous live forever, and their reward is with the Lord. . . . therefore they will receive majestic royalty" (5:16). In this sense we can understand how "the desire for wisdom leads to a kingdom" (6:20). Finally we are told that wisdom guided the righteous man and "showed him the kingdom of God and gave him knowledge of angels" (10:10). The reference is to Jacob. The apparent equation of the "kingdom of God" with the world of the angels is reminiscent of Daniel, and indeed the Wisdom of Solomon is influenced at many points by apocalyptic traditions.[22] It does not, however, retain the expectation of a kingdom on earth, and there is a tendency to identify the kingdom with wisdom and righteousness which are the root of immortality (Wis 15:3).

Other writings of the Diaspora go further in spiritualizing the "kingdom."[23] For 4 Macc 2:23 the mind which follows the law will rule a

---

19. The most complete survey of references to the kingdom of God and related concepts in the "intertestamental" literature is that of Odo Camponovo, *Königtum, Königsherrschaft und Reich Gottes in den frühjüdischen Schriften* (OBO 58; Göttingen: Vandenhoeck & Ruprecht, 1984). See also M. Lattke, "On the Jewish Background of the Synoptic Concept 'The Kingdom of God,'" *The Kingdom of God* (ed. B. Chilton; Philadelphia: Fortress, 1984) 72–91.

20. So Componovo, *Königtum*, 187.

21. So J. A. Goldstein, "How the Authors in I and II Maccabees treated the "Messianic Prophecies," *Judaisms and Their Messiahs* (ed. J. Neusner; Cambridge: Cambridge University, forthcoming).

22. G. W. Nickelsburg, *Resurrection, Immortality and Eternal Life in Intertestamental Judaism* (Cambridge: Harvard, 1972) 68–82; J. J. Collins, "Cosmos and Salvation. Jewish Wisdom and Apocalyptic in the Hellenistic Age." *History of Religions* 17 (1977) 121–42.

23. K. L. Schmidt, $\beta\alpha\sigma\iota\lambda\epsilon\iota\alpha$ ($\tau o\hat{v}$ $\theta\epsilon o\hat{v}$) in Hellenistic Judaism," *TDNT* (1964) 1:574–76.

kingdom characterized by the four cardinal virtues. The idea found in Stoicism that the wise man is a king is also in Philo (e.g. *Migr Abr* 197; *Abr* 261; *De Somniis* (2:244). For Philo, kingdom ($\beta\alpha\sigma\iota\lambda\epsilon\acute{\iota}\alpha$) is the rule of the wise man, and it is established by God (*Abr* 261). "Kingdom" ($\beta\alpha\sigma\iota\lambda\epsilon\acute{\iota}\alpha$) can even be defined as wisdom (*Migr Abr* 197) or as virtue (*De Somniis* 2:244).

The Apocalyptic Kingdom

The apocalyptic idea of the kingdom, developed in Dan 7–12, figures more prominently in the Judaism of the land of Israel, although even there it is not as prevalent as we might expect. The kingdom is not a prominent motif in the early Enoch literature.[24] In the Book of the Watchers (1 Enoch 1–36) God is called the eternal king (9:4; 12:3; 25:3–5, 7; 27:3). When he "comes down to visit the earth for good" (25:3) his throne will be established on a mountain. Then "the chosen" will receive life from the fruit of a tree, "and they will live a long life on earth, as your (Enoch's) fathers lived, and in their days sorrow and pain and toil and punishment will not touch them" (25:6). The reign of God, then, will finally involve a return to a paradisiac state. In view of ch 22 we must assume that the spirits of the dead can also participate in this state, even though it is located on earth. However, the Book of the Watchers does not refer to this eschatological state as "the kingdom of God," God is king of all eternity.

Again in the Book of Dreams (1 Enoch 83–90), God is hailed by prayer as "Lord King, great and powerful in your majesty, Lord of the whole creation of heaven, King of Kings and God of the whole world" (84:2). In the Animal Apocalypse (1 Enoch 90:20) the Lord takes his seat for judgment on a throne "in the pleasant land" (Israel). The transformation that follows the judgment is again located on earth, although it apparently involves a resurrection of the dead. In the Apocalypse of Weeks (1 Enoch 93:1–10; 91:11–17) both the historical temple and the eschatological one are associated with the kingship of God. The final consummation is an exercise of divine sovereignty, but it cannot be equated with the kingdom of God.

The Enochic writing which bears closest resemblance to Daniel is the Book of Similitudes (1 Enoch 37–71), a document of disputed date which most probably comes from around the time of Christ.[25] The expression

24. Camponovo, *Königtum*, 257.
25. D. W. Suter, *Tradition and Composition in the Parables of Enoch* (SBLDS 47; Missoula: Scholars, 1979) 11–38.

"kingdom of God" is not used, and God is called king in only one passage (1 Enoch 63:2-4). However, the theme of kingship is more important than a purely terminological inquiry might suggest. At the center of the Similitudes are God, the "Lord of Spirits" or "Head of Days," and the exalted angelic figure called "that Son of Man."[26] The main function of the Son of Man figure is to judge and destroy the kings and the powerful. "And this Son of Man whom you have seen will rouse the kings and the powerful from their resting places, and the strong from their thrones, and will loose the reins of the strong . . . and he will cast down kings from their thrones and from their kingdoms" (1 Enoch 46:4-5). The Lord of Spirits is ultimately the one "who is king over all kings" (63:4, cf. Dan 4:29), but he sets the Son of Man on his throne of glory (61:8; 62:5) to function as royal judge. The Similitudes do not speak of an earthly kingdom to replace that of "the kings of the mighty." The emphasis is rather on the resting places of the righteous with the angels and holy ones (39:5; cf. 51:4). The kingship of God is viewed primarily in its negative aspect, in the destruction of the kings of the earth. The Son of Man is also called "messiah" (48:10; 52:4) and takes over traditional kingly functions,[27] but his kingdom has an otherworldly character.

The Testament of Moses

Perhaps the clearest example of an "apocalyptic" kingdom of God is found in the Testament of Moses, which is not formally an apocalypse, but is closely related to the "historical" apocalypses in form and theme. In its present form the Testament dates from about the turn of the eras. It is probable, however, that the original document dates from the Maccabean period.[28] The redacted Testament is one of the few compositions that can be dated with confidence to the first half of the first century C.E., and so it is of considerable interest for the context in which Jesus lived.

The Testament of Moses reviews the history of Israel so as to demonstrate a pattern of sin and punishment. In ch 8: "there will come upon them punishment and wrath such as has never happened to them from the creation till that time." The punishment in question looks very much like the persecution of Antiochus Epiphanes. The Testament goes on to tell of a man named Taxo who takes his seven sons and resolves to fast for

---

26. See Collins, The Apocalyptic Imagination, 142–54.

27. J. Theisohn, Der auserwählte Richter (Göttingen: Vandenhoeck & Ruprecht, 1975) 98–99.

28. For the debate on the provenance of the Testament see the essays, Studies on the Testament of Moses (ed. G. W. Nickelsburg; Missoula: Scholars, 1973). For its relation to the apocalypses see Collins, The Apocalyptic Imagination, 102–6.

three days, go into a cave in the open country and die rather than transgress the commandments, "for if we do this and do die, our blood will be avenged before the Lord" (9:7). There follows directly the announcement that "then his kingdom will appear throughout his whole creation" (10:1). The manifestation of the kingdom will be the vengeance of God on his enemies, through the hands of an angel. Israel will be raised up to the heaven of the stars and see her enemies from on high.

As in Daniel and the Similitudes of Enoch, the kingdom here has a strongly destructive aspect. The statement in 10:8 that Israel will mount up above the necks and wings of the eagle breaks the metrical pattern, and so can be shown to involve a redactional change from the Roman period, when the eagle symbolized Rome.[29] The Testament does not speak of a Jewish kingdom to replace the Roman. The exaltation to the stars (10:9) should probably be understood, by analogy with Dan 12, to imply immortality. Otherwise we are given no positive description of the kingdom. Perhaps the most important point to note is that the kingdom is ushered in with no human agency. The contribution of the human Taxo is to purify himself and die—a course of action very similar to the *maskilim*, or wise teachers in Dan 11. In the Testament, as in Daniel and the Similitudes of Enoch, the kingdom of God is brought about by the transcendent power of God and his angels. It is not to be attained by human revolution and does not even involve the earthly career of a messiah.

The Psalms of Solomon

Messianic expectations did persist throughout this period, however.[30] Apart from the Qumran scrolls, the major witness is found in the Psalms of Solomon, from the mid-first century B.C.E. These Psalms were written after the violation of Jerusalem by Pompey in 63 B.C.E. The Psalmist takes the subsequent death of Pompey in Egypt as evidence "that it is God who is great, powerful in his great strength. He is king over the heavens, judging even kings and rulers" (Pss Sol 2:29–30). As in Dan 4, God is the king who disposes of all kingdoms.

The Psalms' theology of kingship is most fully laid out in Pss Sol 17. After an initial declaration that "you, Lord, are our king forevermore" (v 1) and that "the kingdom of our God is forever over the nations in

29. Adela Yarbro Collins, "Composition and Redaction of the Testament of Moses 10," *HTR* 69 (1976) 179–86. Cf. the incident in 4 B.C.E. when two doctors of the law incited some youths to pull down the golden eagle from the temple (Josephus, *JW* 1.33.2–4 [648–55]; *Ant* 17.6.2–3 [149–63]).

30. J. H. Charlesworth, "The Concept of the Messiah in the Pseudepigrapha," *ANRW* 1:12 (ed. W. H. Haase; Berlin: de Gruyter, 1979) 188–218.

judgment" (v 3), the psalm recalls how God chose David as king. "Those to whom you did not make the promise" (the Hasmoneans) set up a kingdom because of their arrogance, and provoked the punishment of God through the hand of the lawless one (Pompey). Now the psalmist prays, "See, Lord, and raise up for them their king, the son of David, to rule over your servant Israel" (Pss Sol 17:21). The kingdom ruled by this messiah is essentially the restoration of a national Jewish kingdom. He will "purge Jerusalem from gentiles" (17:22); and "he will have gentile nations serving him under his yoke" (v 30); and "there will be no unrighteousness among them in his days, for all shall be holy, and their king shall be the Lord Messiah (v 32).[31]

The Psalms of Solomon show the influence of apocalypticism in one important respect: the belief that "those who fear the Lord shall rise up to eternal life" (3:12; cf. 13:11; 14:3; 15:13). The dominant emphasis, however, is on the restoration of a national kingdom where the kingship of God is mediated by a Davidic messiah.

The Testaments of the Twelve Patriarchs

Messianic expression about the turn of the era is not well documented. That is due, at least in part, to the limitation of our sources. The Testaments of the Twelve Patriarchs are widely believed to preserve Jewish material from the second century B.C.E. forward. Perhaps the most notable of these traditions is the association of the messiah with both Levi and Judah. In the present form of the Testaments, one messiah, Christ, is both priest and king, but it is very probable that the earlier tradition envisaged a dual messiahship as we also find at Qumran. According to Test Dan 13:10–13, salvation will arise from Levi and Judah and defeat Beliar. Then the souls of the saints will rest in Eden and rejoice in the new Jerusalem and "the Holy One of Israel will reign over them." The kingdom of God here has a distinctly apocalyptic character insofar as it involves victory over Beliar, resurrection, and a new, rather than restored, Jerusalem. It is also Christian in its present form. Unfortunately, the Testaments do not provide independent evidence of Jewish beliefs but need corroboration from the sources.[32]

---

31. See further Camponovo, Königtum, 200–228; G. Davenport, "The 'Anointed of the Lord' in Psalms of Solomon 17," in Ideal Figures in Ancient Judaism (ed. G. W. Nickelsburg and J. J. Collins; Missoula: Scholars, 1980) 67–92.

32. For an overview of the debate about the Testaments see J. J. Collins, "Testaments," Jewish Writings of the Second Temple Period (ed. M. Stone; Philadelphia: Fortress, 1984) 325–44; "The Testamentary Literature in Recent Scholarship," Early Judaism and its Modern Interpreters (ed. G. W. Nickelsburg and R. A. Kraft; Philadelphia: Fortress, 1986) 268–78.

Messianic Movements in the First Century

We know from Josephus that there were messianic movements in the first century C.E. which did not leave written records of their ideology.[33] A number of these movements developed after the death of Herod, led by such figures as Judas of Galilee, Simon, a servant of Herod, and Athronges, a shepherd.[34] At the time of the first Jewish revolt against Rome further messianic pretenders appeared—Menahem, son of Judas, and most notably Simon Bar Giora.[35] In the early second century the great Diaspora revolt centered on the messianic figure Andreas (Lukuas) and of course Bar Kochba was also a messianic figure. In all of these cases the messianic movements were actively and violently revolutionary, and the objective was to replace Roman rule with a native Jewish kingdom.

Josephus distinguishes these violent revolutionaries from

> another group of scoundrels, in act less criminal but in intention more evil. . . . Cheats and deceivers, claiming inspiration, they schemed to bring about revolutionary changes by inducing the mob to act as if possessed and by leading them out into the wild country on the pretence that there God would give them signs of approaching freedom.[36]

The best known examples of this type, Theudas and the Egyptian,[37] did not claim to be messiahs and are not said by Josephus to have spoken of a kingdom; but, we simply do not know how they conceived their actions. They bear enough similarity to Taxo in the Testament of Moses to merit mention here.[38]

Messianism in the Apocalypses

Messianic expectations were integrated into an apocalyptic schema in the great apocalypses from the end of the first century C.E., 4 Ezra and 2 Baruch.[39] Fourth Ezra draws on the four-kingdom schema of Daniel in the

33. The best account of these movements can be found in R. A. Horsely and J. Hanson, *Bandits, Prophets and Messiahs* (Minneapolis: Winston/Seabury, 1986) ch 3.

34. Judas: *Ant* 17.10.5. (271–72); Simon: *Ant* 17.10.6 (273–76); Athronges: *Ant* 17.10.7 (278–85).

35. Menahem: *JW* 2.17.8–9 (433–48). On the messianic character of Simon see Horsely and Hanson, *Bandits*.

36. *JW* 2.13.4 (258–60).

37. Theudas: *Ant* 20.5.1 (97–99); Acts 5:36. The Egyptian: *JW* 2.13.5 (261–63); Acts 21:38.

38. On the relevance of these figures to discussions of "the kingdom" see E. P. Sanders, *Jesus and Judaism* (Philadelphia: Fortress, 1985) 138.

39. See M. E. Stone, "The Concept of the Messiah in II Ezra," *Religions in Antiquity, Essays in Memory of E. R. Goodenough* (ed. J. Neusner; Leiden: Brill, 1968) 295–312; Müller, *Messias und Menschensohn*, 83–154.

vision of the lion and the eagle in chs 11–12. The eagle symbolizes Rome, "the fourth kingdom which appeared in a vision to your brother Daniel" (12:11). The lion is "the Messiah whom the Most High has kept until the end of days, who will arise from the posterity of David" (12:32). The function of this messiah is to rebuke and destroy the nations, especially Rome, and to deliver "the remnant of my people" (12:34). In 4 Ezra 13, the messiah, identified as "he whom the Most High has been keeping for many ages" (12:26) and "my son" (13:32, 37) rises from the sea on a cloud. He destroys the nations with the breath of his mouth and gathers the lost tribes of Israel.

According to 4 Ezra 7:28–30 the messiah will reign on earth for 400 years, and then die. There will follow seven days of primeval silence, a new creation, and the resurrection of the dead. The traditional hope for a messianic kingdom is thus given a place in the schema, but it is not the ultimate focus of hope.

Second Baruch operates with a similar schema. Here again we find the four-kingdom sequence, in ch 39. The messiah will uproot the fourth kingdom, and "his dominion will last forever until the world of corruption has ended and until the times which have been mentioned before have been fulfilled" (40:3). His reign is nonetheless temporary. The description of his reign in ch 29 is followed by the prediction that "it will happen after these things when the time of the appearance of the Anointed One has been fulfilled and he returns with glory, that then all who sleep in hope of him will rise" (30:1–2). The reign of the messiah marks the end of gentile dominion and brings about the transformation of the earth (cf. chs 72–74), but again the focus of the apocalyptic hope lies beyond the messianic reign in the new age of the resurrection. Neither 2 Baruch nor 4 Ezra uses the expression "kingdom of God" for the messianic age, but their conceptions are evidently of relevance here, especially in view of their use of the four kingdom schema.

The Targums to the Prophets

The Targumic and Rabbinic literature lie outside the scope of this survey. Yet the Targum Jonathan to the Prophets requires some comment, since a number of recent studies have argued that its "kingdom theology may represent first century thinking."[40] The difficulty of dating the Targumic material is notorious. At most, particular exegetical traditions can be

---

40. B. Chilton, *The Kingdom of God*, 22. See also his *The Glory of Israel, The Theology and Provenance of the Isaiah Targum* (Sheffield: JSOT, 1982). The relevance of the Targums for the teaching of Jesus is also urged by Klaus Koch, "Offenbaren wind sich das Reich Gottes," *NTS* 25 (1979) 158–65.

shown to be early by comparison with other, dateable material.[41] The motif of the "kingdom of God" has attracted attention because the phrase is used in a set, standard way, as it also is in Gospels, but not in the Apocrypha and Pseudepigrapha, and because the Targumic use of the phrase contrasts with the Rabbinic use of "the kingdom of heaven" for the rule of the law.

In the Targum of Isaiah the phrase "kingdom of God" or "kingdom of the Lord" is used in place of a reference to God himself: e.g. at Isa 24:23 the MT "because the Lord of hosts will reign on Mt. Zion" is rendered "because the kingdom of the Lord of hosts will be revealed on Mt. Zion."[42] We should not conclude that the kingdom is simply a periphrasis for God himself.[43] The phrase is used in contexts where the MT is already eschatological. The characteristic Targumic phrase "the kingdom of the Lord will be revealed" puts the emphasis on the expectation of an eschatological event. The idea of the "revelation" of the kingdom has its closest parallel in Test Moses 10:1, and the very fact that it is revealed gives it an "apocalyptic" character. Yet the Targum does not show the interest in an angelic transcendent world, characteristic of Daniel or the Similitudes of Enoch. Rather, the kingdom is associated with Mt. Zion.[44] The Targum shows a developed interest in the Davidic messiah, and also associates him with Zion (Targum Isaiah 16:1, 5).[45] In general the eschatology of the Targum looks for a Jewish restoration, but it also includes the resurrection of the dead (Targum Isaiah 26:19). In all of this the "kingdom theology" of the Targum may be compatible with that of the Psalms of Solomon or perhaps (but less clearly) of 4 Ezra and 2 Baruch. As in all of this literature there is a sharp antithesis between the fate of Jerusalem and that of Rome (e.g. Targum Isaiah 54:1). The kingdom of God is, of course, based on the idea of divine sovereignty, but it would seem to

41. See Chilton, The Glory of Israel, 4–12.

42. The references to the kingdom of God, or of the Lord, are laid out clearly by Camponovo, Königtum, 419–28.

43. So Chilton, The Glory of Israel, 77. Cf. his article "Regnum Dei Deus Est." SJT 31 (1978) 261–70. He qualifies the identification however by saying that the periphrasis is "employed in respect of divine and saving revelation, particularly on Mt. Zion." Cf. his clarification of his view in The Kingdom of God, 23: "I have suggested that the future-oriented eschatological aspect of the kingdom is to be acknowledged, but that it stems from Jesus' view of God, and not from a particular expectation of the future."

44. Chilton (The Glory of Israel, 78) finds a discrepancy between an exclusively Zion-associated kingdom in Targum Isaiah and a more universal one in Targum Zechariah, but the biblical Isaiah already conceives of a universal kingdom center on Zion.

45. The references to the messiah in the Isaiah Targum are collected by Chilton, The Glory of Israel, 86–96. In an appendix, 112–17, he concludes that "the other Latter Prophets Targums appear to reflect messianic teaching consistent with that represented in the Isaiah Targum, but not so fully," and that the Jeremiah and Ezekiel targum are closest to that of Isaiah. In Targum Micah 4:7–8 the revelation of the kingdom is explicitly associated with the messiah.

imply the expectation of an earthly kingdom too. Klaus Koch is probably right when he concludes: "the kingdom of God, the kingdom of the messiah and the dominion of Israel (over the nations) belong together for the Targum."[46]

Conclusion

We have seen that the motif of the kingdom of God was a complex one in Judaism in the period 200 B.C.E.–100 C.E. The basic underlying idea of all conceptions of the kingdom was that God is king of the universe, past, present, and future. In some contexts the kingdom could be understood in a moral or spiritual way, especially in the Hellenistic Diaspora. In the great majority of cases, however, especially in the land of Israel, in the first centuries B.C.E. and C.E., it was expected that the "kingship" of God would be manifested in an eschatological kingdom.

The eschatological kingdom could still be conceived in various ways. We may contrast the apocalyptic kingdom of Dan 7–12 or Test Moses 10, which would be brought about by angels, with the more traditional messianic kingdom of Pss Sol 17. These two types however do not remain pure and separate:[47] in 4 Ezra and 2 Baruch the messianic kingdom is accommodated as a transitory stage within an apocalyptic framework. Even the earthly kingdom of the Pss Sol involved the resurrection of the dead, but this belief was not taken up in the Sibylline Oracles of Egyptian Judaism (i.e. Sib Or 3 and 5). Finally we lack direct information about the ideology of the various messianic and prophetic movements mentioned by Josephus, which left no records of their own, but which apparently aimed at the restoration of the Jewish nation. The common denominator of all eschatological formulations of the kingdom, however, in addition to the postulate of divine sovereignty, was rejection of foreign rule. The implementation of the kingdom of God, whether by a messiah or a direct heavenly intervention, implied the destruction of the kings and the mighty of this world.

The material we have reviewed here illustrates the associations which would have been attached to the proclamation of the kingdom of God in the first century. It is of course possible that Jesus departed radically from these ways of understanding the kingdom, but at the very least they provide the context within which his proclamation would have been understood.

---

46. Koch, "Offenbaren," 164.

47. Cf. the classic typology of Jewish eschatology proposed by Sigmund Mowinckel, *He That Cometh* (Nashville: Abingdon, 1955) 281.

7   The Kingdom of God in the Qumran Literature

B. T. Viviano, OP

Professor of New Testament,
École Biblique et Archéologique Française, Jerusalem

THE DESCRIPTION OF QUMRAN eschatological benefits and hopes, among which may be numbered the hope for the kingdom of God, is vexed at the present time by several problems of method. This essay will proceed in the following fashion. I will give a definition of terms (I), then a brief presentation of the current scholarly debate (II). These will be followed by a rather austere inventory of the terms for kingdom or rule of God in the published Qumran texts (III). Next will come a closer look at some passages from one of the main eschatological texts, the War Scroll from Cave 1 (IV). Some larger perspectives will form the conclusion (V).

Definition of Terms

An inquiry into the hope of a future kingdom of God on earth requires a definition of terms. An apocalyptic eschatology contains a view of life which presupposes a God who can and does act in history, not a deistic God who does not intervene in the world's affairs. This God can act directly or through angels, men, natural events, or miracles. Such an eschatology differs from other biblical beliefs in divine intervention in the past, for example at creation or at the exodus from Egyptian bondage or Babylonian exile, in that it believes that God will yet intervene in history in a definitive, major new act that will usher in a period of full justice, peace, and love. In this future period God's sovereignty and kingship will not only be acknowledged in faith and hope, but will be visible and realized in the structures of society. This latter state is referred to as the kingdom of God in its full earthly realization. This kingdom is not to be confused with God's permanent sovereignty in heaven.

In Jewish writings, the establishment of this kingdom is often con-nected with the military triumph of God's elect people and the elimina-tion of its enemies. This kingdom hope is sometimes connected with messianic figures, sometimes not. The establishment of the kingdom is sometimes thought to follow upon the resurrection of the saints to an earthly life; at times it is thought to precede such a resurrection; and on other occasions, as in the Qumran War Scroll, it is not connected with resurrection at all. (Even though in the NT, both a belief in a future kingdom and in the resurrection are held, they are not usually related; 1 Cor 15:20–28 and Rev 20:1–7 are exceptional in this regard.) A belief in the immortality of the soul may be joined to a belief in the resurrection of the body and eternal life with God (this is an early Christian synthesis), but is not so easily combined with the expectation of a kingdom of God on earth. This latter expectation remains characteristically Jewish and Jew-ish Christian.

Apocalyptic eschatology can express its hopes in more or less realistic, more or less utopian, visionary, terms. Indeed, there can be intense combinations of the realistic and the utopian, as in the vision of the restored temple and land in Ezk 40–48 or in the War Scroll of Qumran. The realization of the kingdom may be presented as more dependent on human repentance and cooperation, or less dependent.

The fluidity of apocalyptic eschatology's precise beliefs and its lack of dogmatic consistency have often been noted.[1] But the conclusion that these beliefs were therefore unimportant to those who held them, or to Judaism in general or to early Christianity, is probably wide of the mark. At least for some circles of believers, in some of their moods, they were important, forming the ultimate horizon of their hopes and religious vision. Sapiential and legal literature tend not to mention such hopes, but it is at least possible that one and the same author composed works in all three genres. (See the view of Carmignac mentioned below.) Such hopes and beliefs constitute a unique aspect of Jewish and Jewish Christian literature of the Hellenistic-Roman period, especially in Greco-Roman civilization, whose outlook tends to be more cyclical and deistic, or else pantheistic. This remains true despite the Stoic belief in fiery consum-mation (ἐκπύρωσις) of the present world, since a reconstitution of the present is expected, not a new order. The last judgment scene in Plato's Gorgias (523–26) looks to individual rewards and punishments rather than to a kingdom of God on earth. For our purposes then, a hope for the kingdom of God is a hope for a future divine intervention in history that

---

1. See G. F. Moore, *Judaism in the Tannaitic Period* (Cambridge: Harvard University, 1927) 2:323–95; D. S. Russell, *Method and Message of Jewish Apocalyptic* (Philadelphia: Westminster, 1964) 285–323; E. E. Urbach, *The Sages* (Jerusalem: Magnes, 1979) 649–90; M. Smith, "What is Implied by the Variety of Messianic Figures?" *JBL* 78 (1959) 66–72.

would establish a realm of justice, peace, and love of God and neighbor on earth. The question is, did the Qumran community share such a hope?

Current Scholarship

The preceding set of definitions was made necessary in part by a wave of debates over the use of the term "apocalyptic" in connection with Qumran and over the right methodology in the study of eschatology at Qumran. Jean Carmignac has attacked eschatology as an artificial construction of nineteenth-century scholarship and prefers to avoid the term altogether.[2] To be sure, there is need for caution in investigating ancient texts, lest one impose artificial systems of doctrine upon them or find an artificial unity of thought in works of different authors or in single works of composite authorship. But, in the case of Qumran literature, there can be little doubt that at least several of the sectarian writings share some basic conceptions with the apocalypse genre, and, rightly or wrongly, Carmignac himself holds that the Community Rule, the Thanksgiving Hymns, and the War Scroll were all substantially composed by the same author, the Teacher of Righteousness.[3]

Recently J. J. Collins, in a survey of eschatology at Qumran, continued the tradition of viewing the Qumran community as an "apocalyptic community."[4] For this he has been severely criticized by P. R. Davies.[5] Davies' thesis is that "in the elucidation of Qumran doctrines the only method that offers even the prospect of success is one of *documentary* analysis."[6] In this he follows the path pioneered by Jerome Murphy-O'Connor.[7] Literary analysis must be applied to the Qumran documents, to be sure, but this does not solve all problems.

Davies' own reconstruction of the types of eschatological doctrine into (a) *dualistic* (1QS 3:13–4:26; 1QM 1:15–19); (b) *legalistic* (a reformed Israel will observe a stricter interpretation of the Mosaic law, a solar calendar,

---

2. J. Carmignac, *Le Mirage de l'Eschatologie* (Paris: Letouzey, 1979); idem, "Apocalyptique et Qumran," *RevQ* 37 (1979) 163–92; idem, "Roi, Royauté et Royaume dans la Liturgie Angelique," *RevQ* 46 (1986) 176–86; idem, "Règne de Dieu. Qumran," DBS 10 (1981) 58–61.

3. J. Carmignac and P. Guilbert, *Les Textes de Qumran* (Paris: Letouzey, 1961) 83–86.

4. J. J. Collins, Patterns of Eschatology at Qumran," in *Traditions in Transformation* (ed. B. Halpern and J. D. Levenson; Winona Lake, Ind.: Eisenbrauns, 1981) 331–73.

5. P. R. Davies, "Eschatology at Qumran," *JBL* 104 (1985) 39–55.

6. Davies, "Eschatology," 48.

7. J. Murphy-O'Connor, "La génèse littéraire de la Règle de la Communauté," *RB* 76 (1969) 328–549; his series of analysis of the Damascus Document (in English) in *RB* 77 (1970) 201–29; 78 (1971) 210–32; 79 (1972) 200–216; 344–64; he is followed by J. Pouilly, *La Règle de la Communauté de Qumran: Son Évolution Littéraire* (CahRB 17; Paris: Gabalda, 1976).

and supremacy over the nations [1QM ii–ix; 1QSa]); and (c) *exilic/jubilee* (CD), is not in itself implausible, but leaves many questions open.[8] Are not these three strands capable of being combined? How are we to understand the joining of patterns (a) and (b) in the War Scroll as we know it from the Sukenik manuscript? Arc wc not pcrmittcd to interpret the latest stage of the War Scroll as a unity? How do we account for cols x–xiv of the War Scroll?[9]

These methodological problems, while important, need not prevent us from providing a survey of Qumran word usage. They do not impede a discussion of the War Scroll, since the parts that most concern us are col i, x–xiv, xv–xix, not ii–ix; but they will serve to put us on our guard against sweeping generalizations. They encourage us to concentrate on individual documents or parts of documents.[10]

Terminology

The most elementary task in a study of the kingdom of God in the Qumran literature is a review of the word usage. Beside the main Hebrew word

8. Davies, "Eschatology," 49.

9. In his earlier work, *1QM, The War Scroll from Qumran* (BibOr 32; Rome: PBI, 1977), P. R. Davies provides answers to some of these questions. He analyzes cols x–xiv as containing material—prayers and hymns—of diverse origin, perhaps from a collection of liturgical pieces, "the order of the time [of battle]," and especially two main hymns in cols x–xii. Cols xiii and xiv are independent fragments. Davies understands col i as an introduction which serves to unify the diverse earlier material which follows in cols ii–xix. On this view the author of col i viewed cols ii–xix as a potential unity.

10. In summary of earlier studies of Qumran eschatology, Herbert Braun came to the conclusion in *Qumran und das Neue Testament* (Tübingen: Mohr, 1966) 2:265–86, that the Qumran texts were apocalyptic. In their view the last generation outside the community is evil; a holy war and last judgment are expected; final salvation includes an eschatological temple and a messianic banquet; but the kingdom of God and eternal life are not the central themes, while immortality and very probably resurrection from the dead are not present at all. Eschatological figures include a prophet, a teacher, and two messiahs—though neither suffers. The Son of man is not mentioned (but may be represented by Michael). There is a not inconsiderable analogy to the NT.

John the Baptist's views and activity are particularly close, but he has a different idea of the messiah, a different use of the water rite, and makes his message public, in contrast with the Qumranite esotericism. A comparison with the Synoptic Gospels' portrait of Jesus would show that while Qumran is esoteric, Jesus goes public. Both share a near expectation of a new era of salvation; both erred in this; both believe the process has already begun, and is the fulfillment of Scripture. But for Qumran there is no suddenness of the end, no miracles or atoning death of Jesus as signs of the end's nearness. For both the final generation outside the community is evil and exists at the present time. Regarding the holy war, Jesus does not favor hatred or violence; thus one could say he is anational and apolitical. But, though universal in election, he does have a politics, but it depends on God's supernatural intervention, not on human violence. Both demand conversion in view of the last judgment. The gospel view of final salvation resembles Qumran's in many respects, but differs in respect to the messiah, the resurrection, and the greater emphasis on the kingdom of God.

for kingdom, *malkût*, other synonyms must be noted; *melukāh*, *mam-lākāh*, as well as the words for domination, *memšālāh*, and princely rule, *miśrāh*. Not every occurrence is relevant, however, since the same terms are employed for earthly rulers. We must look for usages which combine a religious with political aspiration. Besides the listings in K. G. Kuhn's Qumran concordance,[11] we must also note the supplementary concordance, in the *Revue de Qumran* for 1963, to texts published after Kuhn's work had appeared. Yadin's elegant edition of the Temple Scroll includes a concordance to that work.

Malkût occurs 15 times though 3 occurrences are uncertain textually; *melukāh* occurs twice, and *mamlākāh* once; *memšālāh* occurs 31 times, *miśrāh* thrice. Moreover the term *melek*, king, is applied to God 11 times. And the corresponding verb *mālak*, reign, is applied to God twice, 1QM 12:3 and 4QFlor 1:3, a citation of Ex 15:18: "The Lord shall reign for ever and ever." There are two further references to the kingdom of God in the Aramaic fragments of the books Enoch found at Qumran,[12] but they are not of special importance.

A fair sample rather than an exhaustive citation of texts must be offered here, but complete references will be given at the end of the paragraphs devoted to each term. We begin with the term *malkût* and where it is most frequent, in the War Scroll (1QM). The high priest's exhortation in the battle liturgy contains a call for divine intervention which begins with this praise: "For thou art (terrible), O God, in the glory of *thy kingdom*, and the congregation of thy holy Ones is among us for everlasting succor" (12:7). This line clearly refers to God's kingdom in its permanent form, which is made presently effective on earth ("among us") by the angels ("thy Holy Ones") as they help God's people overturn earthly kings (the next line makes this clear).[13] The end of col xii is damaged, but in line 15 we may read "Shout for joy, (O daughters of) my people! Deck yourselves with glorious jewels and rule over (the *kingdoms* of the nations!)" or "rule over the kingdom" or "rule over the *queens* of the peoples" (so Carmignac, *in loco*). Here the people of God are exhorted to rule over the nations on earth, which amounts to taking part in God's rule on earth. The next line contains three clear words: "Israel to rule forever." War Scroll 19:7 contains an echo of 12:15, but the part of interest, "rule over the kingdom," is too uncertain textually to be helpful. War Scroll 19:8 echoes 12:16 "Israel for the kingdom forever," but again, it lacks a complete context. Still, one thinks of the everlasting kingdom of Dan 7:14.

In the *Blessings*, Appendix B to the Manual of Discipline (1QSb 3:5), we

---

11. K. G. Kuhn, *Konkordanz zu den Qumrantexten. In Verbindung mit A.-M. Denis, O.P.* (Göttingen: Vandenhoeck & Ruprecht, 1960).

12. J. T. Milik, ed., *The Books of Enoch* (Oxford: University Press, 1976), 266 and 316.

13. There are allusions to Dt 7.21 and Ps 143:11 in the first part of the line.

find this prayer: "May he grant you everlasting peace and the kingdom." This is important because it associates the kingdom with peace, as elsewhere it is associated with justice. These are the kingdom's main moral contents, as Paul knew (Rom 14:17). That the biblical concept of peace is wider than ours is well known, but it still includes the absence of war. In the next column (4:26), part of the priestly blessing runs: "May you attend upon the service in the Temple of the *kingdom* and decree destiny in company with the angels of the presence (*panim*), in common council (with the Holy Ones) for everlasting ages." Here the theology of the renewed temple is related to that of the kingdom of God.

The priests on whom the blessing is invoked are envisaged as serving God in a purified cult, participating in the divine judgment (Mt 19:28; Lk 22:28–30) along with the angels (Mt 23:31).[14] In 5:21 of the same document we read: "The Master shall bless the Prince of the Congregation . . . and shall renew for him the covenant of the community that he may establish the *kingdom* of his people for ever, (that he may judge the poor with righteousness and) dispense justice with (equity to the oppressed) of the land."[15] Here the kingdom is linked with the theology of the covenant and especially with the moral content of justice for the poor and oppressed (Mt 5:3–11; 6:33; Rom 14:17). In the Patriarchal Blessings of Cave 4, Gen 49:10, the blessing by Jacob of Judah, is cited and then interpreted. The *ruler's staff* of Genesis is first interpreted (1:2) as "the *covenant of kingship*" (or "of the kingdom") and this unusual phrase is then repeated in line 4: "For to him (the Davidic messiah) and to his seed was granted the *covenant of kingship* over his people for everlasting generations." This formula is remarkable both because of its link of covenant and kingdom and because of its messianic interpretation of the kingdom concept. God will rule over his kingdom through his anointed one.

In the pesher to Nah 3:10, we find: "Interpreted, this concerns Manasseh in the final age, whose *kingdom* shall be brought low by (Israel)." In the pesher, Manasseh represents the evil and illegitimate king, here perhaps Alexander Jannaeus. His kingdom represents false or sinful Israel, but this is not the same as the kingdom of Satan of Mt 12:26 and Lk 11:18. In the Angelic Liturgy at Qumran (4QS1 39, line 25) we find: "He shall bless all the (companions) of righteousness who endlessly (praise) the kingdom of his glory." Again we see the link with justice and the allusion to Ps 143:11. In the Temple Scroll (39:17, 21), the king's descendants are promised that they will sit on the throne of the kingdom of Israel

14. On the theology of the temple in both testaments, see Y. J. Congar, *The Mystery of the Temple* (Baltimore: Helicon, 1963).

15. The first part may echo 1 Sam 24:20 (HT 21). The lacuna can be supplied from Isa 11:4.

forever. In this document the king functions as the executor of the will of God, but God is not explicitly presented as the heavenly king of the earthly king.

So much then for *melukāh*. The term *melukāh* occurs in the War Scroll once: "And sovereignty shall be to the God of Israel, and he shall accomplish mighty deeds by the saints of his people." This line (6:6) contains echoes of Ob 21 and Num 24:18. It occurs in a section (col ii–ix) which literary criticism commonly assigns to a different author, but it nevertheless shares the same basic hope as the more theological portions. (There is another occurrence of this word in Fragment 25 which I have not been able to examine.)

The synonymous term *mamlākāh* occurs in the Thanksgiving Psalms (6:7) in the plural (and damaged at that): "And I am consoled for the roaring of the peoples, and for the tumult of *k(ing)doms*) when they assemble," but this does not refer to the kingdom of God but to its rivals.

The term *memšālāh*, domination, occurs over thirty times, too often to cite each case in full. I must select some relevant instances.[16] Outside the War Scroll, the most important occurrences are found in the Community Rule. In the first columns the dominion of Belial is mentioned three times. In the theologically crucial Instruction of the Two Spirits (3:13–4:26) the terms occurs five times, mostly in a single passage (3:17–23):

> He has created man to have *dominion* over the world, and has appointed for him two spirits in which to walk until the time of his visitation: the spirits of truth and falsehood. . . . *Dominion* over all the sons of righteousness is in the hand of the Prince of light; they walk in the ways of light. All *dominion* over the sons of perversity is in the hand of the Angel of darkness; they walk in the ways of darkness. And because of the Angel of darkness all the sons of righteousness go astray; and all their sins and iniquities . . . are because of his *dominion*, according to the Mysteries of God until the end appointed by him. And all the blows that smite them . . . are because of the *dominion* of his malevolence.

Here we see first of all man's *dominium terrae*, given him by God in Gen 1:28. Next we notice the dualistic thinking, in which two conflicting spirits are personified as angels who have contrasting moral effects on humanity. The dominions of these spirits are present, interior to man, and moral (or immoral, cf. Mt 12:26). But if one follows the line of thinking of the Instruction, one sees that the struggle between the spirits is not endless, but concludes in the final triumph of the spirit of truth and holiness.

The result for those who walk in this good spirit is described in 1QS 4:6–8, and this is the positive content of the future, final kingdom of God for this document: "It will be healing, abundance of peace (well-being)

16. The complete list of occurrences runs: pHab 2:13; 1QS 1:18, 23; 2:19; 3:17, 20, 21, 22, 23; 4:19; 10:1; 1QM 1:6, 13; 10:12; 13:10; 14:9, 10; 17:3, 7; 18:1, 11: 1QH 1:11, 17; 7:23; 12:6, 9, 23; 13:11; Frag 34, 3, 2, 3; 4QMa 6; pNah 2:4.

for length of days, fruitfulness of seed, with all everlasting blessings and eternal joy in life without end and a crown of glory with a garment of splendor in unending light." This is an excellent description of the kingdom of God, rivaling Rom 14:17, but it fails to mention justice explicitly, because it concentrates on the blessings for the individual, rather than society.

Most of the uses of *memšālāh* in the Thanksgiving Hymns are not relevant because they are not eschatological. But there is one noteworthy exception. In 7:23 the Teacher of Righteousness prays: "My enemies are like chaff before the wind, and my *dominion* is over the sons (of the earth, or, of iniquity)." Dupont-Sommer comments: "The idea announced here is very important: the Teacher of Righteousness will rule; he will be conqueror and lord."[17] Unfortunately, this interpretation, which almost amounts to seeing here a messianic kingdom, is probably an overinterpretation. Most probably no more is meant than that the Teacher of Righteousness expresses his trust that God will vindicate him against his enemies. In any cases it is poor method to build too much on a single line, and a damaged one at that.

The other significant uses of *memšālāh*, as well as the three instances of *miśrāh*, are all in the War Scroll, so they will be treated in the next section.

The Kingdom of God and the War Scroll

The War Scroll resembles a liturgy of holy war, based on Dt 20:1–20 (cf. Num 21:14 which mentions the book of the wars of God, and 1 Sam 1 8:17; 23:28 where defensive wars of God are mentioned) and influenced by the description of almost magical conquest in the Book of Judges. Other important biblical influences are the Gog and Magog oracles of Ezk 38–39 and the vision of the last days in Dan 10–12.

A war of 40 years duration is envisaged (col ii), but 5 of these are years of sabbatical rest. Of the 35 years of effective service, 6 are for preparation and 29 for active campaigning. The scroll reflects an obsessive character of paranoid ideation, a mixture of the really practical and of the utopian, not unlike Ezk 40–48. Even the unreal elements often have a biblical foundation, like the trumpets of col iii which are based on Num 10:1–10. Some aspects are turned into brief reality by the various Jewish revolts of the first and second centuries.

Turning to the issue of the kingdom of God in the Scroll, let us begin by

---

17. A. Dupont-Sommer, *The Essene Writings from Qumran*, (Cleveland: World, 1962), 224, n. 4.

recalling our definition of the kingdom hope as a hope for a future divine intervention in history which would establish a realm of justice, peace, and love. Next, let us look at a significant, longer passage from the War Scroll (12:7–16, repeated in 19:2–8), a passage Carmignac describes as a hymn of enthusiasm, itself part of a longer discourse of the chief priest. The passage is divided into three strophes, each beginning with a vocative: God, hero, Zion. It is debated whether the second strophe is addressed to God or to the Prince of the congregation, but the former seems more likely. The whole hymn draws heavily upon biblical phrases. Because of its importance, we will quote the text in full.

> For thou art terrible, O God, in the glory of thy *kingdom*,
> And congregation of the holy ones is among us for everlasting succor.
> We will despise kings, we will mock and scorn the mighty;
> For our God is holy, and the king of glory is with us
> Together with the holy ones.
> Valiant warriors of the angelic host are among our numbered men,
> And the hero of war is with our congregation;
> The host of the spirits is with our foot-soldiers and horsemen.
> They are as clouds, as clouds of dew covering the earth,
> As a shower of rain shedding *justice* on all that grows on the earth.
>
> Rise up, O hero!
> Lead off thy captives, O glorious one! Gather up thy spoils, O author of mighty deeds!
> Lay thy hands on the neck of thine enemies and thy feet on the pile of the slain!
> Smite the nations, thine adversaries, and devour the flesh of the sinner with thy sword!
> Fill thy land with glory and thine inheritance with *blessing*!
> Let there be a multitude of cattle in thy fields
>   and in thy palaces silver and gold and precious stones!
>
> O Zion, *rejoice* greatly!
> O Jerusalem, show thyself amidst jubilation!
> Rejoice, all you cities of Judah;
> Keep your gates open that the hosts of the nations may be brought in.
> Their kings shall serve you
>   and all your oppressors shall bow down before you;
>   they shall lick the dust of your feet.
> Shout for joy, O daughters of my people!
> Deck yourselves with glorious jewels and *rule* over the *kingdom* of the nations!
> *Sovereignty* shall be to the Lord and everlasting *dominion* to Israel. (1QM 12:7–15)

This hymn gathers together many threads which make up the kingdom theme. It is, especially in its second strophe, a prayer for a future divine intervention in history, based on confidence in God's present and permanent power expressed in the first strophe. This intervention will establish a realm of justice (12:10) and blessing (12:12). This blessing is described as agricultural and mineral prosperity, corresponding to biblical ideas of well-being and peace. The third strophe stresses the theme of joy, expressed as a delight in God and his saving deeds. One component of this joy is contempt for the vanquished enemies. Love of neighbor, of God's people, does not extend to love of enemies. We notice further a bracketing or inclusion: the kingdom dominion is mentioned explicitly in the first and last lines of the hymn. But in the first line it refers to God's permanent reign in heaven, while in the final lines it refers to God's future reign with his people on earth. Despite considerable differences, namely the military imagery and the vindictive tone, one can see the same structure of thought in the hymn as Paul's definition of kingdom of God as justice, peace, and joy in the Holy Spirit (Rom 14:17).

This text and its analysis makes our main point, that there is a kingdom hope at Qumran and that it shares some common presuppositions with the kingdom hope of the NT, while differing from it in several aspects. It remains to look at a few other texts from the War Scroll for additional nuances. The characteristic dualism of the theological framework of the Scroll appears in the mention of Belial and the angels of his empire (1:15 damaged), the dominion of Belial and men of his empire (14:9–10; 18:1, 11) for the opposition, and on the other hand the empire of the saints (10:12), the dominion of Israel (17:7), and most notably the empire of the Prince of light (13:10), who is doubtless to be identified as the angelic agent of divine power, Michael. This we learn by turning to a key but complex passage (17:6–7) where the term *miśrāh* (a cognate of *śar*, a word for prince) occurs twice, alongside other related vocabulary.

> This is the day appointed by him (God) for defeat and overthrow of the prince of the kingdom of wickedness. He will send eternal succor to the company of his redeemed by the might of the princely angel of the kingdom of Michael. With everlasting light he will enlighten with joy (the children) of Israel; peace and blessing shall be with the company of God. He will raise up the kingdom of Michael in the midst of the gods, and the realm of Israel in the midst of all flesh. Justice shall rejoice on high, and all the children of his truth shall jubilate in eternal knowledge. (1QM 17:6–7)

This passage is clearly influenced by Daniel. The role of Michael comes from Dan 10:13 and 12:1; he is the national protecting angel of Israel, as there are national angels for the Persians and the Greeks (Dan 10:20). The kingdom of God is the theme of the entire Book of Daniel. The kingdom is handed over to one like a Son of man in Dan 7:13–14, and this mysterious figure is identified by some scholars with the angel Michael.[18] This will explain why the author of the War Scroll can speak of a "kingdom (or supremacy or principality) of Michael." It is important not to overinterpret the passage, by speaking of the incarnation of an angel, but at least the moral content of the kingdom here contains the same elements as in Rom 14:17, justice, peace, and joy, to which are added the intellectual blessings of knowledge and truth. We may also understand better against this background how the NT can speak of the kingdom of the Son

18. J. J. Collins, *The Apocalyptic Vision of the Book of Daniel* (HSM 16; Missoula: Scholars Press, 1977), 144–46.

of man or of Christ, since the War Scroll can speak of the kingdom of Michael.[19]

Conclusion

Since the kingdom of God theme belongs to the central message of the preaching of Jesus as presented in the Synoptic Gospels, it is of interest to know what were its connotations in the minds of its hearers. We have investigated the Qumran literature, particularly the War Scroll, for the light it can shed on the peculiar NT usage. We have found kingdom of God terminology in the Qumran literature, particularly in the dualistic theology and eschatology of a section of the Community Rule and in parts of the War Scroll. There is no basis for asserting that every document or member of the Qumran community was absorbed by this theme to the exclusion of other biblical or post-biblical themes. But there also is no doubt that this theme was present in the passages mentioned, even if it is not as central or as public as in the Synoptic Gospels.

The kingdom of God as proclaimed by Jesus may be described as social, political, personalistic (respectful of individual freedom), universal in intent, transcendent in origin, earthly in realization, present in sign, future in its fullness. The Qumran kingdom vision is also social and political, but differs as national rather than universal in its aims; militaristic, vindictive, violent, and somewhat more deterministic in its means, with no hint of love of enemies or forgiveness of sins. The agents of its realization are angelic (this is an element of NT expectation too, e.g., Mk 8:38), but not so clearly messianic, expect in 1QSa, though to be sure, there is a messianism at Qumran. Qumran's kingdom is also transcendent in origin, earthly in realization, but it prefers to speak explicitly of Michael as the angelic chief agent rather than of the mysterious Son of man. Despite these differences, it is safe to conclude that if these Qumran ideas were in the air in early first-century Palestinian Judaism, Jesus' preaching, "Repent, for the kingdom of God is at hand," would not have been unintelligible to some of his hearers.[20]

---

19. The main texts for this subtheme are Mt 13:41; 16:28; 20:21; Lk 1:33; 22:29–30; 23:42; Jn 18:36; Eph 5:5; Col 1:13; 2 Tim 4:1, 18; 2 Pet 1:11.

20. For texts and translations I have made eclectic use of Eduard Lohse, *Die Texte aus Qumran* (Munich: Kösel, 1964); Dupont-Sommer, *Essene Writings*; Geza Vermes, *The Dead Sea Scrolls in English* (Harmondsworth: Penguin, 1963); Carmignac-Guilbert, *Les Textes de Qumran*; J. van der Ploeg, *Le Rouleau de la Guerre* (STDJ 2; Leiden: Brill, 1959); B. Jongeling, *Le Rouleau de la Guerre* (Studia Semitica Neerlandica 4; Assen: van Gorcum, 1962); Y. Yadin, *The Scroll of the War of the Sons of Light against the Sons of Darkness* (Oxford: Oxford University, 1962); P. R. Davies, *1 QM, The War Scroll from Qumran.*

8 The Kingdom of God and the Historical Jesus

J. Ramsey Michaels

Professor of Religious Studies
Southwest Missouri State University

IT IS PERHAPS A BLESSING that NT scholarship does not always follow closely its own stated criteria in its quest for the historical Jesus. Take, for example, the famous "criterion of dissimilarity," the notion that sayings attributed to Jesus are to be accepted as authentic to the extent that they differ from the Judaism of his time and from the theology of the Christian movement that followed.[1] There is by no means a consensus among scholars that Jesus referred to himself as Son of Man, even though "Son of Man" as a personal self-designation is attested neither in late Judaism nor in the theology of the early church. Yet there is a near consensus that Jesus addressed God as "Abba," or Father, in spite of the fact that in the NT this term occurs twice in the letters of Paul (Rom 8:15; Gal 4:6) and only once on the lips of Jesus (Mk 14:36).[2] And there is a scholarly consensus that Jesus proclaimed the coming of the kingdom of God, even though this notion appears both in late Judaism[3] and in the teaching of the early Christian church.[4]

In the last instance, the reason for the apparent inconsistency is not hard to find. Common sense takes precedence over formally stated criteria. When a person has surveyed all the references to the kingdom of God in Mark and Matthew, in Luke–Acts, and in John, to say nothing of

1. See, e.g., N. Perrin, *Rediscovering the Teaching of Jesus* (New York: Harper & Row, 1967) 39–43.
2. Cf. J. Jeremias, *New Testament Theology* (New York: Scribner's, 1971) 2.
3. E.g., Dan 2:44; Ps Sol 5:18; 17:3–4; Testament of Moses 10:1; Sib Or 3:46–48; Wisd 10:10; Targum of Isaiah 40:9; Targum of Micah 4:7; also the Jewish Kaddish prayer: "May he establish his kingdom in your lifetime and in your days and in the lifetime of all the house of Israel, even speedily and at a near time."
4. In the NT alone, cf., e.g., Acts 8:12; 14:22; 19:8; 20:25; 28:23, 31; Rom 14:17; 1 Cor 4:20; 6:9–10; 15:24, 50; Gal 5:21; Eph 5:5; Col 4:11; 2 Thes 1:5; Rev 12:10.

Paul's epistles, it is clear that the data are more easily explained on the supposition that Jesus of Nazareth actually proclaimed the coming kingdom than on the supposition that he did not. It appears that the time-honored principle of textual criticism, "That reading which best explains the origin of all the others is preferred," has a certain validity with respect to historical reconstruction as well, a validity that in this instance supersedes the rather arbitrary and hard-to-apply criterion of dissimilarity.

The consensus among scholars about Jesus' proclamation of the kingdom of God ends when (as Rudolf Bultmann might have put it) we move beyond the "Dass" to the "Was."[5] It is certain that Jesus of Nazareth proclaimed the kingdom of God, but what he meant by this expression is not so certain. The aim in this essay is to follow the same method used tacitly by scholars to establish the fact that Jesus actually did proclaim the kingdom of God, and bring it to bear on the further question of what the expression meant to him and to his first hearers. In other words, what use of the image of the kingdom of God in the teaching of the historical Jesus best explains the varied testimonies to his teaching that we find in the earliest Christian literature?

For me, the task carries with it a certain nostalgia. In the mid-fifties I completed a Th.M. thesis investigating the passages in the Gospels commonly used in support of C. H. Dodd's "realized eschatology" (i.e. the theory that to Jesus the kingdom of God had already come). The main ones were Mt 12:28/Lk 11:20, Mt 11:12/Lk 16:16, and Lk 17:21. I concluded that although there was a present aspect to the kingdom of God that truly went back to the historical Jesus, this aspect was derivative in his thinking and not primary. Explicitly, the kingdom Jesus proclaimed was future; only implicitly could it be regarded as present. The content of his proclamation was that the kingdom of God was to come in the very near future, yet the act of proclamation itself, together with acts of healing people and driving out demons, was a sign mediating this essentially future kingdom to Jesus' contemporaries in the present.[6]

Though the years have not changed my basic conclusion in this matter, it is clearer to me now than it was thirty years ago that the question of the time of the kingdom's coming in Jesus' proclamation is not the only question, or even the most significant one, that must be asked. There is also the question of Jesus' terminology—"kingdom of God" or "kingdom of heaven"—and its significance, and there is the question whether the kingdom he proclaimed is to be understood in an ethnic Jewish frame-

5. This terminology comes mostly from Bultmann's discussion of the Gospel of John. See, e.g., his *Theology of the New Testament* (New York: Scribner's, 1955) 2:66.

6. J. R. Michaels, "The Kingdom of God Has Come," Westminster Theological Seminary, Philadelphia (1956); for a summary, see *The New Testament Student* (Philadelphia: Presbyterian and Reformed, 1975), 2:253–54.

work or a universal and transcendent one. Finally, there is the question of Jesus' use of metaphor and parable in describing, even defining, this kingdom—itself a metaphor.[7] What is the relationship between Jesus' varied images and the reality to which they all point?

Terminology

Several questions are involved in any discussion of the kingdom terminology attributed to Jesus. The dominant phrase in every Gospel except Matthew is "kingdom of God." Matthew uses instead, with only four exceptions, the expression, "kingdom of heaven" (the exceptions are 12:28; 19:24; 21:31 and 43). "Kingdom of heaven" (or "the heavens") is the equivalent of the Hebrew expression common in Rabbinic literature, *malkût šāmayim*.[8] It appears to reflect the characteristically Jewish tendency to refer to God only indirectly or by circumlocution. The question of priority between "kingdom of God" and "kingdom of heaven" cannot be decided with certainty. Either "kingdom of heaven" is original with Jesus and "kingdom of God" is simply Mark's and Luke's adaptation for their Gentile audiences, or "kingdom of God" (Aramaic: *malkûta d'elaha*) is original and Matthew has assimilated his terminology to customary Jewish usage. It is even possible that Jesus' own usage varied. In any event, the matter of priority cannot be addressed in isolation from other issues. The important thing about both expressions is that they highlight one crucial feature of the proclamation of Jesus: its God-centeredness.

Mark's designation of the message that Jesus began to proclaim in Galilee after John the Baptist's imprisonment as "the gospel of God" (Mk 1:14) does not in itself prove the God-centered character of Jesus' proclamation. Mark's terminology may simply mirror that of the church's mission to the Gentiles after Jesus' resurrection. Paul too refers to the message he brought to the Gentiles at Thessalonica as "the gospel of God" (1 Thes 2:2, 8, 9; cf. Rom 1:1) and summarizes the experience of Gentile Christians: "how you turned to God from idols, to serve a living and true God, and to wait for his Son from heaven, whom he raised from the dead, Jesus who delivers us from the wrath to come" (1 Thes 1:9–10).

Though this language is obviously shaped by the Gentile experience of coming to know the God of the Jews for the first time, it also coheres to a

7. On the kingdom of God as a metaphor, see esp. N. Perrin, *Jesus and the Language of the Kingdom* (Philadelphia: Fortress, 1976).

8. See H. L. Strack and P. Billerbeck, *Kommentar zum Neuen Testament aus Talmud und Midrasch*, (Munich: C. H. Beck, 1956) 1:172–84; G. Dalman, *The Words of Jesus* (Edinburgh: T. & T. Clark, 1902) 96–101.

remarkable extent with the emphasis of the Gospel tradition—not only of Mark but of the so-called Q material as well. Whether by chance or by design, both the God-centeredness and the strongly future orientation of Jesus' own proclamation of the kingdom are clearly visible in the brief Pauline summary in 1 Thes 1. In particular, Paul's specific statement that Jesus "delivers us from the wrath to come" (v 10b) recalls certain Q material attributed to John the Baptist (Mt 3:7/Lk 3:7; cf. Jesus' words in Mt 23:33). In Paul's epistles generally the God-centeredness and the futurity of the kingdom go together.[9] Paul speaks several times of "inheriting the kingdom of God" as a future experience (1 Cor 6:9, 10; 15:50; Gal 5:21; cf. Eph 5:5), and otherwise indicates by his language that he thinks of it as realized only at the end of the age (1 Thes 2:12; 2 Thes 1:5; Col 4:11; cf. 2 Tim 4:1, 18). When Paul wants to focus on the present manifestation of the kingdom, he tends either to introduce the term "justice" or "righteousness" along with "kingdom" (Rom 14:17) or in place of it (Rom 1:17; for the close association of the kingdom and justice of God, cf. Mt 6:33), or (alternatively) to connect the kingdom with Jesus Christ rather than God the Father (Col 1:13). The latter tendency becomes explicit in 1 Cor 15:

> Then comes the end, when he [i.e. Christ] delivers the kingdom to God the Father after destroying every rule and every authority and power. For he must reign until he has put all his enemies under his feet. . . . When all things are subject to him, then the Son himself will also be subjected to him who put all things under him, that God may be everything to everyone (vv 24–25, 28).

The God-centeredness of Jesus' own proclamation in the Gospels is just as unmistakable. In the Q tradition, when Jesus is put to the test by Satan in the desert, he answers, "Man shall not live by bread alone, but by every word that proceeds from the mouth of God" (Mt 4:4; cf. Lk 4:4); "You shall not tempt the Lord your God" (Mt 4:7/Lk 4:12); and "You shall worship the Lord your God and him only shall you serve" (Mt 4:10/Lk 4:8). Though the three responses are all quotations from Deuteronomy, they are at the same time pronouncements that Jesus has claimed as his own, like the first of the two great commands of the law: "You shall love the Lord your God with all your heart and with all your soul and with all your mind . . ." (Mk 12:30/Mt 22:37/Lk 10:27, perhaps originally present in both Q and Mark). Both Matthew and Luke represent Jesus in the Lord's Prayer as teaching his disciples to pray to God the Father, "Hallowed be thy name, Thy kingdom come"—another indication that he saw the kingdom as both God-centered and future-oriented.

Even in the rare instances in which the future kingdom is portrayed as already at work in the present, its power is clearly identified as the power of God: "But if it is by the Spirit [or finger] of God that I cast out demons,

9. See K. P. Donfried, "The Kingdom of God in Paul," 175–90 in this volume.

then the kingdom of God has come upon you" (Mt 12:28/Lk 11:20). The fact that Matthew departs here from his usual "kingdom of heaven" for the sake of the word-play on "God" strongly suggests that the God-centered emphasis is important and integral to this saying from the Q tradition. In other instances, however, the "heaven/earth" terminology itself testifies to the God-centeredness of Jesus' teaching, whether in specific connection with the kingdom imagery or not. A number of these are Matthean: e.g. the address to the Lord's Prayer, "Our Father in heaven" and the petition, "Thy will be done, as in heaven so on earth" (Mt 6:9, 12); also the binding and loosing pronouncements in Mt 16:19 and 18:18 (cf. v 19). Some, however, are paralleled in Luke and can be assigned with some confidence to Q: e.g. Mt 6:19/Lk 12:33; Mt 11:25/Lk 10:21.

The preceding survey includes no instance of Jesus proclaiming himself as king in the process of announcing the near advent of the kingdom of God. The Gospel writers (esp. John, and esp. in the passion narratives) make unmistakably clear their belief that he was in fact both Messiah and king of the Jews (Paul and Silas at Thessalonica were accused of "saying that there is another king, Jesus," Acts 17:7). But for the most part the Gospels are content to let that conclusion remain implicit in the story they tell rather than putting it explicitly on the lips of Jesus. The kingdom remains primarily theological rather than christological in its significance, and this may be part of the reason it is not as central in Paul and in later Christian thought as it is in the teaching of the historical Jesus. A fully present or realized kingdom requires a present and reigning king, and the mission of Jesus in history seems to have been closer to that of a teacher or prophet than a king. At most his proclamation, his healings, and his exorcisms were signs of the kingdom's power, and perhaps signs of his own kingship—or proprietorship of his Father's kingdom. The Gospel writers, however strong their christological interests, seem to have been unwilling to claim more than this. In those few passages in Paul's letters where the kingdom is seen as present, the terminology for it tends to change. In one case at least (1 Cor 15:20–28) Paul distinguishes between God's kingdom and Christ's and attempts to integrate the two into a single eschatological perspective.

Ethnicity

A question curiously neglected in the study of the kingdom of God in Jesus' teaching is the question of the ethnicity of the kingdom that he proclaimed to his contemporaries. Along with the usual alternatives— kingdom of heaven or kingdom of God; present or future; God-centered

or Christ-centered—there is one more that is seldom discussed. Was the
kingdom of God in the proclamation of Jesus essentially Jewish in its
orientation and centered in Jerusalem, or was it universal in scope? To
some extent, this is a false dichotomy (i.e. Why can't it be both?), yet no
more so than the other three. In some sense, as we have seen, the
kingdom of which Jesus spoke was *both* kingdom of God and kingdom of
heaven, *both* present and future, *both* God-centered and Christ-centered.
In each instance, however, a certain priority could be discerned (only in
the case of kingdom of God vs. kingdom of heaven was the priority
difficult to assign). These priorities can be stated in terms of what is
explicit and what is implicit: the kingdom that Jesus proclaimed was
explicitly future and implicitly present, explicitly God-centered and
implicitly centered on Jesus the Son of Man, its messenger.

The ethnicity of the kingdom of God in the teaching of Jesus is perhaps
most appropriately viewed against the background of another much-
discussed dichotomy or alternative not yet treated in this paper: rule vs.
realm. There is fairly general agreement that the meaning of βασιλεία is
abstract rather than concrete. This Greek word, like the Hebrew *malkût*
or the Aramaic *malkûta*, means first of all the rule, reign, or sovereignty of
a king or queen.[10] Yet there is no disputing the fact that "rule" in this
abstract sense requires and implies a specific realm in which it is
exercised. The question of ethnicity is one way of posing this question of
realm. What was the scope and territory of the kingdom of God that Jesus
announced as being at hand? Was it earth or heaven or both? Was it the
whole world or the world of the Jews, centered in Jerusalem? The Jewish
background of Jesus' kingdom proclamation suggests that this too is a false
dichotomy: the kingdom intimated in the Book of Daniel, for example, or
in the Pharisaic Psalms of Solomon from the first century B.C.E. is universal
in scope, yet no less Jewish for all its universality. It is the kingdom of
God, and at the same time the kingdom of Israel (see, e.g. Ps Sol 17:3–4).

The tendency of much Christian scholarship has been to minimize the
Jewishness or ethnicity of Jesus' vision of the kingdom of God with the
observation that he had no interest in a political kingdom, or one that
could be established by military might or rebellion against Rome rule.
The tacit assumption is that nonpolitical means nonnationalistic, which in
turn means nonethnic and non-Jewish, but instead "spiritual" and "universal." Actually the kingdom of God in Jewish expectation was *both*
spiritual and national, *both* universal and ethnic.[11]

10. See e.g., G. E. Ladd, *The Presence of the Future: The Eschatology of Biblical
Realism* (Grand Rapids: Eerdmans, 1974) 122–48.
11. This was a significant contribution of the work of the dispensationalist A. J.
McClain, in *The Greatness of the Kingdom* (Grand Rapids: Zondervan, 1969).

Because of the rejection of the early church's message about Jesus by most of the Jews and the widespread acceptance of it by the Gentiles, we would expect the church and the Gospel writers to play down the distinctively Jewish elements in Jesus' teaching about the kingdom. Yet the Gospels agree that Jesus singled out exactly *twelve* of his disciples, with the expectation (at least in the Q tradition) that they would "sit on twelve thrones, judging the twelve tribes of Israel" (Mt 19:28; cf. Lk 22:30). When one of the original Twelve committed suicide, it was important, according to Luke, that the vacancy be filled (Acts 1:15–26). Jesus at his trial was charged with threatening to destroy and rebuild the Jewish temple in Jerusalem (Mk 14:58). Even though John interprets the saying as a reference to Jesus' own body (Jn 2:19), what was heard even in that Gospel was a statement about the temple. When Jesus and his disciples drew near to Jerusalem, some of them got excited because they "supposed that the kingdom of God was to appear immediately" (Lk 19:11). After the resurrection, according to the Book of Acts, Jesus' disciples asked him (even after he had instructed them for forty days about the kingdom of God!): "Lord, will you at this time restore the kingdom to Israel?" (Acts 1:6). Jesus' reply gives no hint that this nationalistic expectation was in any way wrong or misguided, only that the time of restoration was set in God's authority alone.[12] Though there is no proof that these traditions are authentic, they are certainly dissimilar to what soon became the dominant emphasis of the growing church, and therefore difficult to explain away as inventions after the fact.[13]

Parable

Our brief survey has characterized Jesus of Nazareth as an apocalyptic prophet of the restoration of Israel. His proclamation centered initially not on himself, but God; not on the present, but the future; not on the whole world, but on Jerusalem and the nation of Israel. That is what his ministry was all about explicitly. But first appearances are partial and potentially deceptive, for in the course of his ministry some implications about the present as well as the future, and some implicit claims about himself as well as God came to the surface. Things are not always exactly—or exclusively—what they seem. It was the implicit more than

12. See D. L. Tiede, "The Exaltation of Jesus and the Restoration of Israel in Acts 1," *Society of Biblical Literature 1985 Seminar Papers* (Atlanta: Scholars Press, 1985) 369–75 (though Tiede focuses on the Lukan perspective, his argument virtually requires that the hope of Israel's restoration belonged to pre-Lukan tradition as well).
13. Cf. B. F. Meyer, *The Aims of Jesus* (London: SCM, 1979) 174–219.

the explicit meaning of Jesus' proclamation of the kingdom that interested the early Christian church in the decades following Jesus' death and resurrection. Aside from Jesus' self-designation as Son of Man, the principle vehicle for this implicit meaning seems to have been his use of parables and metaphors.

It has often been remarked that in the Gospel tradition Jesus never defines the kingdom that he proclaims; at one level the reason for this is that he assumes a traditional definition understood by his hearers on the basis of the Hebrew Scriptures and Jewish tradition. But in another sense, he does define the kingdom; he defines it in parables by juxtaposing the traditional metaphor of the kingdom with other, sharply contrasting metaphors ("The kingdom of God is like . . ."). The political or military image of a "kingdom" is put side by side with gentler images of planting and growth, fishing, women baking bread, landowners finding treasures, or merchants buying pearls.[14] In many different ways, Jesus affirms the traditional Jewish expectations, yet he gives them at the same time what Henry James would call a "turn of the screw," a new twist that shocks his hearers and in some respect calls their behavior and world-view into question—note, e.g., his apocalyptic vision of the final kingdom according to Mt 8:11–12 (cf. Lk 13:28–29): "I tell you, many will come from east and west and sit at table with Abraham, Isaac, and Jacob in the kingdom of heaven, while the sons of the kingdom will be thrown into the outer darkness." In apocalyptic sayings of this kind, and in many of his parables, we see Jesus at his most radical. If Jesus heralded a restored Israel, he heralded also a transformed, a topsy-turvy Israel, for he came, as he said, "not to call the righteous, but sinners" (Mk 2:17).

Even if the specific saying in Mt 8:11–12/Lk 13:28–29 is suspect as an attempted justification of the church's mission to the Gentiles, still the surprise twist or "turn of the screw" that it contains is characteristic of the Jesus of history. Jesus' expectation is well within the framework of contemporary Jewish messianic and apocalyptic expectations, but almost always with a reversal or surprise of some kind—whether the reversal of tax collectors and prostitutes on the one hand and scribes and Pharisees on the other, or the reversal of Jews and Gentiles. But even with the radical reversal—a reversal evident already in the repentance preaching of John the Baptist (e.g. Mt 3:9/Lk 3:8, Mt 21:31, Lk 7:29–30; cf. Mt 11:12/Lk 16:16), the kingdom that Jesus heralded remains an ethnic Jewish kingdom, and Jesus remains, like John before him, an essentially Jewish prophet and seer.

14. Cf. J. R. Michaels, *Servant and Son: Jesus in Parable and Gospel* (Atlanta: John Knox, 1981) 86–92.

Conclusion

The reality of what Jesus is, beyond being simply an apocalyptic prophet, is revealed in the Synoptic Gospels more indirectly than directly. The study of the historical Jesus and the kingdom of God must always reckon with the distinction between what is explicit and what is implicit. The tendency has often been to by-pass the former in favor of the latter in order to make Jesus more of a "Christian" and his kingdom more "spiritual." This practice is not wedded to any particular ideology: it was (and is) characteristic both of traditional orthodoxy and of the optimistic liberalism of the late nineteenth century. Recent literature produced by the Jesus Seminar, under the leadership of Robert W. Funk, shows a similar movement in the direction of a noneschatological Jesus.[15] In the latter instance, the result is not so much to "Christianize" Jesus (the Seminar's commitment for the most part to the criterion of dissimilarity tends to prevent that, at least in theory), as to paint him in the colors of a Hellenistic teacher of wisdom, or even a Gnostic before his time—anything but a Jewish prophet who expected the imminent end of the world![16]

It has become almost routine to distinguish between a "husk" of ethnic Jewish nationalism and a "kernel" of spiritual truth that remarkably anticipates the best thinking of the nineteenth—or the twentieth—century. But can the "husk" (if it is that) be so easily discarded? Can the search for the "real" Jesus and for what is implicit in his message afford to ignore that which is explicit? A possible alternative is to adopt what may loosely be called a "sacramental" approach to the evidence of the Gospels: i.e. to assume that what is implicit ("real," if you like) in Jesus' message is to be found "in, with, and under" what is explicit. The kingdom's present reality is only to be understood by coming to terms with its literal futurity; its Christ-centeredness only against the backdrop of its God-centeredness; its universality only when justice has been done to its

15. As an example, cf. M. Borg, "A Temperate Case for a Non-eschatological Jesus," *Society of Biblical Literature 1986 Seminar Papers* (Atlanta: Scholars Press, 1986) 521–35.

16. The Jesus Seminar is forthright about its own ideological/political agenda. One member is quoted to the effect that "'The new view' definitely undercuts the picture of Jesus who will come as the Son of man to rescue the world from its failures," and that this is good because "Jesus' image as a returning world-rescuer has contributed to the feeling by many American Christians that the nuclear arms race is a part of an inevitable Armageddon but that believers will be saved for the coming Kingdom of God . . ." *Westar News* (Westar Institute: Sonoma, Calif., December 1986) 5. Clearly, the logic could just as easily cut in the opposite direction: it is when we are *no longer* convinced that Jesus is going to return from heaven to punish the enemies of God that we decide it is up to us to do the job for him!

particularity and its Jewishness. Modern scholarship is not free from its fears and taboos, whether of Jesus the Jew, Jesus the wild-eyed fanatic, Jesus the millennialist, or Jesus the political revolutionary. Scholars no less than other people want a Jesus who is "presentable," a person one could invite to tea and converse with about "the brotherhood of man," or "human potential," or "the inner life." Sometimes we "love Jesus" too much to read the Gospels straight, and indeed it is not difficult to love something of our own making! Perhaps the Jesus of history was—and is— rather more like Eliot's "Christ the Tiger" than some may care to admit.

9   The Kingdom of God in the Gospel of Matthew

Ron Farmer

Assistant Professor of Religious Studies
University of Missouri-Columbia

Introduction

IN HIS BOOK *The Kingdom of God in the Teaching of Jesus*, Norman Perrin traced the modern discussion of the kingdom of God. In his summary chapter, he set forth the three major questions that have arisen in the course of that discussion: (1) is kingdom of God an apocalyptic concept in the teaching of Jesus? (2) is the kingdom present or future? and (3) what is the relationship between eschatology and ethics in Jesus' teaching?[1]

With regard to the first question, Perrin reported that the (1963) scholarly consensus was that the kingdom of God was an apocalyptic concept in the teaching of Jesus. In spite of this consensus as to the background for Jesus' use of the expression, there was considerable disagreement as to the meaning and use of kingdom of God in apocalyptic literature. Although a consensus had not emerged concerning the second question, Perrin remarked that most scholars viewed the kingdom as somehow both present and future. How one should understand this tension between present and future, however, was a source of considerable difference of opinion. Regarding the relationship between eschatology and ethics—the third question—Perrin observed that there was little scholarly agreement. The *Interimsethik* (interim ethic) approach—which views the kingdom as future—had been accepted, rejected, and modified.

---

1. Norman Perrin, *The Kingdom of God in the Teaching of Jesus* (London: SCM, 1963) 158.

Likewise, the relationship between the kingdom as present and Jesus' ethical teachings had been expressed in various ways.[2]

Perrin's 1963 review of the modern discussion of the kingdom of God and summary of the scholarly conclusions remained current until 1976 when he published *Jesus and the Language of the Kingdom: Symbol and Metaphor in New Testament Interpretation*. With this book the modern discussion turned a corner.[3] In this study, Perrin argued that the kingdom of God should be viewed as a "symbol" rather than a "concept." This new approach to the kingdom has profound implications for many areas of Gospel studies, but in light of the fact that the Gospel of Matthew contains so much material of an ethical nature, I will restrict myself primarily to the impact Perrin's proposal has for understanding the Matthean ethical teachings.[4]

The Kingdom of God as Symbol

According to Perrin, the roots of the symbol "kingdom of God" lie in the Jewish consciousness of themselves as the people of God. This consciousness was based largely upon two OT themes: the kingship of God and Salvation History. The kingship of God, a myth[5] common to all the peoples of the ancient Near East, dealt primarily with God creating the world, annually renewing the fertility of the earth, and sustaining his people. The enthronement psalms—Pss 47, 93, 96, 97, 98, and 99—demonstrate Israel's adoption and adaptation of this ancient myth in its annual New Year festival. Salvation History, expressed in confessional summaries such as Dt 26:5-9, is the history of the saving activity of God on behalf of Israel. These two originally separate traditions were brought

---

2. Ibid., 158-60.

3. The year 1976 also witnessed the doctoral thesis by Bruce Chilton, later published as *God in Strength: Jesus' Announcement of the Kingdom* (Freistadt: Plöchl, 1979). Chilton's conclusion, based on Targumic studies and a redaction-critical reading of Jesus' kingdom proclamations, was that the kingdom of God referred to God's redemptive self-revelation. Thus, Jesus was proclaiming his conviction that God was acting and would act in strength on behalf of the people. The similarities between Chilton's historical reconstruction and Perrin's literary findings could suggest that scholarship is on the verge of a new consensus as to the meaning of the kingdom of God in the message of Jesus.

4. I agree with the majority view that in Matthew "kingdom of heaven" is synonymous with "kingdom of God." For a recent attempt to distinguish between the two expressions see Margaret Pamment, "The Kingdom of Heaven according to the First Gospel," *NTS* 27 (1981) 211-32.

5. He adopted Alan Watt's definition: "Myth is to be defined as a complex of stories— some no doubt fact, and some fantasy—which, for various reasons, human beings regard as demonstrations of the inner meaning of the universe and of human life" (*Myth and Ritual in Christianity* [New York: Macmillan, 1954]) 7.

together in various ways in the OT, thus setting the stage for the emergence of the symbol, kingdom of God.

> At the level of language the symbol is derived from the myth of the kingship of God, for *malkuth*, "reign" or "kingdom," is an abstract noun formed from the root *m-l-k* "reign, be king." At the level of immediate reference, however, the symbol evokes the features of the Salvation History. What happened was that the two myths came together to form one, the myth of God who created the world and is active on behalf of his people in the history of that world, and the symbol evolved to evoke that myth.[6]

Perrin derived his understanding of the nature and function of symbols from Philip Wheelwright's *Metaphor and Reality* and Paul Ricoeur's *The Symbolism of Evil*. According to Wheelwright, "a symbol, in general, is a relatively stable and repeatable element of perceptual experience, standing for some larger meaning or set of meanings which cannot be given, or not fully given in perceptual experience itself."[7] Wheelwright categorized symbols into two distinct types, "steno-symbols" and "tensive symbols."[8] A steno-symbol has "a one-to-one relationship to that which it represents, such as the mathematical symbol *pi*"; a tensive symbol has "a set of meanings that can neither be exhausted nor adequately expressed by any one referent."[9]

In light of the history of the origin and use of the symbol kingdom of God, it is clear that although it was often understood as a steno-symbol in Jewish apocalyptic—for example, it was expected that God would intervene during the Maccabean Revolt, the Jewish War, and the Bar Kochba Revolt, and each time this intervention was thought to be the beginning of the End—at heart the kingdom of God is a tensive symbol. Its meaning could never be exhausted or adequately expressed by any one referent.

According to Perrin, the reason for the current impasse in the modern discussion of the kingdom is that consistently scholars have viewed the kingdom of God as a "conception" or an "idea" rather than as a symbol. "As a symbol it can *represent* or *evoke* a whole range or series of conceptions or ideas, but it only becomes a conception or idea if it constantly represents or evokes that one conception or idea."[10] To call the kingdom a conception or an idea is to prejudge a whole range of impor-

---

6. Perrin, *Jesus and the Language of the Kingdom*, 20–21. Perrin cited Ps 145:10–14; Ex 15; Isa 33:22; 52:7–12; Zeph 3:14–15; the *Assumption of Moses* 10; the War Scroll (1QM 6:6; 12:7); and the Kaddish prayer to illustrate the meaning and use of the symbol in Jewish literature and worship.

7. Philip Wheelwright, *Metaphor and Reality* (Bloomington: Indiana University Press, 1962) 92.

8. Ibid., 93–96.

9. Perrin, *Jesus and the Language of the Kingdom*, 30. Ricoeur makes a similar distinction between "sign" and "symbol" (*The Symbolism of Evil* [Boston: Beacon Press, 1967] 15).

10. Perrin, *Jesus and the Language of the Kingdom*, 33.

tant issues, to assume that there is one consistent, well-defined idea in the Gospels represented by the expression kingdom of God. In short, to call the kingdom a conception or an idea is to make it a steno-symbol.

The Kingdom of God and Eschatology

In the course of the modern discussion of the kingdom of God, there were problematic passages for all interpreters who tried to force a unified idea or static concept out of the tensive symbol. For the view of Johannes Weiss and Albert Schweitzer[11] that the kingdom should be interpreted from the standpoint of "thoroughgoing or future eschatology," passages such as Mt 11:11-13, 12:28, and the parables of the kingdom[12] proved to be insurmountable obstacles. For the opposing position espoused by C. H. Dodd[13] that the kingdom should be interpreted from the standpoint of "realized eschatology," passages such as Mt 4:17, 10:7, 16:28, and 26:29 presented equally insuperable difficulties.[14]

As a result of the difficulty in understanding the kingdom as entirely future or entirely present, most interpreters began to view the kingdom as somehow both present and future. In general, two schools of thought exist. One school—represented by scholars such as Joachim Jeremias, Werner Georg Kümmel, and Oscar Cullmann[15]—maintains that the tension between present and future is to be understood temporally. Jeremias suggested that Dodd's realized eschatology should be modified to "eschatology in the process of realization," a modification Dodd later endorsed.[16] Kümmel related present and future as present fulfillment carrying with it the certainty of future promise. Cullmann advocated an "inaugurated eschatology" in which the Christ-event is "D-Day" and the parousia is "V-Day."

The other school views the tension between present and future as a dialectic tension and interprets it existentially rather than temporally. Post-Bultmannians such as Ernst Käsemann, Günther Bornkamm, and

11. Johannes Weiss, *Jesus' Proclamation of the Kingdom of God* (Philadelphia: Fortress, 1971); Albert Schweitzer, *The Quest of the Historical Jesus* (London: Black, 1911).
12. The modern discussion of the parables has demonstrated that the challenge of the parables implies the presence of the kingdom.
13. C. H. Dodd, *The Parables of the Kingdom* (New York: Charles Scribner's Sons, 1935, 1948, 1961).
14. Dodd's suggestion that ἤγγικεν should be translated "has come" rather than "is at hand" failed to establish itself.
15. Joachim Jeremias, *The Parables of Jesus* (New York: Charles Scribner's Sons, 1954); Werner Georg Kümmel, *Promise and Fulfilment* (Naperville Ill.: Allenson, 1957); Oscar Cullmann, *Christ and Time* (London: SCM, 1967).
16. C. H. Dodd, *The Interpretation of the Fourth Gospel* (Cambridge: University Press, 1953) 447, n. 1.

Ernst Fuchs[17] broke with their mentor in that they viewed the kingdom as being fulfilled in part in history, in the ministry of Jesus. The decisive event which confronts humanity with the crisis of decision took place in the ministry of Jesus.

If the kingdom is viewed as a static concept—as it has been by both schools just mentioned—then the tension between present and future remains somewhat enigmatic. If, however, the kingdom is approached as a tensive symbol evoking the myth of the salvific, kingly activity of God, then the fact that some passages depict the kingdom as present while others portray the kingdom as future is not at all surprising. The meaning of a tensive symbol is not exhausted in any one referent. If the symbol of the kingdom of God evokes the expectation of the redemptive activity of God on behalf of the individual and/or community, then it is obvious that God could manifest redemptive activity in the person and mission of Jesus, again at the consummation, and at any and all points between.[18] "The Kingdom of God is neither present nor future. It is both at the same time."[19] It is a way of expressing the immanence of God without losing the transcendence of God.

The Kingdom of God and Ethics

One of the major questions that has arisen in the course of the modern discussion of the kingdom of God concerns the relationship between eschatology and ethics. Nineteenth-century Protestant liberalism—which optimistically looked for some approximation of the kingdom of God on earth through human effort—may have been able to dispense with the eschatological as mere "husk" (a nonessential) surrounding the "kernel" (the essential) of Jesus' religious and ethical teachings,[20] but twentieth-century scholarship as a whole has viewed the eschatological as inseparably intertwined with the ethical. This relationship has been expressed in a variety of ways, as the following representative survey testifies.

17. Ernst Käsemann, "Das Problem des historischen Jesus," "Sackgassen in Streit um den historischen Jesus," and "Zum Thema der urchristlichen Apokalyptik" in *Exegetische Versuche und Besinnungen* (Göttingen: Vandenhoeck & Ruprecht, 1964); Günther Bornkamm, *Jesus of Nazareth* (New York: Harper & Row, 1960); Ernst Fuchs, *Zur Frage nach dem historischen Jesus* (Tübingen, 1960).

18. At this point I depart from Perrin. According to him, viewing "kingdom of God" as a tensive symbol means that present and future are improper categories for its discussion (*Jesus and the Language of the Kingdom*, 40). I agree that as a tensive symbol the kingdom of God should not be conceived of as exclusively present or exclusively future, but I see no reason to eliminate the category of time altogether.

19. Douglas Ezell, "Eschatology and Ethics in the New Testament," *Southwestern Journal of Theology* 22 (1980) 79.

20. See Adolf von Harnack, *What Is Christianity?* (New York: G. P. Putnam, 1901).

For those convinced by Albert Schweitzer's thoroughgoing eschatology, Jesus' ethical teachings were not laid down as timeless truths intended for the guidance of the moral life of countless generations to come. Rather, Jesus' teachings were an "interim ethic" for the period between his preaching and the imminent coming of the kingdom of God. Jesus called for repentance—that is, moral renewal as expressed in the Sermon on the Mount—to prepare for this coming kingdom. Following the moral teachings of Jesus made one fit for the kingdom.

C. H. Dodd, the chief proponent of realized eschatology, disagreed with Schweitzer's contention that Jesus taught an interim ethic in preparation for the coming kingdom. Rather, Jesus' ethical teaching is the way people are to live who have already entered the kingdom of God. For Dodd, Jesus' ethical teaching has a twofold function. First, the absolute standards of the kingdom call people to repentance as they see how short they have fallen of God's demand. Second, once people enter the kingdom, the ethical teaching challenges them to new obedience and a new outlook on life.

Like Schweitzer, Rudolf Bultmann advocated a futuristic interpretation of Jesus' understanding of the kingdom, but his interpretation is quite different. Although Jesus shared the eschatological ideas of his contemporaries—the myth that the world was about to end—this was merely the form or husk in which the real meaning of Jesus found its outward expression. Bultmann proposed to "demythologize" the message of Jesus, that is, to disclose the existential, nontemporal meaning of the eschatological myth.

According to Bultmann, Jesus' real concern was his understanding of human existence. He proclaimed his hour as the last hour, but by this he was expressing his understanding of human existence, namely, that every hour is the last hour. Jesus' message that the kingdom is at hand calls people to "decision." This decision is a call to repentance, to what Bultmann described as "radical obedience."[21]

In light of frequent criticism against Bultmann for his failure to recognize the present aspect of the kingdom in the teachings of Jesus, the post-Bultmannians began to see a dialectic tension between the present and future aspects which they interpreted existentially. For example, Günther Bornkamm contrasted Jesus' call for repentance with that of John the

---

21. Bultmann did not see Jesus as a teacher of ethics; he set forth neither rules nor principles. Jesus demanded only one thing, decision in light of the existential imminence of the kingdom—a decision for God's will with one's whole being. Because this moment of decision contains all that is necessary for the decision, Jack T. Sanders (*Ethics in the New Testament* [Philadelphia: Fortress, 1975] 12) labeled Bultmann's understanding of this demand for decision "existential contextualism" due to its lack of rules or principles from which particular concrete requirements can be derived.

Baptist. In the preaching of John, repentance was a means of preparation for the future redemptive act of God; in the message of Jesus, however, repentance was the means to lay hold of present salvation. Jesus' call to repentance was a call to decision and action by the individual, but it had been preceded by a decision and action of God in manifesting the kingdom in Jesus. Moreover, those who respond to the will of God in the "Now" of salvation must also respond to the will of God as expressed in Jesus' ethical teachings.

Finding fault with the existing interpretations, Amos Wilder[22] set forth an approach which stressed the symbolic nature of apocalyptic language. Jesus felt himself to be an instrument of and witness to a great redemption-transaction being effected by God in his generation. To lend urgency to his message, Jesus used apocalyptic language which should be understood symbolically not literally, an imaginative way of describing the ineffable and expressing confidence that the final outcome would be decided by the power of God. For Wilder, the relationship between eschatology and ethics is twofold. First, eschatology serves as a secondary (not primary) sanction/motive for Jesus' ethical teaching. Second, since the kingdom comes through the ministry of Jesus, his ethical teaching expresses the lifestyle which is relevant to and made possible by the present kingdom. It is an ethic of the time of salvation, a discipleship ethic.

Two points should be noted about the preceding survey of methods of relating eschatology and ethics: (1) each attempt recognizes a connection between the kingdom of God and Jesus' ethical teaching, and (2) with the possible exception of Wilder's interpretation,[23] each attempt assumes that the kingdom of God is a static concept. Although the second point represents an understanding of the kingdom that is highly questionable in light of Perrin's work, the first point remains valid. Jesus' ethic is a "kingdom ethic."

This leads to an important—albeit obvious—observation: a term common to the study of both eschatology and ethics is the kingdom of God. This observation suggests that a more productive way to approach the relationship between eschatology and ethics is through this common term rather than through a particular eschatological theory. Approaching the relationship through a particular eschatological theory—which will be

22. Amos N. Wilder, *Eschatology and Ethics in the Teaching of Jesus* (New York: Harper & Row, 1950).

23. Although Wilder considered the kingdom of God to be a symbol "loosely used," he confined its reference to the present new age (beginning with Jesus) which he distinguished from the future resurrection life. "At some point the resurrection life and the life of the Kingdom meet," but they are "two [distinct] lines of eschatological conviction" (*Eschatology and Ethics*, 60). Thus, his understanding of the kingdom is closer to Wheelwright's steno-symbol than tensive symbol.

the case if one views the kingdom as a static concept—means that ethics must be subsumed under eschatology. "Eschatological ethics" will result. Approaching the relationship through the tensive symbol kingdom of God does not subsume ethics under eschatology and will result in "theocentric ethics."[24] This approach does not deny that eschatology has an impact on ethics and vice versa. As Wilder demonstrated, judgment is a secondary sanction for ethics, especially in Matthew. At the same time, one's vision of the future is a projection of one's values in their ultimate fulfillment. What this approach does argue, however, is that both eschatology and ethics are derived from the nature and character of the God in whom one believes. The God of Matthew is revealed in the tensive symbol "kingdom of God."

The Kingdom of God: A Common Term between Eschatology and Ethics

That the focus of Jesus' preaching and teaching was the kingdom of God is universally acknowledged. Therefore, it is logical to assume that in this integrating stackpole, eschatology and ethics find their point of union. If kingdom of God is a tensive symbol, then it is incorrect to interpret Jesus' message from any one eschatological viewpoint—futuristic, realized, inaugurated, or existential. Jesus announced the good news of the saving activity of God (the proclamation of the kingdom). His proclamation challenged his hearers to recognize the kingly activity of God as a present reality in their personal experience as well as a future hope. For as Amos Wilder observed,

> A true metaphor or symbol is more than a sign, it is a bearer of the reality to which it refers. The hearer not only learns about that reality, he participates in it. He is invaded by it. . . . Jesus' speech had the character not of instruction and ideas but of compelling imagination, of spell, of mythical shock and transformation.[25]

But the saving activity of God proclaimed by Jesus demands a response from people if they are to enter into a dynamic relationship with their Redeemer (the ethic of the kingdom). Jesus' ethical teaching set forth the response proper for one who has been gripped by Jesus' proclamation, one who has experienced the immanence of God.[26]

---

24. Cf. Hans Bald, "Eschatological or Theocentric Ethics? Notes on the Relationship between Eschatology and Ethics in Jesus' Preaching," *The Kingdom of God* (ed. Bruce Chilton; Philadelphia: Fortress, 1984).

25. Amos Wilder, *Early Christian Rhetoric: The Language of the Gospel* (Cambridge, Mass.: Harvard University Press, 1971) 84.

26. In this respect Jesus' ethical teaching resembles the "taking upon oneself the yoke of the kingdom of God" found in the Rabbinic literature (cf. Mt 11:28–30).

These twin elements—the saving activity of God and the human response—did not originate with Jesus. At its heart the OT is not a "law" to be fulfilled in order to achieve right standing with God but rather a "gospel" of the saving activity of God to which people respond and by responding enter into relationship with God.[27]

What this means is that the ethic of Jesus is neither a call to repentance in light of an imminent, future kingdom nor is it a blueprint for bringing about the perfect society on earth. Rather, Jesus' ethic is a response ethic, the proper response of people who have experienced the gracious, saving activity of God. This is also the conclusion reached by Joachim Jeremias in his study of the Sermon on the Mount.[28] That Jeremias reached essentially the same conclusion by a totally different approach (a historical reconstruction of the composition of the Sermon on the Mount) strengthens one's confidence that the Matthean ethic is indeed a response to grace.

Many passages could be chosen by way of illustration, but the following are representative of the various kingdom passages in Matthew.[29] Before examining individual kingdom sayings, one extended passage will be analyzed, Mt 4:17–9:35.

In what could be called the prologue to the ministry of Jesus (4:17–25), the evangelist summarized Jesus' activity as teaching, preaching, and healing (4:23).[30] As many commentators have noted, the essence of Jesus' preaching is expressed in the opening verse of the prologue (4:17), his teaching is summarized in the Sermon on the Mount (5–7), and his healing activity is illustrated in chapters 8 and 9.

In fulfillment of the prophetic hope (4:14–16), Jesus appeared proclaiming the good news that the kingdom of God was at hand (4:17). A significant element in his proclamation was a call for repentance. What constituted genuine repentance the evangelist expressed by means of a composite summary of Jesus' teachings[31] set forth as the Sermon on the

27. For example, the preface to the Decalogue (Ex 20:2) briefly rehearses the saving activity of God on behalf of Israel (cf. Ex 19:4–8). The experience of God's redemptive activity precedes the demand for ethical response.

28. Joachim Jeremias, *The Sermon on the Mount* (Philadelphia: Fortress, 1963).

29. The word "kingdom" occurs 55 times in Matthew, 50 of which are pertinent to the present study: kingdom of heaven (32), kingdom of God (4), gospel of the kingdom (3), word of the kingdom (1), his (the Father's) kingdom (1), thy (the Father's) kingdom (1), kingdom of my (Jesus') Father (1), kingdom of their Father (1), his (the Son of Man's) kingdom (2), thy (the Son of Man's) kingdom (1), sons of the kingdom (2), the kingdom having been prepared for you (1). Of the 50 occurrences, 45 are on the lips of Jesus; others who use the term are John the Baptist (1), the disciples (1), the mother of the Zebedees (1), and the narrator (2).

30. A distinction between preaching and teaching is implied by this threefold summary.

31. The Sermon on the Mount is bracketed by expressions indicating that the Sermon represents the teaching rather than the preaching of Jesus (5:2; 7:28–29).

Mount (5–7). Thus far my analysis sounds much like that of Schweitzer's, but two observations result in a radically different understanding of ethics.

The first observation is that by means of the literary device of inclusion —9:35 is almost a verbatim repetition of 4:23—the evangelist indicated that the Sermon on the Mount (5–7) and the miracles of Jesus (8–9) are to be read as a unit. The second observation concerns the import of the miracles of Jesus. Many scholars understand 12:28 as indicating that Matthew saw in Jesus' ability to cast out demons the presence of the kingdom of God. If one adopts this reading of 12:28, then the same can be said of the miracles found in Mt 8–9. In Jesus' person and ministry the kingdom of God is present. People can experience the saving activity of God not only as a future hope, but also as a present reality. Therefore, the use of inclusion (4:23; 9:35) suggests that the ethical demands of the Sermon on the Mount represent the proper response not only to the kingdom as a future hope (4:17) but also as a present experience (8–9). Thus, the ethic of the kingdom is a response ethic, a response to the gracious, salvific activity of God.

In Mt 6:9–13, the address, "Our Father," expresses the new relationship with God made possible by acceptance of the proclamation of the kingdom. "Thy kingdom come" is a call for God to become active in the experience of the petitioner, present as well as future. Acceptance of the divine activity results in a desire for and a doing of the will of God—"Thy will be done" (cf. 7:21). Futhermore, the experience of divine forgiveness results in a corresponding forgiving attitude—"As we also have forgiven our debtors" (cf. 6:14–15; 18:23–35).

Matthew 7:21–23, along with other "entry sayings," refers to the experience of joy in the presence of God, not to some static "state" secured for the redeemed.[32] Only those doing God's will can experience (appropriate) the joy of God's presence in their lives and hope for it in the future ("on that day"). The redemptive activity of God demands a response if a relationship is to exist. Those who have been gripped by Jesus' proclamation of the kingdom, those who have come to recognize the redemptive activity of God as a personal experience and a future hope, respond by doing God's will and thereby appropriate the joy of God's redemptive presence. Neither pious profession ("Lord, Lord") nor religious activity ("prophecy," "exorcism," and "mighty works") will suffice. The proper response is "doing the will of the Father."

The twin parables of the Hid Treasure (13:44) and the Pearl of Great

---

32. Chilton, *God in Strength* 285. Cf. Mt 19:16, 17, and 23 where "to have (experience) eternal life," "to enter life," and "to enter the kingdom of Heaven" are parallel expressions.

Price (13:45–46) stress the response necessary to "possess" the kingdom of heaven. In the former parable, the motivation for the response was the great joy in discovering the treasure, though obviously the value of the treasure stimulated the joy. No price was considered too high for a treasure that brought such joy, even if the man must sell all he had to raise the funds. When might he again have such an opportunity? In the latter parable, the response grew out of an appreciation of the great value of the pearl, though doubtless its discovery brought the merchant great joy. No price was considered too high for this most valuable pearl, even if the merchant must sell all he had to raise the funds. When might he again have such an opportunity?

In parabolic fashion, the case is the same with the kingdom of God. The kingdom is of great value and brings great joy; consequently, no price is too high to "possess" it. Moreover, the price cannot be called a sacrifice since the kingdom is of more value than any price paid.[33] As with the man who found the treasure and the merchant who found the pearl, Jesus' hearer is given an unique opportunity which must be seized. Of special importance for the present study, however, is the fact that in both parables the striking behavior was motivated by the splendor of the discovery. Likewise, the ethical demands of Jesus are preceded by the proclamation of the kingdom of God.

The point of this study is illustrated vividly in 21:28–32, a passage unique to Matthew. In context, this is the first of three parables condemning the religious leaders for rejecting God's messengers. Following the reading of the twenty-sixth edition of the Nestle-Aland text, the first son, defiantly disobedient at first, later repented and did what his father had asked. The second son, although at first paying polite lip service, did not fulfill his father's request. When asked which son did the will of the father, Jesus' hearers, the chief priests and elders of the people (cf. 21:23), correctly replied, "the first." Jesus pointed out that in their answer they condemned themselves; moreover, "the tax collectors and the prostitutes are going[34] into the kingdom of God before you." By means of an addition to the parable (v 32, cf. Lk 7:29–30), Matthew linked the parable to the preceding passage. Despite their pious professions, the chief priests and elders of the people failed to repent at the preaching of John the Baptist. In stark contrast, tax collectors and prostitutes, whose lives were far from God's will, repented in response to John's proclamation of the kingdom. The point is clear. Saying "yes" to God verbally yet failing to do the will of

---

33. Cf. Eta Linnemann, *Parables of Jesus: Introduction and Exposition* (London: SPCK, 1966) 100.

34. If the present tense is taken at face value, it denotes a present experience of the kingdom. It could, however, be understood as a futuristic present.

God excludes one from the kingdom (cf. 7:21). The gracious, redemptive activity of God demands a response of radical obedience.

Conclusion

Norman Perrin's most significant contribution to the modern discussion of the kingdom of God has been his demonstration that the kingdom is a tensive symbol. This new approach to the kingdom has profound implications for various areas of Gospel studies, not the least of which is an understanding of the nature of the ethical teaching. In light of the myth that the kingdom symbol evokes, the phrase "kingdom ethic" should not bring to mind an eschatological theory—be it futuristic, realized, inaugurated, or existential—but rather the proper human response to the gracious, redemptive activity of God.

10 The Kingdom of God in Mark

M. Eugene Boring

A. A. Bradford Professor of Religious Studies
Texas Christian University

THE FOLLOWING DISCUSSION is not concerned with the meaning of the phrase ἡ βασιλεία τοῦ θεοῦ ["the kingdom of God"][1] as a central element of the message of the historical Jesus, nor with the variety of ways in which the term was understood in early Christianity, but is strictly limited to its meaning in the Gospel of Mark.[2] Without claiming to settle disputed points of definition arbitrarily and in advance, for purposes of clarity I would like to indicate how I am using the key term of this discussion. I presuppose apocalypticism as the primary context within which early Christianity's use of the term "kingdom of God" is to be understood.[3] I consider "kingdom of God" to be tensive symbolic language.

The "kingdom of God" is thus
    (1) that tensive (not "steno-") symbol (not "concept")
    (2) which evokes the myth
       (a) of God the creator

1. The English translations provided for the convenience of the Greekless reader are from the RSV. They do not take into account the subtleties of translation necessary for exegesis.

2. The priority of Mark is presupposed throughout.

3. But of course the definition of "apocalypticism" is itself a disputed point. I am using it in the sense of "a worldview which anticipates the end of the present cosmos in the near future as the fulfillment of the purpose of God." Some scholars would simply use "eschatology" for this meaning. But existentialist interpretation has so blurred the meaning of "eschatology" that I prefer "apocalyptic" to emphasize the cosmic and imminent aspects of the type of eschatology here presupposed.

I will not rehearse the various options advocated as the context for understanding "kingdom of God" in the NT. For a survey of the field and key essays representing the various options, see Bruce Chilton, ed., *The Kingdom of God* (Philadelphia: Fortress, 1984). For a good exposition of apocalyptic as the setting of Mark, see Howard Clark Kee, *Community of the New Age*, (Philadelphia: Westminster, 1977) esp. 70ff.

(b) who has been active in history to preserve his people, and
(c) who will soon act definitively at the denouement of history to defeat the powers which he has hitherto permitted to operate in the cosmos and reassert his rule over his rebellious creation which is at present *de jure* his kingdom, but will become *de facto* his kingdom only through this eschatological act.

The elements of this definition may be briefly elaborated:

(1) I am using "tensive" symbol in the sense popularized by Philip Wheelwright, i.e. as that form of metaphorical language which sets up a tension within the mind rather than simply serving as a shorthand symbol for the object it is intended to represent. "Kingdom of God" language is the language of symbol, which means that one should ask how it *functions* as a *symbol* rather than for a single conceptual content of the term.

(2) Such symbols function by evoking a mythical structure as a whole. The myth evoked by "kingdom of God" has the following primary elements:

(a) God the creator. "Creation" and "apocalyptic" are not alternatives. The confidence that God will act to restore his rule over his creation is grounded in the faith in God the creator. Apocalypticism does not abandon the creation and hope only for the salvation of individual souls out of the world, but holds on to faith in God the creator despite the evil of the present world. Its hope is for the salvation *of* the world, not *from* the world. It is thus precisely apocalyptic which "is grounded in the soteriological dimension of the doctrine of creation. The world, even in its present, distorted condition, is still God's creation when seen from the viewpoint of a faith that includes confidence in God's creative activity, both present and future."[4] I consider this true of apocalyptic thought in general, and particularly true of Mark.[5]

4. These are the words of Hans Bald, "Eschatological or Theocentric Ethics," in Chilton, *Kingdom*, 146. Bald considers this an argument that creation can thus not "be devalued in the apocalyptic manner." But Bald's own premises point rather to the conclusion that apocalyptic is not necessarily a "devaluation" of creation, but can be a courageous affirmation of it.

5. The verb κτίζω ["create"] is used in the Gospels only in Mk 13:19 (and in Mt 19:4, where it reflects the parallel κτίσις ["creation"] in Mk 10:6). Note that Mark emphasizes the idea of creation by repetition (ἀπ᾽ ἀρχῆς κτίσεως ἣν ἔκτισεν ὁ θεός, "from the beginning of creation which God created"), and that this emphasis on creation is in a very apocalyptic context. Κτίζω, though not used elsewhere in the Gospels, is found three times in Revelation (4:11 2x, and 10:6), as frequent as any other NT book. Κτίσις ["creation"] is found in the Gospels only in Mk 10:6 and 13:19. Again, though not found in any other Gospel text, Revelation uses it (3:14). Likewise, γῆ ["earth"] in the sense of "creation" is found in Mk 13:27, 13:31, again in an apocalyptic passage.

Mark's apocalypticism does not preclude an emphasis on the doctrine of God the creator; it is rather an expression of it. "Creation or eschatology" is not only a false alternative, eschatology is only understood when it is seen as an aspect of the doctrine of creation. And the doctrine of God-the-creator is only understood when it is seen in eschatological terms rather than in static ontological terms.

(b) The imminent eschatological act of God which is an element of the myth evoked by the symbol ἡ βασιλεία τοῦ θεοῦ is in continuity with the acts of God in the past and present of the people of God. The eschaton is not a historically discontinuous cataclysm, but the denouement of a story which has been continuing for generations. Eschatological faith is the ultimate expression of faith in the God who acts, a faith which does not arise as escape from the harsh realities of this world, but arises out of the faith generated by the God who acts in this world.

(c) When the kingdom arrives, it is not the case that God will then assert his kingship over new territory. A spatial understanding of the kingdom, especially in the sense that the kingdom begins in a limited territory and then expands to become more comprehensive, is alien to Mark's understanding.[6] God is at present king over the whole creation. But although God is at present the rightful king over his own creation, his kingship has been usurped by hostile powers. God's *de facto* kingship will thus mean his mighty reestablishment in fact of a kingship which is presently real but not actualized.

Although the above is my own formulation, my dependence on that stream of NT interpretation represented by Rudolf Bultmann,[7] Norman Perrin,[8] and Werner Kelber (see n. 6) is clear. With Kelber, I am particularly grateful to Norman Perrin and the manner in which he has developed Bultmann's insights. Using Perrin's work as a point of departure, I would refine my own understanding of the kingdom of God in Mark by demurring from his recasting of Bultmann's insights on this subject in three primary respects:

First, Perrin considers the apocalyptic hope of the kingdom of God to be "hope for a deliverance from history itself."[9] This seems to me to be too "gnostic" a way of expressing both the problem (as though history itself were the problem for the apocalyptists) and the solution which the kingdom of God brings (deliverance "*from* history" [emphasis mine]). To be sure, neither is the hope for the coming kingdom of God a hope for a deliverance within history, as though the kingdom would come and history would continue as before, but now under the reign of God (as American Social Gospel liberalism tended to understand it). In that apocalyptic Judaism, which formed the context of early Christianity and

---

6. I thus have difficulty with the territorial and spatial aspects of Kelber's understanding in *The Kingdom in Mark: A New Place and a New Time* (Philadelphia: Fortress, 1974). Kelber is helpful in illuminating the connection between geography and the preaching of the kingdom in Mark. But is this best expressed by regarding the kingdom, in Mark's view, as having a "Jewish part" (57) which is then expanded geographically to include a "Gentile part" (61)? Cf. also 105, 121, 130.

7. *Theology of the New Testament* (New York: Scribners, 1951) 1:4–11.

8. *Jesus and the Language of the Kingdom* (Philadelphia: Fortress, 1976) 15–34.

9. Perrin, *Language*, 27.

the Gospel of Mark, I understand the referent of the symbol "kingdom of God" to be the myth of God's deliverance *of* history, i.e. the redemption of history which makes the historical process itself meaningful, rather than a deliverance from history. In my opinion, those apocalyptists who looked for the coming kingdom of God should not be accused of giving up on history and of flight into some a- or anti-historical other world. Precisely the opposite is the case: they held on to the meaningfulness of history as the arena of God's rule, even in the face of all empirical evidence to the contrary. The affirmation of the apocalyptic hope of the kingdom of God is the affirmation of history, not its denial.

Second, while I agree with Perrin that "kingdom of God" is a tensive symbol rather than a steno-symbol, I would question his using the terms "transparent" and "opaque" to express this. It is the latter word to which I object. While "transparent" is a good term to express the way steno-symbols are supposed to function—they are simply transparent windows through which one may without distortion view the realities to which the symbol points—the term "opaque" does not express what I understand Perrin to intend to say. Tensive symbols are not transparent, but neither are they opaque. An opaque symbol only allows one to look *at* it, to see its surface, or worse, to see in it the reflection of one's own convictions or prejudices. I consider the symbol of the kingdom of God, like all such tensive symbols, to be a *translucent* symbol. The symbol "kingdom of God" (and the mythical imagery it evokes) does not clearly and straight-forwardly communicate what it wants to express in a 1:1 fashion like the mathematical symbol π, as through a transparent window. But neither does it obstruct our vision, or reflect our own views, as would an opaque wall or a window on which a scene had been painted. Rather, it lets us "see" the eschatological realities of the ultimate victory of God in reestab-lishing his kingship over his creation, but not in any objectifying, concep-tual way." Ἐκ μέρους γὰρ γινωσκόμεν . . . βλέπομεν γὰρ ἄρτι δι᾽ ἐσόπρου ἐν αἰνίγματι" ["For our knowledge is imperfect . . . for now we see in a mirror dimly"] (1 Cor 13:9, 12).[10]

The third modification of Perrin's view which I propose is that to regard the kingdom of God as a tensive symbol does not make irrelevant ques-tion of the time of the kingdom's arrival. This question is dealt with below, pp. 140–43.

In the preceding discussion, I have attempted to present the way in which I see the symbol "kingdom of God" to have functioned for Jews with an apocalyptic orientation, therefore representing the context within

10. We must not be misled by the "mirror" metaphor Paul uses, for Paul is not thinking of looking at himself in a mirror, but uses the distortion one received from an ancient mirror as analogous to our "seeing" the ultimate realities expressed by such metaphors as "kingdom of God."

which the preaching of Jesus and, to some extent, the Gospel of Mark, are to be interpreted.[11] But for interpreting the Gospel of Mark, these general considerations can only be a point of departure. Whether Mark adopted, adapted, or rejected this meaning can, of course, only be determined from study of the Gospel of Mark itself, and it is to that task that we now turn.

Our study cannot be limited to the results of lexicon and concordance, but it had best begin there (since even some of our best commentaries and studies tend to talk about the kingdom of God in *Mark* with information derived from the other Gospels[12]). We thus need first to note what is there and what is not there, on a lexical basis. The data are as follows:

Βασιλεία ["kingdom"] occurs nineteen times in the Gospel of Mark, fourteen of them in the phrase ἡ βασιλεία τοῦ θεοῦ ["the kingdom of God"]:

1:14–15—Μετὰ δὲ τὸ παραδοθῆναι τὸν Ἰωάννην ἦλθεν ὁ Ἰησοῦς εἰς τὴν Γαλιλαίαν κηρύσσων τὸ εὐαγγέλιον τοῦ θεοῦ καὶ λέγων ὅτι Πεπλήρωται ὁ καιρὸς καὶ ἤγγικεν ἡ βασιλεία τοῦ θεοῦ. ["Now after John was arrested, Jesus came into Galilee, preaching the gospel of God, and saying, 'The time is fulfilled, and the kingdom of God is at hand.'"]

3:24—καὶ ἐὰν βασιλεία ἐφ᾽ ἑαυτὴν μερισθῇ, οὐ δύναται σταθῆναι ἡ βασιλεία ἐκείνη. ["If a kingdom is divided against itself, that kingdom cannot stand."]

4:11—Ὑμῖν τὸ μυστήριον δέδοται τῆς βασιλείας τοῦ θεοῦ· ἐκείνοις δὲ τοῖς ἔξω ἐν παραβολαῖς τὰ πάντα γίνεται. ["To you has been the given the secret of the kingdom of God, but for those outside everything is in parables."]

4:26—Οὕτως ἐστὶν ἡ βασιλεία τοῦ θεοῦ ὡς ἄνθρωπος βάλῃ τὸν σπόρον ἐπὶ τῆς γῆς. ["The kingdom of God is as if a man should scatter seed upon the ground."]

4:30–31—Πῶς ὁμοιώσωμεν τὴν βασιλείαν τοῦ θεοῦ ἢ ἐν τίνι αὐτὴν παραβολῇ θῶμεν; ὡς κόκκῳ σινάπεως ["With what can we compare the kingdom of God, or what parable shall we use for it? It is like a grain of mustard seed."]

6:23—καὶ ὤμοσεν αὐτῇ [πολλά], Ὅτι ἐάν με αἰτήσῃς δώσω σοι ἕως ἡμίσους τῆς βασιλείας μου. ["And he vowed to her [many things], 'Whatever you ask me, I will give you, even half of my kingdom.'"]

9:1—Ἀμὴν λέγω ὑμῖν εἰσίν τινες ὧδε τῶν ἑστηκότων οἵτινες οὐ μὴ γεύσωνται θανάτου ἕως ἂν ἴδωσιν τὴν βασιλείαν τοῦ θεοῦ ἐληλυθυῖαν ἐν δυνάμει.

11. Though Mark is a document of the Hellenistic church, "Jewish" apocalyptic is not alien to it. Apocalyptic should not be thought of as an isolated phenomenon in a cultural backwater, but as part of the lively interchange between Judaism and Hellenism in the Hellenistic Age. Cf. Kee, *Community*, 70, who refers to Martin Hengel, *Judaism and Hellenism* (Philadelphia: Fortress, 1974) 1:210–12.

12. E.g. Eduard Schweizer, *The Good News According to Mark* (Richmond: John Knox, 1970) 45–47.

["And he said to them, 'Truly, I say to you, there are some standing here who will not taste death before they see that the kingdom of God has come with power.'"]

9:47—καὶ ἐὰν ὁ ὀφθαλμός σου σκανδαλίζῃ σε, ἔκβαλε αὐτον· καλόν σέ ἐστιν μονόφθαλμον εἰσελθεῖν εἰς **τὴν βασιλείαν τοῦ θεοῦ** ἢ δύο ὀφθαλμοὺς ἔχοντα βληθῆναι εἰς τὴν γέενναν ["And if your eye causes you to sin, pluck it out; it is better for you to enter the kingdom of God with one eye than with two eyes to be thrown into hell."]

10:14—Ἄφετε τὰ παιδία ἔρχεσθαι πρός με, μὴ κωλύετε αὐτά, τῶν γὰρ τοιούτων ἐστὶν **ἡ βασιλεία τοῦ θεοῦ**. ["Let the children come to me, do not hinder them; for to such belongs the kingdom of God."]

10:15—ἀμὴν λέγω ὑμῖν, ὃς ἂν μὴ δέξηται **τὴν βασιλείαν τοῦ θεοῦ** ὡς παιδίον, οὐ μὴ εἰσέλθῃ εἰς αὐτήν. ["Truly, I say to you, whoever does not receive the kingdom of God like a child shall not enter it."]

10:23—Πῶς δυσκόλως οἱ τὰ χρήματα ἔχοντες εἰς **τὴν βασιλείαν τοῦ θεοῦ** εἰσελεύσονται. ["How hard it will be for those who have riches to enter the kingdom of God!"]

10:24—Τέκνα, πῶς δύσκολόν ἐστιν εἰς **τὴν βασιλείαν τοῦ θεοῦ** εἰσελθεῖν. ["Children, how hard it is to enter the kingdom of God!"]

10:25—εὐκοπώτερόν ἐστιν κάμηλον διὰ [τῆς] τρυμαλιᾶς [τῆς] ῥαφίδος διελθεῖν ἢ πλούσιον εἰς **τὴν βασιλείαν τοῦ θεοῦ** εἰσελθεῖν. ["It is easier for a camel to go through the eye of a needle than for a rich man to enter the kingdom of God."]

11:10—Εὐλογημένη ἡ ἐρχομένη **βασιλεία** τοῦ πατρὸς ἡμῶν Δαυίδ ["Blessed is the kingdom of our father David that is coming."]

12:34—Οὐ μακρὰν εἶ ἀπὸ **τῆς βασιλείας τοῦ θεοῦ**. ["You are not far from the kingdom of God."]

13:8—ἐγερθήσεται γὰρ ἔθνος ἐπ᾽ ἔθνος καὶ **βασιλεία** ἐπὶ **βασιλείαν** ["For nation will rise against nation, kingdom against kingdom."]

14:25—οὐκέτι οὐ μὴ πίω ἐκ τοῦ γενήματος τῆς ἀμπέλου ἕως τῆς ἡμέρας ἐκείνης ὅταν αὐτὸ πίνω καινὸν ἐν **τῇ βασιλείᾳ τοῦ θεοῦ**. ["I shall not drink again of the fruit of the vine until the day when I drink it new in the kingdom of God."]

15:43—ἐλθὼν Ἰωσὴφ [ὁ] ἀπὸ Ἀριμαθαίας εὐσχήμων βουλευτής, ὃς καὶ αὐτὸς ἦν προσδεχόμενος **τὴν βασιλείαν τοῦ θεου** ["Joseph of Arimathea, a respected member of the council, who was also himself looking for the kingdom of God"]

Βασιλεύς ["king"] occurs twelve times in Mark, as follows: [References to Jesus as **βασιλεύς** are in bold type.]

6:14—Καὶ ἤκουσεν ὁ βασιλεὺς Ἡρῴδης ["King Herod heard of it"]

6:22—εἶπεν ὁ βασιλεὺς τῷ κορασίῳ ["and the king said to the girl"]

6:25—καὶ εἰσελθοῦσα εὐθὺς μετὰ σπουδῆς πρὸς τὸν βασιλέα ᾐτήσατο ["And she came in immediately with haste to the king, and asked"]

6:26—καὶ περίλυπος γενόμενος ὁ βασιλεύς ["And the king was exceedingly sorry"]

6:27—καὶ εὐθὺς ἀποστείλας ὁ βασιλεὺς σπεκουλάτορα ["And immediately the king sent a soldier"]

13:9—ἐπὶ ἡγεμόνων καὶ βασιλέων σταθήσεσθε ἕνεκεν ἐμοῦ ["you will stand before governors and kings for my sake"]

15:2—καὶ ἐπηρώτησεν αὐτὸν ὁ Πιλᾶτος, Σὺ εἶ ὁ **βασιλεὺς τῶν** Ἰουδαίων; ["And Pilate asked him, 'Are you the King of the Jews?'"]

15:9—ὁ δὲ Πιλᾶτος ἀπεκρίθη αὐτοῖς λέγων, θέλετε ἀπολύσω ὑμῖν τὸν **βασιλέα τῶν** Ἰουδαίων; ["And he answered them, 'Do you want me to release for you the King of the Jews?'"]

15:12—ὁ δὲ Πιλᾶτος πάλιν ἀποκριθεὶς ἔλεγεν αὐτοῖς, Τί οὖν [θέλετε] ποιήσω [ὅν λέγετε] **τὸν βασιλέα τῶν** Ἰουδαίων; ["And Pilate again said to them, 'Then what shall I do with the man whom you call the King of the Jews?'"]

15:18—καὶ ἤρξαντο ἀσπάζεσθαι αὐτόν, Χαῖρε, **βασιλεῦ τῶν** Ἰουδαίων ["And they began to salute him, 'Hail, King of the Jews!'"]

15:26—καὶ ἦν ἡ ἐπιγραφὴ τῆς αἰτίας αὐτοῦ ἐπιγεγραμμένη, Ὁ **βασιλεὺς τῶν** Ἰουδαίων ["And the inscription of the charge against him read, 'The King of the Jews.'"]

15:32—ὁ χριστὸς ὁ **βασιλεὺς** Ἰσραὴλ καταβάτω νῦν ἀπὸ τοῦ σταυροῦ, ἵνα ἴδωμεν καὶ πιστεύσωμεν ["Let the Christ, the King of Israel, come down now from the cross, that we may see and believe."]

Related words are not found in Mark at all are: βασιλεύω ["rule"] (!), βασιλικός ["royal"], βασίλειος ["royal"], and βασίλισσα ["queen"].

Some phenomena which appear to be significant concerning Mark's usage of this vocabulary become immediately apparent:

1. In Mark, ἡ βασιλεία τοῦ θεοῦ, although used in all cases (except the vocative), is an absolutely fixed phrase. Markan usage stands out all the more when it is contrasted with that of the other evangelists. Although Mark uses κύριος for "God" (5:19; 11:9; 12:11, 29, 30, 36; 13:20), and knows οὐρανός ["heaven"] and πατήρ ["father"] as circumlocutions for "God" (8:38; 11:30–31; 13:32; 14:36), he never has ἡ βασιλεία τῶν οὐρανῶν ["the kingdom of heaven"] (often in Matthew) or ἡ βασιλεία τοῦ πατρός ["the kingdom of the father"] (Mt 13:43; 26:29).[13] No one ever addresses God with a reference to ἡ βασιλεία σου ["your kingdom"] (cf. Mt 6:10). Mark never has any phrase representing the kingdom as belonging to the Son of Man, the Christ, or Jesus (cf. Mt 13:41; 16:28, Lk 1:33), nor does he ever have anyone address Jesus with a reference to ἡ βασιλεία σου (cf. Lk 23:42), nor have Jesus refer to ἡ βασιλεία ἡ ἐμή ["my kingship"] (Jn 18:36; cf. Lk 22:29–30). Mark never uses βασιλεία in the absolute when referring to the kingdom

---

13. "Their" (=the righteous') Father in Mt 13:43, and "my" (=Jesus') Father in 26:29.

of God (cf. Lk 12:32); nor does he ever use βασιλεία alone as a modifier for some other substantive (e.g. no εὐαγγέλιον τῆς βασιλείας ["gospel of the kingdom"], as in Mt 4:23, or use λόγος τῆς βασιλείας ["word of the kingdom"] as in Mt 13:19).[14] When referring to the kingdom of God, Mark consistently has this absolutely fixed phrase, ἡ βασιλεία τοῦ θεοῦ, and is unique in this regard not only among the Gospels, but in the NT as a whole. This means that Mark does not formulate his kingdom language ad hoc. For him, ἡ βασιλεία τοῦ θεοῦ is an objectively real entity always represented by its specific designation.

2. Βασιλεύς ["king"] is used twelve times, but with only two referents: six times of hostile kings (including five times of Herod, 6:14–27) and six times of Jesus. Thus, contrary to what we would be led to expect from the manner in which the βασιλεία vocabulary is used, the βασιλεύς vocabulary does not present us with the kingdoms of this world over against the kingdom of God, but rather, over against the hostile kings of this world is placed Jesus as king. This in turn leads the reader of Mark to inquire if there is some connection between the kingdom of God and Jesus as king. And this in turn leads to the result that *if* there is any such connection, it must be veiled and presented in an ironic mode, since all the references to Jesus as king are ironic or mocking, and since all such references are found in the context of Jesus' trial and crucifixion. But the *question* is raised for the reader simply by the terminology used and its distribution in the Markan Gospel.

3. No one in the story uses the phrase "kingdom of God," or makes any reference to God's kingdom except Jesus himself. The kingdom is preached by Jesus and only by Jesus; not by John the Baptist (contrast Mt 3:1); not by the disciples, either before Easter (contrast Mt 10:7) or after (contrast Mt 24:14; Acts 8:12 etc). This is another indication that "king" and "kingdom" are bound together for Mark.[15]

Although no one in the story uses the phrase except Jesus, after Jesus' death the narrator himself uses ἡ βασιλεία τοῦ θεοῦ once, as the object of Joseph of Arimathea's προσδέχεσθαι ["looking for"], 15:43. This probably indicates that it is not by chance that the phrase is reserved for Jesus' own words in the Gospel. Rather than having Joseph himself or someone else

14. Mk 4:11 is somewhat peculiar in this regard: here Mark does have τὸ μυστήριον . . . τῆς βασιλείας τοῦ θεοῦ ["the mystery . . . of the kingdom of God"] but this is still an instance of the intact phrase ἡ βασιλεία τοῦ θεοῦ, and is probably an epexegetical genitive—the mystery which the kingdom is—rather than a phrase modifying μυστήριον.

15. Although Kelber, *Kingdom*, correctly makes the important point that "from beginning to end Jesus is the proclaimer and bringer of the Kingdom" (p. 74), he does not seem to notice that Jesus is the *only* one who does this, and thus weakens his argument by inserting *kingdom* preaching into the mouths of others besides Jesus, something which Mark does not do. (Commenting on the healed demoniac, for example, Kelber describes him as required to "spread the news of the Kingdom throughout the Decapolis," p. 51.)

in the story express Joseph's hope for the coming kingdom of God, the narrator interjects it into the story himself. This final occurrence of the phrase in 15:43 also seems to indicate that the author himself, represented by the narrator, believes in the futurity of the kingdom, i.e. that the expectation of a future kingdom is not merely the misunderstanding of persons in the story, but that even after the cross, ἡ βασιλεία τοῦ θεοῦ is still something to be anticipated in the future.

4. The grammatical structures into which ἡ βασιλεία τοῦ θεοῦ fits in Markan usage are revealing. With reference to how ἡ βασιλεία τοῦ θεοῦ fits into subject-verb-object structures, there are three categories:

A. In the most frequent pattern (six of the fourteen occurrences of ἡ βασιλεία τοῦ θεοῦ) ἡ βασιλεία τοῦ θεοῦ is the object of active verbs, of which human beings are the subjects, all of which occur in the section 9:47–10:25, where εἰσέρχομαι ["enter"] is the verb, plus 15:43, where προσδέχομαι ["look for, wait for, expect"] is the verb. One could get a surface impression that the kingdom in Mark is thus primarily the object of human action—but this would be a misunderstanding. Again, this is clear in the last occurrence of ἡ βασιλεία τοῦ θεοῦ in 15:43, where the narrator himself speaks. Although Joseph is the subject of προσδέχομαι, obviously he is not the subject who acts to bring the kingdom for which he can only wait. In the other five of these six instances where ἡ βασιλεία τοῦ θεοῦ is the object of human action, the verb is εἰσέρχομαι (9:47; 10:15 [+ δέχομαι {"receive"}], 23, 24, 25). In these fives cases, εἰσέρχομαι is not used in the sense of human initiative and action, but of being permitted to enter, with God, of course, being the hidden subject who permits or denies.

There are several reasons why this cluster of texts in which human beings seem to be the actors are, in fact, to be understood in the sense that God is the hidden actor. First, the conditional nature of the sentences so indicates. This is sometimes explicitly expressed in the grammar, as in 10:15 (ὃς ἄν ["whoever"]), but is the case even where the grammar is not explicit, due to the "entrance requirement" form of the sayings.

Second, it is clear that Mark understands human beings to be passive recipients of the kingdom of God in that the cluster of sayings where ἡ βασιλεία τοῦ θεοῦ is linked with εἰσέρχομαι in 10:23–25, "enter the kingdom of God" is equated with ζωὴν αἰώνιον κληρονομήσω ["inherit eternal life"], a passive idea though the grammar is active, in 10:17, and the passive verb σωθῆναι ["be saved"] in 10:26.

Third, the entire section 10:15–25 is preceded by the incident in which the children who "ἔρχεσθαι" ["come"] into τὴν βασιλείαν τοῦ θεοῦ (v 14), which seems to be active enough, are in fact brought to him (προσέφερον, v 13, an active verb with a very passive picture of the children). This section in which the cluster of sayings about entering the kingdom is found is then concluded with the affirmation: Παρὰ ἀνθρώποις ἀδύνατον, ἀλλ᾽ οὐ παρὰ θεῷ πάντα γὰρ δυνατὰ παρὰ τῷ θεῷ ["With men it is impossible, but not with God; for all things are possible with God."]. Thus God is the hidden actor, even in those sentences which have a human subject and ἡ βασιλεία τοῦ θεοῦ as the object of an active verb.

B. In another category, ἡ βασιλεία τοῦ θεοῦ is itself the subject of active verbs. There are two instances of this: 1:15, where ἤγγικεν ["is at hand"] is the verb, and 9:1, where the perfect participle ἐληλυθυῖαν ["has come"] is the verb. The kingdom comes of itself (αὐτομάτη, 4:28). There is no text in Mark where God or the Messiah is the subject and the kingdom is the object. The βασιλεία τοῦ θεοῦ is itself the subject. But this simply means that in the Gospel of Mark ἡ βασιλεία τοῦ θεοῦ is a primary means of talking about God.[16]

C. In a third category ἡ βασιλεία τοῦ θεοῦ neither acts nor is acted upon, but "descriptive" statements are made about it. It is equated with (or perhaps characterizes, depending on how one takes the genitive) the μυστήριον ["secret"] which God gives to the disciples (4:11). I say "God gives" in this instance, taking δέδοται ["has been given"] to be the "divine passive." Again, God is the hidden actor, even in a statement in which ἡ βασιλεία τοῦ θεοῦ is grammatically neither subject nor object. The kingdom of God is described as somehow like sowing or seed (4:26; 4:30). Again, there is no action attributed to the kingdom of God, but the picture is of God the author, albeit the hidden actor.

In 10:14, ἡ βασιλεία τοῦ θεοῦ is composed of, or belongs to (depending, again, on how one takes the genitive), the παιδία ["children"]. The remaining two statements, like 15:43 already discussed, have to do with the time of the kingdom of God: it is future. In 12:34, the scribe who had answered well is told that he is "not far" from the kingdom of God. Although this is often taken in a spatial sense, in view of the overwhelming temporal orientation of the kingdom of God sayings in Mark (to be discussed below), it is better to take this, at the Markan level, in a temporal sense as well. The remaining saying, 14:25, speaks of ἡ βασιλεία τοῦ θεοῦ as that future reality beyond Jesus' death and resurrection in which people will drink wine together, i.e. celebrate the Messianic Banquet.

Two issues have come to light in this study which need to be pursued: the time of the kingdom and the relationship of the kingdom of God to the kingship of Jesus as "king of the Jews (and/or Israel)."

In this connection I take up the third point on which I dissent from the line of interpretation represented by Perrin, i.e. the temporal aspect of the

16. This is a lacuna in Markan studies on which John Donahue, "A Neglected Factor in the Theology of Mark," *JBL* 101 (1982) 563–94, has recently done constructive work, as has Bruce D. Chilton, *God in Strength: Jesus' Announcement of the Kingdom* (Studien zum Neuen Testament und seiner Umwelt, B: 1; Freistadt: Verlag F. Plöchl, 1979).

kingdom. When does Mark expect the kingdom to come? Was it present in Jesus? Is it present in Mark's own time? Is it to come only in the (near) eschatological future? Is it some combination of these, dialectical or otherwise?

There is no text in Mark which clearly declares that the kingdom is present, even in some hidden way. There are texts which clearly indicate that the kingdom is future. And there are texts which *could* be understood in terms of a present, but hidden, kingdom.[17] Before pursuing this question, we must first ask if the question itself is misplaced. Perrin argues that the question "present or future?" even if answered with a dialectical both/and, is still simply *posed* wrongly.[18] In Perrin's view, so long as the kingdom of God is thought of as a "concept," then the question of the time of its coming is a legitimate, indeed, a necessary question. But when one ceases to attempt to investigate Mark's (or Jesus') "concept" of the kingdom of God, and instead begins to ask *how a symbol functions*, then the question of time is not only no longer appropriate, but positively misleading. Perrin's argument is that whoever understands kingdom of God in temporal terms has [mis-]understood it as a steno-symbol, and since kingdom of God is a tensive symbol, any temporal understanding is a category mistake and is a priori wrong.[19]

But why should this be the case? Mark does seem to grasp the tensive symbolic nature of the language of the kingdom of God, and thus avoids descriptions and setting timetables. But this by no means necessitates eliminating the category of time as such from the symbolic function of kingdom language. Mark seems rather to emphasize the futurity of it. But it is still not a calculable future, one that can be reckoned with in steno-language terms. It is that future which already impinges on the present, while remaining outside the present. "Ηγγικεν (1:15) captures this perfectly. This first verb Mark uses of the kingdom of God expresses a real future, just as does the last verb he uses, προσδέχομαι. In both cases, a real,

17. That Mark understands the time between Jesus' earthly life and his reappearance as the apocalyptic Son of Man as the time in which the kingdom is present, but hidden, has been argued by the two recent major studies of the kingdom in Mark. Aloysius M. Ambrozic, *The Hidden Kingdom: A Redaction-Critical Study of the References to the Kingdom of God in Mark's Gospel* (CBQMS 2; Washington: Catholic Biblical Association, 1972), and Kelber, *Kingdom*.

18. *Language*, 39–40.

19. Kee, *Community*, 209–10 seems to be correct that it is Perrin's existentialism [*existential* rather than *existentiell*] which keeps him from incorporating the temporally future dimension of the kingdom of God in Mark, or leads him to eliminating it by means of the "steno-symbol" label.

Chilton, *Kingdom*, 124ff., argues somewhat analogously to Perrin in that it is the misunderstanding of the kingdom as a spatial realm which misleadingly generates questions as to the time of its coming. But thinking in terms of the act of God, as advocated by Chilton, is not an atemporal category. I see no reason to avoid the temporal aspects of the coming of the kingdom, either in Mark or elsewhere in the NT.

chronological future is intended, but not a speculative future which may be "reckoned." It is rather that future which, while remaining future, is "near" and therefore affects the present.

Nor does the language of hiddenness (4:26–32, cf. esp. κρυπτός ["hidden"] in 4:22) necessarily mean that the kingdom of God is *present*, not even in a presence understood in some hidden way. One might rather understand the seed parables, at the Markan level, as indicating that the decisive action ("sowing") which shall bring the kingdom has already been taken, and that the harvest shall certainly come (though not by human doing), but not that the kingdom is present but hidden like seed in the ground. This latter is hardly a symbol of *presence*. The present is rather an in-between-time of *absence*. Kelber well describes "the Markan people who live between seedtime and harvest." But I think Kelber's seminal treatment of this subject could be sharpened: It should be made clear that for Mark's own time, the kingdom is not present. Kelber's statements that Mark affirms "the reality of the Kingdom now" (e.g., 39) blur this important point. Discussing the seed parables of the kingdom, Kelber uses such phrases as "the present hiddenness of the kingdom" (e.g., 38), though he also uses the metaphors of "embryonic" (40) and "prenatal" (42). The latter metaphors are actually nearer to what I understand Mark to be saying, in that embryonic life, though real, is still thought of as a future reality rather than a present one. I think what Kelber is properly concerned to affirm in his language about the "presence" of the kingdom is that for Mark it is no longer merely a hope which looks toward the future, but is based on a reality which has already entered history in Jesus. Kelber is thus very illuminating in speaking of the Markan Christians as living "between Kingdom and Kingdom" (140). What Kelber does not do is to describe the present "betweenness" as the time of the *absence* of the kingdom. Kelber's (and Mark's) view could thus be stated more pointedly as follows:

There is a three-act drama in Mark's understanding of the kingdom:

I. (Past) The kingdom appears in Jesus (the kingdom is where the king is).

II. (Present) The kingdom is absent because the king is absent. This is the experience of the Markan community. To speak of the kingdom as present-but-hidden violates the parallel Mark draws between king and kingdom.

III. (Future) The kingdom will re-appear when Jesus reappears in apocalyptic power.

I would thus see "present/absent/present" as better rubrics for Mark's "history of the Kingdom" than "appeared/concealed/manifest."[20] My sug-

---

20. *Kingdom*, 42.

gested terminology allows the "history" of king and kingdom to be described together, and this is important for Mark's understanding of the kingdom.

To describe people as living "between seedtime and harvest" means that they live in the time between remembrance and hope, not in the time when the kingdom is present even in a hidden manner. When one has seed, and when one has harvest, something is present. But between seedtime and harvest, although the decisive act has already been accomplished, it is a time of absence, waiting, and hoping. Just as Mark views the present as the time of the absence of Jesus, not of his hidden presence, so it is with the kingdom. This brings us to the final issue to be discussed, that of the connection between the kingdom of God and the kingship of Jesus.

In this connection, I wish to make only one suggestion, and that in relation to a recent dissertation by Frank J. Matera.[21] Matera summarizes his view of Mark's understanding of the kingship of Jesus (p. 149):

1. Kingship is inseparable from rejection and suffering.

2. Kingship possesses a glorious aspect which will be revealed when the only Son returns in his capacity as the Son of Man. But this kingship cannot be disclosed until Jesus has completed his suffering and death.

3. Kingship finds its supreme title in "Son of God" but no one can make this proclamation until the temple curtain has been torn. This event, the result of Jesus' death, allows the Markan community and all believers to confess Jesus as God's Son.

There can be no doubt that "Son of God" is a, if not the, key christological term for Mark. It was probably present in the original text of 1:1, despite its absence from some good manuscripts. And it is certainly present at key junctures of the book, when Jesus is confessed as "Son of God" by the heavenly voice (1:11; 9:7), by Jesus himself (14:62), and by the centurion at the cross (15:39). Matera has done us the service of showing that there is a "royal" dimension to this title. But he seems to understand "Son of God" predominantly, if not exclusively, in this tradition.[22] He thus finds it necessary to downplay the Son of Man understood in an apocalyptic sense, interpreting Son of Man in royal terms. And especially, he ignores the $\theta\epsilon\hat{\iota}os\ \dot{a}v\dot{\eta}\rho$ ["divine man"] connotations of "Son of God" in the Markan miracle stories. (I am here not making a case for the term $\theta\epsilon\hat{\iota}os$ $\dot{a}v\dot{\eta}\rho$, but use it only as a convenient modern label for that charismatic miracle-worker endowed with superhuman power.) "Son of God" in this sense certainly plays a role in Mark's situation and in his own Chris-

21. The Kingship of Jesus: Composition and Theology in Mark 15 (SBLDS 66; Chico, Calif.: Scholars, 1982).

22. Cf. my critique of this position as represented by Jack D. Kingsbury, in my review of his The Christology of Mark's Gospel (Philadelphia: Fortress, 1983) in JBL 104 (1985) 732–35.

tology, but not simply as his negative reaction to his opponents' Christology.[23] The miracle-working "θεῖος ἀνήρ" Son of God plays a major role as a positive dimension of Mark's own Christology. Chapter 15 of Mark seems to be concerned precisely with this understanding of "Son of God"/Christ/king of Israel. It is this interpretation of "Son of God" as a miracle-worker filled with divine power with which Mark is wrestling (15:32), rather than with "opponents who argued that Jesus did not fulfill the messianic expectations of the Old Testament," as Matera claims.[24]

Thus I would argue that for Mark, "king of the Jews/Israel" does not function to interpret the meaning of "Son of God," but functions ironically.[25] Just as it is very important to note that "kingdom of God" occurs only on the lips of Jesus (and once by the narrator, but by no one except Jesus in the story), so it is important to note that "king of the Jews/Israel" occurs only in the mouth of Jesus' opponents, unbelievers who misunderstand him. Thus what they say is true, but *ironically* true.

It is not the case that "king of the Jews" serves to explicate the meaning of the key title "Son of God," in such a way that "Son of God" could be *reduced* to "royal messianism." There is too much connection between the miracle stories—a major part of the content of Mark—and "Son of God" Christology for that. And these two, miracle (or the lack of it) and Christ (=Son of God, cf. 14:61) are conjoined ironically again in the final scene (15:32).[26] "King of the Jews" stands in ironical relation to the major topic of Jesus' proclamation: the kingship of God. Jesus proclaimed the kingdom to come, and what came was the kingship of (the crucified!) Jesus. The kingdom of God, now absent (not "hidden") because the crucified king is absent,[27] but to come in glory in the future when the

---

23. Contra Theodore J. Weeden, Mark—Traditions in Conflict (Philadelphia: Fortress, 1971).

24. Kingship, 151.

25. On Mark's use of irony, including specifically with reference to the above topic and text, cf. David Rhoads and Donald Michie, Mark as Story: An Introduction to the Narrative of a Gospel (Philadelphia: Fortress, 1982) 59–62. I do not understand the claim of Ambrozic, Hidden Kingdom, 32, that "irony . . . is not one of his characteristics."

26. With this scene as point of contact, I have attempted to show how Mark affirms both the Christology expressed in the miracle stories and the Christology of the weakness of Jesus expressed in the passion story, without compromising either, in Truly Human/Truly Divine: Christological Language and the Gospel Form (St. Louis: CBP Press, 1984).

27. Werner Kelber, "Conclusion: From Passion Narrative to Gospel," in Werner Kelber, ed., The Passion in Mark: Studies on Mark 14—16 (Philadelphia: Fortress, 1976) 164: "The absence of Jesus is . . . a presiding feature in the Markan Gospel." On the absence of Jesus as a Markan theme, cf. the essays by Vernon K. Robbins and J. Dominic Crossan in The Passion in Mark, Kelber's later work in The Oral and Written Gospel: The Hermeneutics of Speaking and Writing in the Synoptic Tradition, Mark, Paul and Q (Philadelphia: Fortress, 1983); J. Dominic Crossan, "A Form for Absence: The Markan Creation of Gospel," in Semeia 12 (1978); Weeden, Mark, 83–89, 106–11, 115.

crucified king returns in glory, is indeed the eschatological act of God to deliver his people. In the Gospel of Mark, the kingdom of God, presently absent but still to come in power, is inseparable from the kingship of Jesus, and that means that the eschatological act of God is inseparable from the crucified Jesus.

11 The Kingdom of God in Luke–Acts

Robert O'Toole, SJ

Professor of Theology
St. Louis University

THE PURPOSE OF THIS ESSAY is to describe as accurately and completely as possible what Luke, the author of Luke–Acts, means by "the kingdom of God." Like every presentation, this one, too, has its assumptions. First, it is based on the understanding of Luke's theology which I have established in my recent book.[1] Second, Luke addresses not any given fictional audience but the actual readers of his two-volume work. Third, another important observation is that Luke's use of "kingdom of God" cannot be studied apart from the related concepts: "kingdom," "king," "reign," "Jesus' Davidic lineage," "the Christ," "seated on a throne," "Lord," "Son of God," and "the Son of Man." Finally, as this article will clarify, "kingdom of God" for Luke is not an univocal term.[2] Its meaning varies with the contexts, and it is one of the major ways in which Luke moves from "Jesus the preacher" to "Jesus the preached."

The methodology employed is a type of redaction criticism which might more appropriately be called composition criticism. Luke writes of "the kingdom of God" and its related terms, and at times concentrates these

---

1. R. F. O'Toole, *The Unity of Luke's Theology: An Analysis of Luke–Acts* (Wilmington: Michael Glazier, 1984). Please consult the brief bibliography of that book for further information.

2. I am not totally comfortable with N. Perrin's "tensive symbol" in *Jesus and the Language of the Kingdom: Symbol and Metaphor in New Testament Interpretation* (Philadelphia: Fortress, 1976) 2–3, 28–34, 77–78, 197–99, 202–4. Perrin is concerned that the mythology of Jesus not be discredited by the subsequent course of history; however, his "tensive symbol" tends toward a relativity. For instance, how much meaning can one drop from "the kingdom of God" before it ceases to be a "tensive symbol"? Perrin has not attended sufficiently to the objective content or limited nature of a symbol. A symbol cannot say everything, nor can it be deprived of some definite content.

expressions.[3] However, rather than study each of the terms related to "the kingdom of God" in detail, the best approach is to unify the presentation by reviewing what themes "the kingdom of God" and its related concepts convey for Luke.[4]

God the Father Brings About the Kingdom

The "kingdom of God" is God's action and gift. This is the primary import of the genitive, "of God," in Luke–Acts.[5] This fact is established from the very beginning. The angel Gabriel promises Mary, "and the Lord God will give him the throne of his father David" (Lk 1:32). Jesus responds to those who claim that he casts out demons through the power of Beelzebub, "But if it is by the finger of God that I cast out demons, then the kingdom of God has come upon you" (Lk 11:20). At the Last Supper Jesus assures his apostles, "I assign to you, as my Father assigned to me, a kingdom, that you may eat and drink at my table in my kingdom" (Lk 22:29–30). Thus, the Father brings the kingdom. It is the Father's good pleasure to give the disciples the kingdom (Lk 12:32), and they are to pray that it comes (Lk 11:2). The exact time of its coming depends radically on the Father, as Jesus, at the beginning of Acts, explains to his apostles, "It is not for you to know times or seasons which the Father has fixed by his own authority" (1:7).

3. For example, see Lk 18:16–17, 24–25, 29; 19:11–12, 14–15, 27; 22:16, 18, 29–30; 23:2–3, 37–38, 42, 51. The Bible translation followed in this article is: *The New Oxford Annotated Bible with the Apocrypha: Revised Standard Version* (ed. H. G. May and B. M. Metzger; New York: Oxford, 1977). I only vary from that translation when I believe it to be incorrect or misleading.

4. Some of the recent literature on the "kingdom of God" in Luke includes: A. del Aqua Pérez, "El cumplimiento del Reino de Dios en la misión de Jesús: Programma del Evangelio de Lucas (Lc 4,14–44)," *EstBib* 38 (1979–80) 269–93; C. H. Dodd, *The Parables of the Kingdom* (London: William Collins Sons & Co., 1961) 29–35, 62–63, 80–83, 142–45, 150–54; A. George, "La royauté de Jésus selon l'évangile de Luc," *ScEccl* 14 (1962) 57–69; W. W. Glover, "'The Kingdom of God' in Luke," *BT* 29 (1978) 231–39; A. R. C. Leaney, *A Commentary on the Gospel According to St. Luke* (London: A. & C. Black, 1958) 6–7, 34–37, 74–75, 152; I. H. Marshall, *Luke: Historian and Theologian* (Grand Rapids: Zondervan, 1971) 88–93, 128–36; O. Merk, "Das Reich Gottes in den lukanischen Schriften," *Jesus und Paulus*, Fs. W. G. Kümmel (ed. E. E. Ellis and E. Grässer; Göttingen: Vandenhoeck & Ruprecht, 1975) 201–20; F. Pereira, *Ephesus: Climax of Universalism in Luke–Acts: A Redactional-Critical Study of Paul's Ephesian Ministry (Acts 18:23–20:1)* (Jesuit Theological Forum 10/1; Anand: Gujarat Sahitya Prakash, 1983) 118–27; R. Schnackenburg, *God's Rule and Kingdom* (New York: Herder and Herder, 1965) 83–86, 93–94, 117, 122–27, 132–42; M. Völkel, "Zur Deutung des 'Reiches Gottes' bei Lukas," *ZNW* 65 (1974) 57–70; G. Voss, *Die Christologie der lukanischen Schriften* (StudNeot 2; Paris: Desclée de Brouwer, 1965) 25–97, 131–53; A. Wainwright, "Luke and the Restoration of the Kingdom to Israel," *ExpTim* 89 (1977) 76–79; T. Weiser, *Kingdom and Church in Luke–Acts* (Diss. Union Theological Seminary, New York 1962).

5. Lk 1:32–33; 12:32 and Acts 1:7 are unique to Luke.

The Holy Spirit and the Kingdom of God

Through the Holy Spirit Jesus becomes the Son of God and Mary's son and will reign over the house of Jacob forever (cf. Lk 1:26–37).[6] And, although it is not explicitly stated in Luke, Jesus' baptismal scene in Lk 3:21–22 may well reflect this kingly reign of Jesus. The Holy Spirit does descend on Jesus, and the voice from heaven identifies him, "You are my beloved Son, with whom I am well pleased."

The only other Lucan passage which clearly conveys a special relationship between the Holy Spirit and the kingdom of God is Acts 2:30–36. The Pentecost speech speaks of the oath to David that there would be a descendant on his throne. This Davidic descendant is the risen Jesus, and exalted at God's right hand as Lord and Christ, he has received from the Father and poured out the promise of the Holy Spirit. This Lucan understanding doubtless explains the connection between the kingdom and the Holy Spirit in Acts 1:7–8. Consequently, both at Jesus' birth and exaltation, Luke portrays the Holy Spirit as related to the kingdom. Probably, this emphasis on the Spirit is not stronger because for Luke the risen and enthroned Jesus is also active.

The Kingdom of God is also Jesus' Kingdom

The kingdom also belongs to Jesus. As mentioned above, Jesus is to receive the throne of David and reign over the house of Jacob forever (Lk 1:32–33), and he assigns to his apostles as his Father assigned to him a kingdom (Lk 22:29–30). In the latter passage Jesus speaks of eating and drinking at table "in my kingdom." A number of other Lucan passages make this same point. For instance, as he enters Jerusalem, his disciples shout, "Blessed is the king who comes in the name of the Lord" (Lk 19:38). The Jews of Thessalonica accuse Jason and those with him of acting against the decrees of Caesar because they say, "that there is another king, Jesus" (Acts 17:7). Ironically, Jesus is called a king or associated with the kingdom of God a number of times during his passion (Lk 23:2–3, 37–38, 42, 51). All but Lk 23:3, 38 are unique to Luke. Of course, Luke intends

6. Certainly, Luke sees a relationship between the kingdom of God and the Holy Spirit, but this relationship is not that fully developed in Luke–Acts, despite the contention of J. D. G. Dunn, "Spirit and Kingdom," *ExpTim* 82 (1970) 37–40, and of S. S. Smalley, "Spirit, Kingdom and Prayer in Luke–Acts," *NovT* (1973) 59–71. See also G. E. Rice, "Luke 3:22–38 in Codex Bezae: The Messianic King," *Andrews University Seminar Studies* 17 (1979) 204–8.

these verses for his Christian readers who recognize Jesus as the king of the Jews and therefore the sharp irony in the treatment given him.

Jesus' Davidic lineage includes his having a kingdom. Elsewhere[7] I have argued that the promise to David helps to explain the thought of the Pentecost speech and of Paul's speech at Pisidian Antioch. According to the Pentecost speech, Jesus is the one who sits on David's throne at the right hand of God (Acts 2:30–35; cf. Lk 22:69). Luke, in Paul's Pisidian Antioch speech, similarly brings up the notion of kingdom, "And when he had removed him, he raised up David to be their king. . . . Of this man's posterity God has brought to Israel a Savior, Jesus, as he promised" (Acts 13:22–23; cf. Lk 1:31–33; 2:11).

Two Lucan passages link the "kingdom of God" to Jesus' presence and actions. When accused of casting out devils in the name of Beelzebub, Jesus ends his answer with, "But if it is by the finger of God that I cast out demons, then the kingdom of God has come upon you" (Lk 11:20). Jesus' presence and actions also explain why he can say to the Pharisees who asked him when the kingdom of God is coming, "The kingdom of God is not coming with signs to be observed; nor will they say, 'Lo, here it is!' or 'There!' for behold the kingdom of God is with you" (Lk 17:20–21).

Luke certainly identifies the following of Jesus with the kingdom of God. Jesus' comment on the rich ruler's unwillingness to follow him (Lk 18:18–30) is, "How hard it is for those who have riches to enter the kingdom of God" (v 24), and so he identifies following himself with entry into the kingdom. Luke repeats this idea within a few verses (cf. vv 28–29), where he alone of all the synoptics speaks of "the kingdom of God." Actually, Luke has already united Jesus with the kingdom of God in the previous story. The disciples are trying to prevent people from bringing children to Jesus. But Jesus calls them to him, "Let the children come to me, and do not hinder them; for to such belongs the kingdom of God" (Lk 18:16). Coming to Jesus relates to belonging to the kingdom.

Luke, in verses which are unique to him, has introduced this idea of the following of Jesus connected with the kingdom. In the narrative about the claims of discipleship, we read, "'but as for you, go and proclaim the kingdom of God.' Another said, 'I will follow you, Lord; but let me first say farewell to those at my home.'" Jesus responds, "No man who puts his hand to the plow and looks back is fit for the kingdom of God" (Lk 9:60b–62). The parable about the pounds (Lk 19:11–27) should be included here because only in Luke is Jesus the king to whom those who received the pounds must given an account and who punishes his enemies who did not want him to reign over them.[8]

---

7. See my "Acts 2:30 and the Davidic Covenant of Pentecost," *JBL* 102 (1983) 245–58.
8. For further discussion of this parable see Dodd, *Parables*, 114–21; J. Jeremias, *The*

The fact that Luke interchanges "Jesus" with "the kingdom of God" (cf. Lk 14:26; 18:29) shows that he views them as somehow identical.[9] In addition, if Lk 18:29 is compared with Mk 10:29 (Mt 19:29), one will note that Luke has substituted "for the sake of the kingdom of God" for Mark's "for my sake and for the gospel." Luke speaks of Jesus and the kingdom of God together (Acts 8:12; 28:23, 32); he probably does not intend two different realities, but is rather using one of his favorite literary devices, a double expression, and is simply repeating the one idea in the other. This claim of some identity between "the kingdom of God" and "Jesus" is confirmed by the fact that Luke can refer to the whole gospel message as Jesus alone (e.g. Acts 5:42; 8:35; 11:20; 17:3) or as only the kingdom of God (e.g. Lk 4:43; 8:1; 9:2, 11, 60; 10:9, 11; 16:16, Acts 1:3; 19:8; 20:25).

Certain Characteristics of the Kingdom of God

The kingdom of God which the Father and Jesus bring has itself certain characteristics. First of all, it is not like the kingdoms of this world. It is a kingdom of service (Lk 22:24–27). Consequently, Jesus rejects Satan's offer of the authority and glory of all the kingdoms of the world (Lk 4:5–8).

Since the kingdom of God can summarize the whole of the Christian message, it can take on many of its characteristics. The kingdom of God is mysterious, but its secrets have been revealed to Jesus' disciples (Lk 8:10).[10] Yet they do not know when the Father will establish it (Acts 1:6–7). Like a mustard seed or leaven in flour, it appears insignificant, but becomes very significant (Lk 13:18–21).

The kingdom of God confers dignity on its members. He who is least in it is greater than John the Baptist (Lk 7:28). Jesus, before he tells the parable of the Great Banquet, accepts the blessing which one of his table companions attributes to those who eat bread in the kingdom of God (Lk 14:15). Moreover, the kingdom of God is universal. It will include Gentiles. The end of the parable about the narrow door demonstrates this (Lk 13:28–30). Doubtless, the same point is being made in the last words of the parable of the Great Banquet: "For I tell you, none of those who were invited shall taste my banquet" (Lk 14:24).

Parables of Jesus (New York: Charles Scribner's Sons, 1963) 58–63, 67, 95, 166; B. Noack, *Das Gottesreich bei Lukas: Eine Studie zu Luk. 17,20–24* (SynBU 10; Uppsala: C. W. K. Gleerup, 1948) 48–49; F. D. Weinert, "The Parable of the Throne Claimant (Luke 19:12, 14–15a, 27) Reconsidered," *CBQ* 39 (1977) 505–14.

9. I am indebted for this example to Pereira, *Ephesus*, 122.

10. S. Brown, "Secrets of the Kingdom of God [Mark 4:11]," *JBL* (1973) 66, is correct when he comments on Matthew's and Luke's use of Mark, ". . . they may simply be bringing out what was already implicit in their source."

The parable of the Great Banquet reveals another characteristic of the kingdom of God. It is directed toward the disadvantaged. The householder instructs his servant, "bring in the poor and maimed and blind and lame" (Lk 14:21). This direction of the kingdom of God toward the disadvantaged forms part of the message in Lk 4:14-44. Luke 4:14-44 is a unit, for Lk 4:14-15 constitute a transition and introduction while 4:42-44 form a conclusion and another transition. Moreover, Lk 4:18, "The Spirit of the Lord is upon me, because he has anointed me to preach good news (εὐαγγελίσασθαι) to the poor," marks an inclusion with Lk 4:43, "I must preach the good news (εὐαγγελίσασθαι) of the kingdom of God to the other cities also; for I was sent for this purpose."[11] Luke in this unit intends his readers to understand the good news about the kingdom of God (v 43) in terms of Jesus' preaching good news to the poor and proclaiming release to the captives and recovery of sight to the blind, of his freeing of the oppressed (v 18). Since Lk 4:14-44 is programmatic for the whole of Luke-Acts, particular significance should be given to its portrayal of the importance of the disadvantaged for the kingdom of God.

Likewise, the kingdom is a source of hope and encouragement to the Christians, as the activity of Paul and Barnabas in Lystra, Iconium, and Antioch shows us (Acts 14:22). Whoever seeks the kingdom of the Father will receive the other things he might be anxious about, such as clothing, possessions and what one is to eat and drink (Lk 12:31; cf. 12:22-34). In short, the kingdom of God is beneficial. In his speech to the Ephesian elders, Paul speaks the message of the kingdom of God (v 25) shortly after he claims that among them he did not shrink from declaring everything which was profitable (Acts 20:18-20).

In one sense, the kingdom of God does not come with signs which one can observe (Lk 17:20); in another, there will be definite signs that will indicate when the kingdom of God and our redemption are near (cf. Lk 21:25-31). When the Son of Man brings the kingdom of God, he will come in a cloud with power and great glory (Lk 21:27; cf. 9:26), and the joyful contentment of the kingdom is portrayed by banquet scenes (Lk 14:15-24; 22:28-30).

The Kingdom of God Indicates a Union between Jesus and the Christians

Luke unites Jesus with the Christians. One of the ways in which he does this is through the kingdom of God. Jesus now reigns over the Christians,

---

11. I am indebted to A. del Aqua Pérez ("El cumplimiento del Reino de Dios," 271-73) for this insight. See also Völkel, "Reiches Gottes," 63.

who are the house of Jacob (Lk 1:32–33; cf. Acts 2:30–36; 13:22–37) and the twelve tribes whom the apostles are to judge (Lk 22:29–30). Both of these passages belong to a Lucan theme that the Christians are the true Israel. Jesus is the Christians' king.[12]

Something should be said here about the fact that in his Last Supper narrative (Lk 22:14–38) Luke twice refers to both the kingdom of God (vv 16, 18) and to kingdom (vv 29–30). The latter verses were just interpreted as linking Jesus with the Christians who as the true Israel constitute his kingdom. The former verses stand in the same unity (Lk 22:14–38) as vv 28–30, and so the kingdom which the Father has assigned Jesus is to be understood as the kingdom of God. Also, the Lord's Supper prefigures the kingdom. It unites Jesus with the Christians because it represents the kingdom which the Father assigns him and in which the Christians are ultimately to be joined with their king.

Preaching About "The Kingdom of God" Summarizes the Ministry of Jesus and That of His Followers

Jesus says to the people, "I must preach the good news of the kingdom of God to the other cities also; for I was sent for this purpose" (Lk 4:43). A similar summary of Jesus' activity is to be found in Lk 8:1. In much the same words Jesus assigns their ministry to the apostles, "he sent them (the Twelve) out to preach the kingdom of God and to heal" (Lk 9:1–2; cf. v 6) and to the disciples, "heal the sick in it and say to them, 'The kingdom of God has come near to you'" (Lk 10:9; cf. v 11; 9:60). Paul, in his speech to the Ephesian elders, recapitulates his ministry as, "to testify to the gospel of the grace of God. And now, behold, I know that all you among whom I have gone preaching the kingdom will see my face no more" (Acts 20:24–25). Preaching about the kingdom of God, then, sums up the ministry of Jesus, the apostles, disciples, and Paul.

The Christian Message Can Be Summarized in the Phrase, "the Kingdom of God"

It is no secret that Luke uses any number of expressions for the Christian message. Often when Jesus or one of his apostles or disciples is said to preach, Luke designates this activity further only as "the kingdom of God" (Lk 4:43; 8:1; 9:2, 11, 60; 10:9, 11; 16:16; Acts 1:3; 19:8; 20:25). Of course, Lk 4:43; 8:1 (but see Mt 9:35); 9:11, 60; 10:11; Acts 1:3; 19:8; 20:25 are unique to

12. I explore this in detail in, *The Unity*, 17–24.

Luke. Luke, in 4:43, adds "the kingdom of God" to Mk 1:38, "that I may preach there also," and in 9:11 to Mk 6:34, "and he began to teach them many things." Through the introduction (Lk 4:43; 16:16) or use (Acts 8:12) of εὐαγγελίζεσθαι, "to preach the gospel," Luke explicates the gospel dimension of "the kingdom of God." Therefore, "the kingdom of God" not infrequently stands for the whole Christian message. At times Luke has introduced it into Mark's thought and uses εὐαγγελίζεσθαι to tie the "kingdom of God" more closely with the gospel message.

The Kingdom of God is a Present Reality

The kingdom of God is somehow present. Earlier, when an effort was made to link the kingdom with Jesus, two passages (Lk 11:20; 17:21–22) were considered. Jesus' expelling of demons proves that the kingdom of God has come upon his audience,[13] and apparently, Jesus' very presence means that the kingdom is a reality.[14]

The Pentecost speech gives every evidence that it is reporting the fulfillment of the promise of the angel Gabriel to Mary (Lk 1:31–33). David has a descendant upon the throne; the risen Jesus is exalted as Lord and Christ at God's right hand. Consequently, the kingdom of God and its king were already a reality for Luke's readers, even if that reality has not yet found total actualization.

Luke 7:28, "I tell you, among those born of women none is greater than John; yet he who is least in the kingdom of God is greater than he," is puzzling.[15] No matter to whom "least" refers, the passage views the kingdom of God as at least partially present, for no one can belong to the kingdom of God unless it is somehow present.

13. Schnackenburg, God's Rule, 124–25. See also Dodd, Parables, 28–29.

14. C. H. Roberts, "The Kingdom of Heaven (Lk. XVII.21)," HTR 41 (1948) 1–8; see also Dodd; Parables, 62–63; H. Hartl, "Die Aktualität des Gottesreiches nach Lk 17,20f," Biblische Randbemerkungen Fs. R. Schnackenburg (ed. H. Merklein and J. Lange; Augsburg: Echter, 1974) 26–29; Noack, Das Gottesreich, 1–50; Schnackenburg, God's Rule, 134–36.

15. For interpretations of this verse, see F. W. Danker, Jesus and the New Age: According to Luke (St. Louis: Clayton, 1976) 97; E. E. Ellis, The Gospel of Luke (NCB; Greenwood: Attic, 1974) 119–20; J. A. Fitzmyer, The Gospel According to Luke (I–IX): Introduction, Translation and Notes (AB 28; Garden City: Doubleday, 1981) 670–76; W. Grundmann, Das Evangelium nach Lukas (THKNT 3; Berlin: Evangelische Verlagsanstalt, 1971) 166; Leaney, St. Luke, 58–59; Schnackenburg, God's Rule, 132–34.

Perhaps, equally problematic is the interpretation of "the kingdom of God has come near to you" (Lk 10:9, 11; cf. Mt 10:8). It may be that even though Luke uses a Greek present perfect in both instances, all that we should conclude is that the kingdom "is near." Since it is not clear that these verses convey a present reality to the kingdom of God, they are not treated in this section. Cf. Schnackenburg, God's Rule, 140–42 and Dodd, Parables, 29–30.

The two growth parables of the mustard seed and of the leaven, which Luke (13:18–21) shares with Mark and Matthew, picture the kingdom of God as a present reality. After all, according to these parables, the grain of mustard seed is sown and growing, and the leaven hidden in the three measures of flour has begun its function.[16]

There is no doubt that Luke viewed the kingdom of God as, in part, a present reality.

The Kingdom of God Means the Destruction of Satan's Reign and Salvation for the Christians

---

Luke sees the world as divided between darkness and light, between the power of Satan and the power of God (cf. Acts 26:18). Miracles demonstrate that the reign of Satan is being overcome. This is why Jesus, when he is accused of casting out demons by Beelzebub, says,

> And if Satan is divided against himself, how will his kingdom stand? For you say that I cast out demons by Beelzebub. And if I cast out demons by Beelzebub, by whom do your sons cast them out? Therefore they shall be your judges. But if it is by the finger of God that I cast out demons, then the kingdom of God has come upon you. (Lk 11:18–20; cf. 4:40–43)

This explains, too, Jesus' words about the cure of the woman with an infirmity in Lk 13:16, "And ought not this woman, a daughter of Abraham whom Satan bound for eighteen years, be loosed from this bond on the sabbath day?" In a similar manner, Luke joins the preaching of the kingdom of God with power and authority over demons and to cure diseases (4:40–43; 8:1–3; 9:1–2, 11; 10:9).[17]

Luke associates the kingdom of God with salvation. When the rich official refuses to give up his possessions and follow him, Jesus observes, "'How hard it is for those who have riches to enter the kingdom of God. For it is easier for a camel to go through the eye of the needle than for a rich man to enter the kingdom of God.' Those who heard it said, 'Then who can be saved?'" (Lk 18:24–26). In order that these verses make sense, "to enter the kingdom of God" has to be the equivalent of "being saved." Within a few verses, Luke again associates the kingdom of God and salvation in Jesus' answer to Peter. Jesus assures him, "there is no one who has left house or wife or brothers or parents or children, for the sake of the kingdom of God, who will not receive manifold more in this time,

---

16. For further comment on these growth parables, cf. Dodd, *Parables*, 152–56. Also, in this volume, R. H. Hiers, "Pivotal Reactions to the Eschatological Interpretations," this volume, pp. 15–33.

17. By contrast with the parallels, Luke has introduced "the kingdom of God" into 4:43; 8:1; 9:11; 10:9.

and in the age to come eternal life" (Lk 18:29–30). "Eternal life" surely means salvation.[18] Interestingly, this pericope begins and ends with "eternal life" (18:18, 30).

The next relevant passages are Lk 21:28, 30. Verse 28 parallels v 30 where "the kingdom of God" appears instead of "your redemption." The Lucan implication is that "the kingdom of God" means redemption. Luke does identify "redemption" with "salvation" and interchanges these terms in Lk 1:68–70 (cf. 2:38; 24:21).

Luke has so structured Paul's speech to the Ephesian elders at Miletus that it contains a number of summary statements of Paul's proclamation of the gospel (Acts 20:20–21, 24–25, 27, 32), and for all practical purposes, these summary statements are interchangeable. In one of these statements, Paul speaks of accomplishing his ministry and states, "to testify to the gospel of the grace of God. And now, behold, I know that all you among whom I have gone preaching the kingdom will see my face no longer" (vv 24–25). A later summary statement reveals that "the kingdom" is to be associated with salvation, "And now I commend you to God and to the word of his grace, which is able to build you up and to give you the inheritance among those who are sanctified" (v 32). Again, the kingdom is associated with salvation.

Luke, in Acts 28:23–31, again associates the kingdom of God with salvation. Paul addresses the leaders of the Roman Jews with the words, "testifying to the kingdom of God and trying to convince them about Jesus both from the law of Moses and from the prophets" (v 23). But they disagreed about what he had to say; so Paul, using the words of Isa 6:10, concludes, "Let it be known to you then that this salvation of God has been sent to the Gentiles; they will listen" (v 29). When Paul thereafter continues his work in Rome, he is seemingly again announcing this salvation, but all that Luke writes of him is, "preaching the kingdom of God and teaching about the Lord Jesus Christ quite openly and unhindered" (v 31).

A number of other Lucan passages also interrelate the kingdom of God and salvation. For instance, the good thief asks, "Jesus, remember me when you come into your kingdom," to which Jesus replies, "Truly, I say to you, today you will be with me in Paradise" (cf. Lk 23:42–43). Furthermore, in the same context of the passion narrative Luke directs the following irony to his readers:

> but the rulers scoffed at him, saying, "He *saved* others; let him *save* himself, if he is the *Christ* of God, his Chosen One!" The soldiers also mocked him, coming up and offering

18. For a consideration of our resurrection as part of Luke's concept of salvation and as affected by Jesus' resurrection, see my "Christ's Resurrection in Acts 13:13–52," *Bib* 60 (1979) 361–72.

him vinegar, and saying, "If you are the *King of the Jews save* yourself!" There was also an inscription over him, "This is the *King of the Jews*." One of the criminals who were hanged railed at him saying, "Are you not the *Christ? Save* yourself and us." (Lk 23:35–39)

Finally, as earlier proposed, there is a relationship between "the kingdom of God" and Jesus' Davidic lineage. Two relevant Davidic passages refer to salvation: "for to you is born this day in the city of David a Savior who is Christ the Lord" (Lk 2:11) and "Of this man's (David's) posterity God has brought to Israel a Savior, Jesus, as he promised" (Acts 13:23).

The Kingdom of God is an Eschatological Kingdom

For Luke, the "end-times" start with the arrival of Jesus, the Christ (Messiah); messianic times are eschatological times. The final coming of the kingdom, the Parousia, marks the last event of the end-times.[19] Consequently, even though the kingdom of God is already in some sense present for Luke, it is still eschatological (messianic) because these are the end-times. This section will investigate those Lucan passages which regard the kingdom of God as a future event.

Two statements of Jesus apparently look to an imminent realization of the kingdom of God. They are:

"But I tell you truly, there are some standing here who will not taste death before they see the kingdom of God." (Lk 9:27)
"So also, you see for yourself and know that when you see these things taking place, you know that the kingdom of God is near. Truly, I say to you, this generation will not pass away till all has taken place." (Lk 21:31–32)

In the first citation, Luke drops Mark's (9:1), "has come with power," and he inserts, "the kingdom of God" into the second citation (cf. Mk 13:29; Mt 24:33) and thus ties kingdom of God to the coming of the Son of Man. Generally, interpreters have associated the first citation with the Transfiguration, and not without reason, because the glory of the Son of Man mentioned in Lk 9:26 appears again in 9:32. They explain the second citation by asserting that "this generation" cannot possibly refer to Jesus', which is already past when Luke wrote, and so, it must refer to a later generation or epoch.[20] For the purposes of this essay, it suffices to note that in so far as kingdom of God in the first citation refers to Jesus' Trans-

---

19. For a more complete presentation of this position, see my *The Unity*, 149–59.
20. For these and other understandings of these two passages, cf. Danker, *Jesus and the New Age*, 114–15, 216; Fitzmyer, *Gospel According to Luke*, 786, 789–90; Ellis, *Gospel of Luke*, 141–42, 246–47; Grundmann, *Das Evangelium nach Lukas*, 190–1, 385; Leaney, *St. Luke*, 166; E. Schweizer, *Das Evangelium nach Lukas* (NTD 3; Göttingen: Vandenhoeck & Ruprecht, 1982) 103, 214–19; C. H. Talbert, *Reading Luke: A Literary and Theological Commentary on the Third Gospel* (New York: Crossroad, 1982) 108.

figuration, Luke would be giving it a present dimension, but other than that, these two passages relate to the future.

There are a number of other passages in Luke–Acts which look to the future coming of the kingdom. Jesus directs the disciples, in the Lord's Prayer, to pray, "Thy kingdom come" (Lk 11:2), informs them that people will come from east and west, and from north and south, and sit at table in the kingdom (Lk 13:29), and does not correct his table companion's declaration. "Blessed is he who shall eat bread in the kingdom of God" (Lk 14:15)! Only Luke, in the parable of the Pounds, speaks of a nobleman who is going to a far country to receive his kingdom and introduces the parable with, "he (Jesus) proceeded to tell a parable, because he was near to Jerusalem, and because they supposed that the kingdom of God was to appear immediately" (Lk 19:11). The kingdom will come, but first the nobleman must obtain it, and his servants, in the meantime, are to trade with the pounds which he gave them (cf. Acts 14:22). It has already been shown, in the section on the unity of the Christians with Jesus, that the narrative of the Last Supper (Lk 22:16, 18, 29–30) deals with the coming of the kingdom of God, and Jesus' answer to the good thief, "Truly, I say to you, today you will be with me in Paradise," does not necessarily indicate an immediate realization of the kingdom because "today" (cf. Lk 2:11; 4:21; 5:26; 19:5, 9; Acts 26:29) for Luke deals more with the realization than with a temporal designation of when salvation will be received.

The most important Lucan passage on the ultimate coming of the kingdom, the Parousia, is Acts 1:6–7 (cf. 3:19–21): "So when they had come together, they asked him, 'Lord, will you at this time restore the kingdom to Israel?' He said to them, 'It is not for you to know times or seasons which the Father has fixed by his own authority.'" The kingdom of God is coming, but only the Father knows when! Luke has reinforced this presentation through his Ascension scene in Acts 1:9–11. The emphasis in this scene is on the apostles and their reactions. They are not to remain gazing into heaven in hopes of seeing Jesus return. He will return, but their Christian living must get underway. Luke does not say much more in Acts about the Parousia, and this very lack of attention establishes his conviction that it is delayed.

Luke connects the coming of the Son of Man with the kingdom of God. This can be discovered in Lk 21. When the connection between the kingdom of God and salvation was discussed, it was noted that Lk 21:28 paralleled 21:31. Actually, the evidence in the text is more complicated than has been explicated up till now. Let us look at this in more detail

"And then they will see the Son of Man coming in a cloud with power and great glory. Now when these things begin to take place, look up and raise your heads because your redemption is drawing near." (Lk 21:27–28)

"when you see *these things taking place*, you know that the kingdom of God is near." (Lk 21:31)

"But watch at all times, praying that you may have strength to escape all *these things that will take place*, and to stand before the Son of Man." (Lk 21:36)

In the first of these verses, the coming of the Son of Man is one of "these things" which precede redemption and the kingdom of God. But in v 36 standing before the Son of Man happens after "these things" and is located in much the same place as are "redemption" and "the kingdom of God" in the previous verses. This does not necessarily mean that these three ideas are identical, but they certainly are interconnected.

Jesus is designated as the Son of Man in the narrative of the Last Supper, which, as was seen above, likewise speaks of the kingdom of God (Lk 22:16, 18) and of the kingdom (Lk 22:29–30) the Father assigned Jesus. Of course, the Son of Man will rise and be seated at the right hand of the power of God (Lk 22:69; cf. Acts 7:55–56), the kingly position of David's descendant, Jesus (Acts 2:33–36; cf. Lk 20:41–44). So, "Son of Man" naturally relates to "the kingdom of God" and "kingdom" in the institutional narrative.

The kingdom of God brings the eschatological judgment. The harsh words of the king in Lk 19:27 are clear, "But as for these enemies of mine, who did not want me to reign over them, bring them here and slay them before me." In addition, a judgment scene is probably portrayed when Luke writes, "But watch at all times, praying that you may have strength to escape all these things that will take place, and to stand before the Son of Man" (Lk 21:36).

The kingdom of God is, then, for Luke, an eschatological kingdom whose final establishment takes place at the Parousia. Although some of the evidence is puzzling, there are abundant data which reveal that the kingdom of God is still to come. Only the Father knows the exact time. When it does come, it will be associated with the coming of the Son of Man and ultimate judgment.

To Enter the Kingdom of God One Must Have the Correct Attitude

In Lk 18:9–30, Jesus himself says, "Let the children come to me, and do not hinder them; for to such belongs the kingdom of God" (v 16). But what precisely is it about children which makes them such apt candidates for the kingdom? The other characters in the pericope help to answer this question. The Pharisee trusts in himself that he is righteous. He despises others and exalts himself (vv 9–12, 14). He is not an apt candidate for the kingdom. On the other hand, the tax collector has the good sense to pray, "God, be merciful to me a sinner" (v 13)! He humbles himself and so will be exalted (v 14). The rich ruler in the latter part of the pericope has lived a good life but cannot part with his possessions so that he can follow Jesus (vv 22–23). Consequently, being like a child is to be humble and dependent on God and not attached to anything (which possessions can symbolize) which would keep one from following Christ.

We find these same attitudes recommended for the kingdom of God elsewhere in Luke–Acts. The Lucan Jesus says, "Blessed are you poor, for yours is the kingdom of God" (Lk 6:12), not, "Blessed are the poor in spirit" (Mt 5:3). Joseph of Arimathea depended on God because he was a "good and righteous man, who had not consented to their purpose and deed, and he was looking for the kingdom of God" (Lk 23:50–51). Finally, the good thief is humble. He recognizes his guilt and trusts in Jesus, and consequently prays, "Jesus, remember me when you come into your kingdom" (Lk 23:42).

When the kingdom of God is preached, one should listen. Luke can call this listening "seeing and hearing," but one must see and hear correctly. The end of Acts testifies to this fact. The Gentiles have the right attitude— they will listen (Acts 28:23–31; cf. Lk 8:10).

Other appropriate responses to the proclamation of the kingdom are repentance, faith and baptism. Above, it was claimed that Paul's speech to the Ephesian elders at Miletus has a number of interchangeable gospel summaries in it. One of these is "preaching the kingdom" (Acts 20:25) but another is "testifying both to Jews and to Greeks of repentance to God and of faith in our Lord Jesus Christ" (v 21). That Luke regarded the latter statement as an appropriate response to preaching about the kingdom of God is obvious from Acts 8:12–13:

> But when they believed Philip as he preached good news about the kingdom of God and the name of Jesus Christ, they were baptized, both men and women. Even Simon himself believed, and after being baptized he continued with Philip.

Other attitudes toward the kingdom of God are attended to by Luke. One is to give priority to the kingdom, to seek it first, and other things like clothing, food and drink will be given besides (Lk 12:31). One is to watch and pray (cf. Lk 11:2) and thus escape any of the signs of the end of times and stand with confidence before the Son of Man (Lk 21:36). The parable of the ten pounds proves to be even more practical. The pound, which symbolizes what one has received from the Lord, is to be used to good effect. One is to be a faithful servant (cf. Lk 19:11–27). Or, as Luke notes during the Last Supper, Jesus' kingdom is one of service, not of lording it over others (Lk 22:24–27). Paul and Barnabas furnish a summary statement of how the Christians are to live, "exhorting them to continue in the faith, and saying that through many tribulations we must enter the kingdom of God" (Acts 14:22).

Conclusion

This article has provided a redactional (compositional) criticism of Luke's use of "the kingdom of God" and related terms. For Luke, "the kingdom of God" is not an univocal term. Significantly, "kingdom of God" appears at the beginning and end of Luke–Acts (Lk 1:31–33; Acts 28:23, 31; cf. Lk 4:43; Acts 1:3, 6). The Father brings the kingdom. At Jesus' birth and at Pentecost, the Holy Spirit is associated with the kingdom of God, but Luke places most emphasis on Jesus and the kingdom. Jesus is the king, and following him leads to the kingdom. Luke can refer to the whole gospel message as either "Jesus" or "the kingdom of God." At times, he adds εὐαγγελίζεσθαι, "to preach the gospel," to the message about the kingdom.

Luke has given the kingdom of God certain characteristics. It is not of this world; it is a kingdom of service. It is mysterious, and only the Father knows when it will ultimately come. At first, the kingdom of God appears insignificant, but it fulfills Jewish hopes, confers a radical dignity on its participants, and is universal and particularly open to the disadvantaged. The kingdom of God is beneficial; to eat bread in the kingdom is a blessing. The kingdom of God can be a source of encouragement in times of hardship, and one who seeks it need be anxious about nothing else. The kingdom brings joy. The kingdom of God also shows a unity between Jesus and the Christians.

"The kingdom of God" summarizes the ministry of Jesus and his followers. Jesus and his actions make the kingdom of God present. Certain parables bring out this presence of the kingdom, and at Pentecost, Jesus is enthroned as its king. The kingdom of God begins the destruction of Satan's reign and brings salvation to the Christians. The miracles and power and authority over demons witness to this. Whoever belongs to the kingdom is saved.

Eschatology for Luke begins with Jesus' birth. So, the kingdom of God is surely eschatological. But the Parousia, Jesus' second coming, marks the last event of eschatological times. Acts 1:6–7 are very significant in this regard because they indicate that Luke accepts a delay of the Parousia and recognizes our ignorance of the time and the final establishment of the kingdom. Needless to say, the Son of Man is associated with the final establishment of the kingdom.

To enter the kingdom of God we must have the correct attitudes. We are to be like children who do not trust in themselves and despise others. We are not to be attached to anything which keeps us from God or Christ, but to recognize our dependence on them. We should see and listen to the message and seek the kingdom of God above all else. Repentance, faith and baptism, watching and praying are appropriate responses to the kingdom of God. Until the final establishment of the kingdom, we should be found faithful servants, willing to serve and to move through tribulations to the kingdom.

12   The Kingdom of God in the School of St. John

Robert Hodgson, Jr.

Associate Professor of Religious Studies
Southwest Missouri State University

Introduction

THIS STUDY WILL PROVIDE in a programmatic way an explanation for the virtual absence of the theme of the kingdom of God from the Gospel and the three letters of John, and its survival in the noncanonical literature of the School of St. John.[1]

The first point to be made is that different intellectual and religious forces competed within the School of St. John over the correct understanding of traditions in the Fourth Gospel, since that understanding assured a privileged position in the life of the School. The second point is that two wings of the School, represented by the Acts of John and Sethian

---

1. R. Brown, *The Community of the Beloved Disciple*, (New York: Paulist, 1979) 171–82 summarizes studies of the Johannine School to 1979. All include founder figures, disciples, editors, opponents of various stripes, and successive phases of development in the School's history and theology. I envision the School as the driving force behind a network of originally Syrian congregations with satellite communities in Ephesus and Alexandria. The records of the School's life and faith survive in both canonical (Gospel of John, letters of John, Apocalypse of John) and noncanonical (Acts of John, Apocryphon of John, apocryphal Apocalypses of John) writings. The special problem of the kingdom in the canonical Apocalypse of John must be studied against the backdrop of persecution under the Flavian emperors, and in the interest of space is not treated here. Following N. Perrin, "Jesus and the Language of the Kingdom," *The Kingdom of God* (Issues in Religion and Theology 5; ed. B. Chilton, Philadelphia: Fortress, 1984) 97. I understand the kingdom as a tensive symbol, that is, a symbol capable of several levels of meaning in early Christianity. The tendency to treat the kingdom as a steno-symbol, that is, a symbol with only one level of meaning appears in the 1980 Heidelberg dissertation by A. Zabala, "The Encounter of God and Man in the Trial of Jesus: John 18:28–19:16a," 64–69.

gnostic literature respectively, claimed the kingdom for their theological, mythological, and astrological lore, thus transmuting the kingdom into a symbol or idea whose meaning was unacceptable to that part of the School responsible for the final form of the Fourth Gospel and the letters of John.

The Kingdom of God in the Fourth Gospel

The expression "kingdom of God" ($\beta\alpha\sigma\iota\lambda\epsilon\iota\alpha$ $\tau o\hat{v}$ $\theta\epsilon o\hat{v}$) appears only twice in the Fourth Gospel (3:3, 5). By contrast it (and its equivalent, the kingdom of heaven in Matthew) turns up over seventy times in the Synoptic Gospels and Acts and nine times in the Pauline literature. The expression "my kingdom" ($\dot{\eta}$ $\beta\alpha\sigma\iota\lambda\epsilon\iota\alpha$ $\dot{\eta}$ $\dot{\epsilon}\mu\dot{\eta}$, that is the kingdom of Christ, appears only three times in the Fourth Gospel (18:36), although some thirteen times in the rest of the NT. The letters of John do not mention the kingdom in any form.

At Jn 3:3, Jesus tells Nicodemus, a ruler of the Jews, "Truly, truly, I say to you, unless one is born from above, he cannot see the kingdom of God." At Jn 3:5 Jesus repeats this sentiment, "Truly, truly, I say to you, unless one is born of water and the Spirit, he cannot enter the kingdom of God." Recent research has detected several levels of meaning in these two sayings and in John 3 in general. On one level, for example, Nicodemus represents Jews intrigued by Johannine Christianity but not yet members.[2] On another level, Jn 3:5 and 3:9–15 explain the Johannine community's understanding of baptism and Jesus' heavenly origin.[3]

A recent study of Jn 18:36 ("my kingdom is not of this world") and Rev 11:15 ("the kingdom of the world has become the kingdom of our Lord and of his Christ") has concluded that Jesus' kingdom is otherworldly and insulated from the ideologies and institutions of this world.[4] C. K. Barrett's reading of this passage as a metaphor that "is spatial rather than temporal"[5] makes the same point. Missing from these and other studies of Jn 18:36 is any sense of wonder at the appearance in this text of the kingdom—a theme which, apart from Jn 3:3, 5, is conspicuously absent

2. Brown, Community, 35, 61, 72.

3. R. Schnackenburg, The Gospel According to John (New York: Crossroad 1982) 1:529–42; W. Meeks, "The Man from Heaven in Johannine Sectarianism," JBL 91 (1972) 44–72. Bultmann (Das Evangelium des Johannes [Meyer; Göttingen: Vandenhoeck & Ruprecht, 1978,] 93), calls Jn 3:3 "ein überliefertes Herrenwort" which reveals "das Geheimnis der Wiedergeburt."

4. U. Vanni, "Regno 'non da questo mondo' ma 'regno del mondo.' Il regno di Christo dal IV Vangelo all 'Apocalisse," Studia Missionalia 33 (1984) 325–58.

5. C. K. Barrett, The Gospel According to St. John (London: SPCK 1962) 447.

from the Fourth Gospel. Nor does the literature on John consider it noteworthy that between John 3 and John 18 the proprietorship of the kingdom has shifted from God to Jesus, that is to say, from a theological apocalyptic image to a christological one.[6]

There are, of course, certain common explanations for the lack of references to the kingdom in John's Gospel. Barrett urges that the evangelist took a dim view of Jewish apocalyptic hopes that linked the kingdom to a renaissance of ancient Israel's glory.[7] An older view saw the reality of the kingdom present in the narrative of the Fourth Gospel but expressed in fresh images such as eternal life or truth.[8] Beasley-Murray says that the importance of the kingdom of God is assumed by the evangelist and need not be directly stated.[9] Missing from these explanations is any feeling for historical forces in the history of the Johannine School that may have contributed to the elimination of the concept of the kingdom from the Fourth Gospel with the exception of John 3:3, 5 and 18:36.

On a literary and theological plane there is much to commend these explanations for the virtual loss of the kingdom of God from the Fourth Gospel. After all, Jesus is identified early on in the Gospel (1:49) as the king of Israel, an honorific title that the jubilant crowd applies to Jesus at 12:13. Jesus the king is one of the most frequent double entendres in a gospel full of this literary device (cf. 6:49; 18:33, 37a, 37b, 39; 19:2, 3, 12, 14, 15a, 15b, 19, 21). Two points may be made here. First, it should not be overlooked that the vast majority of the references to the kingdom in the Synoptic Gospels, Acts, and Pauline literature are to the kingdom of God, or to God as king. John (with the exception of 3:3, 5) identifies the proprietor of the kingdom as Jesus and Jesus as king. Second, NT scholarship has not yet fully exploited what it already knows of the history of the Johannine community or school in an effort to illumine either the shift in the proprietorship of the kingdom in the Fourth Gospel or the special problem posed by the loss of the concept of the kingdom of God in the Fourth Gospel.

Thus, despite the attractiveness of the literary-theological account of the kingdom's disappearance, substantive questions remain: If the kingdom was indeed a central theme in the preaching of Jesus why does it appear only on the fringe of John's Gospel? If Jesus is king, why is John

6. Cf. recent surveys by B. Chilton, *Kingdom*, 1–26 and R. Schnackenburg, *God's Rule and Kingdom* (London: Burns and Oates 1965) 358–76.

7. Barrett, 173.

8. R. H. Lightfoot, *St. John's Gospel* (Oxford: Clarendon, revised 1956 edition) 130.

9. G. R. Beasley-Murray, "John 3:3, 5. Baptism, Spirit, and the Kingdom," *ExpTim* 97 (1986) 167–70.

reluctant to speak of his kingdom? Why has John transferred the proprietorship of the kingdom from God to Jesus? The hypothesis of a School
of St. John riddled by competing ideologies may aid in the solution of
these problems.

The Kingdom of God in the Acts of John

According to the most recent editors of the Acts of John, Junod and
Kaestli,[10] the surviving portions of the Acts of John include two major
sources: the first is an aretology and biography of John the Zebedee (chs
18–93; 103–108; 110–115); the second is a summary of John's preaching
that includes a discourse on the cross of light and the famous hymn of the
dance (chs 94–102; 109). Junod and Kaestli have broken fresh ground with
regard to the date of the Acts of John. Despite late manuscript evidence,
they have detected internal evidence that suggests a date around 130 c.e.
for the composition of the two sources, and about 150 c.e. for the collating
of the sources into something like our present Acts of John. By their
reckoning, individual pericopae in each of the sources may reach back
into the first decades of the second century c.e., thus into the period when
the Johannine letters witness to a lively, acrimonious debate in the School
over the correct interpretation of the Johannine heritage.

Junod and Kaestli correctly believe that the Acts originated in eastern
Syria and Egypt. To place the Acts of John in this region is to bring it very
close geographically to the place where recent research has located the
drafting and editing of the Fourth Gospel[11]: in the kingdom of Herod
Agrippa II. G. Strecker[12] has correctly identified the origin and bench-
mark of the ancient school tradition, including the School of St. John, in
the magnetism and authority of a founding father whose identity, language, and ideology are perpetuated in the writings of subsequent generations of disciples.[13]

The presence of John the Zebedee as a founding father in the Acts of
John provides thus an important first clue to its participation in the debate
mirrored in the Johannine letters. Beyond this one can point out certain

10. E. Junod and J. D. Kaestli, *Acta Johannis*, (CC Series Apocryphorum 2; Brepols:
Turnhout, 1983).

11. K. Wengst, *Bedrängte Gemeinde und Verherrlichter Christus* (Biblisch-theo-
logische Studien 5; Neukirchen-Vluyn: Neukirchener Verlag, 1981). Clement of Alexandria (*Comments on 1 John*; ANF, II, 574) quotes with approval a tradition that sounds
very much like the Acts of John. One is inclined to think that Clement knows of the
diversity within the School of St. John.

12. G. Strecker, "Die Anfänge der johanneischen Schule," *NTS* 32 (1986) 31–47.

13. Cf. R. A. Culpepper, *The Johannine School*, (SBLDS 26; Missoula: Scholars Press,
1975).

pericopae which appear to be literary echoes of the controversy in the Johannine School over the Fourth Gospel.

In a pericope modeled on John 13, the footwashing scene, the Zebedee explains to his followers how he first experienced Jesus' polymorphism:

> And he had another strange quality; when I reclined at the table he would take me to his own breast, and I held him fast; and sometimes his breast felt smooth to me and soft, othertimes hard like a rock. (Acts of John 89)

Leaving aside the nature of Jesus' polymorphism, the most striking feature of this text lies in its identification of John the Zebedee with the beloved disciple of Jn 13:22. If this identification is lost on the casual reader, then its repetition in a subsequent pericope would not be:

> Another time he took me and James and Peter to the mountain where he used to pray, and we saw on him a light such that a man who uses mortal speech cannot describe.... Again he took us three likewise up the mountain, saying "Come with me." And again we went.... Then I, since he loved me, went quietly up to him. (Acts of John 90)

These accounts of the footwashing and transfiguration stories provide a ready support for a thesis advanced by Culpepper[14] that the writer of 1 John cannot appeal to the authority of the beloved disciple to enforce discipline and a correct interpretation of the Fourth Gospel because the opponents have already claimed this figure. These two pericopae show how the Acts of John has accomplished this through the insertion of the figure of the beloved disciple into two scenes from the life of Jesus.

The clearest indication that the Acts of John has helped stir up theological strife within the School emerges from a text in which the Acts of John directly attacks the form of tradition and authority championed by 1 John. The prologue to 1 John trades on characteristic themes from the prologue to the Fourth Gospel,[15] laying claim to a certain form of authority and fellowship with God (cf. also 1 Jn 1:1–4).

According to this test, fellowship with God turns on acceptance in faith of the testimony which the author gives to the word of life—a testimony whose validity is secured through an appeal to empirical and verifiable forms of testimony. Compare with 1 John's vision of authority, tradition, and fellowship the claim that the Acts of John makes in a pericope that concludes its description of John's preaching:

> Now my brothers since we have seen the grace of the Lord, and his affection toward us, let us worship him, since we have obtained mercy from him; not with our fingers, or with our mouths, nor with our tongues, nor with any member of our body but with the disposition of our soul let us worship him ... since he is with us in prisons, tombs, bonds, and dungeons, in reproaches, and insults. (Acts of John 103)

---

14. Ibid., 282.
15. R. Schnackenburg, *Die Johannesbriefe* (HTKNT 13; Freiburg: Herder, 1963) 52–72.

Van Unnik[16] believes that the whole of chs 94–102, in which the famous dance of Jesus is featured, reflects actual and ancient liturgical practice in the religious circles represented by the Acts of John. If he is correct, then the summary text quoted from ch 103 above is a defense of the fellowship, authority, and tradition which is under siege by other circles within the School of St. John and its network of churches.

Against this backdrop of the School of St. John divided within itself[17] the kingdom and kingship of Jesus in the Acts of John take on fresh import, for it may well belong to the ideological tug-o-war raging within the School. If one recalls that in the Acts of John, Christology and theology are merged (Jesus is God, king, and the sole proprietor of the kingdom), then the reticence of the Fourth Gospel and letters of John to speak of the kingdom may be interpreted as a response to the aggressive use of the language of the kingdom in the Acts of John. In one of its many miracle stories the Acts report that John is moved to pray to Jesus for the resurrection of the dead Cleopatra:

> We therefore ask of thee, O King, not gold or silver, not substance or possessions, nor any of the perishible things upon earth but two souls. (Acts of John 22)

In the section of the Acts known as the Metastasis (or John's departure) the apostle prays during a final earthly worship service:

> My brethren and fellow-servants, joint-heirs and partners with me in the kingdom of God, you know the Lord, how many great works he has granted you through me. . . . though they are not seen with these eyes nor heard with these ears. (Acts of John 106)

A final kingdom text is worth citing because it attests to the perseverance of the idea of the kingdom in the noncanonical wing of the School. Its evidential value is limited, however, because it belongs to what Junod and Kaestli believe to be a third or fourth-century addition to the Acts of John. John is in Ephesus standing before the emperor Domitian, accounting for his faith. The question that prompts John to his defense comes from the emperor: "Are you John who prophesies that my kingdom ($\beta a\sigma\iota\lambda\epsilon\iota a$) will topple and that another will rule ($\beta a\sigma\iota\lambda\epsilon\acute{v}\epsilon\iota v$) in my place, namely Jesus?" (Acts of John 8).

16. W. C. van Unnik, "A Note on the Dance of Jesus in the 'Acts of John,'" VC 18 (1964) 1–5.

17. Cf. the studies of J. Painter, "The 'Opponents' in 1 John," NTS 32 (1986) 48–71 who identifies the opponents as gentile Christians unsympathetic to the Jewish roots of the Johannine tradition; and J. Blank, "Die Irrlehrer des ersten Johannesbriefes," Kairos 26 (1984) 166–93 who identifies the opponents with the spiritualistic, charismatic Christians of the Corinthian sort.

Sethian Gnosticism within the School of St. John

The word "gnostic" has been frequently applied to the opponents of 1 John.[18] Brown, for instance, believes that the secessionist Johannine Christians "ultimately became a Gnostic sect." The evidence suggests rather that the opponents or secessionists already belonged to emerging Gnosticism. To the extent that the opponents faith can be reconstructed from the raw material of 1 John, they held to a view of Jesus as heavenly redeemer; to a view of their own sinlessness; to a notion of the material world as fallen and beyond redemption; and to a special fellowship (κοινωνία) with God to which they alone held title.[19] Thanks to the discovery of the Nag Hammadi Library and the cooperative effort of an international fellowship of scholars it has been possible to recover a form of Gnosticism hitherto lost except for isolated references to it in Irenaeus, Epiphanius, Pseudo-Tertullian, and Filastrius: Sethian Gnosticism.[20]

Among the tractates of the Nag Hammadi Library, ten are associated with Sethian Gnosticism: three different versions of the *Apocryphon of John*: the *Hypostasis of the Archons*; the *Gospel of the Egyptians*; the *Apocalypse of Adam*; the *Three Steles of Seth*; *Zostrianos*; *Melchizedek*; the *Thought of Norea*; *Allogenes*; and the *Trimorphic Protennoia*. Five themes control this literature and may be taken as typical of Sethianism. There is first an elaborate speculation on the person and mission of Sophia or Dame Wisdom; second, a selective reading of Gen 1–6 with a special emphasis attached to the narratives of Creation, Eve, Tree of Knowledge, Birth of Cain, Abel, and Seth, and Flood; third, a baptismal ideology; fourth, the identification of Christ with actors in the Genesis drama such as Seth; and fifth, an increasing dependence upon the mythology, numerology, and metaphysics of Pythagoreanism and Platonism.

In the course of its literary and social history Sethianism began as a non-Christian baptismal sect (ca. 100 B.C.E. to 100 C.E.) but evolved into one of the many forms of early Christian faith, principally by merging the

18. Cf. R. Brown, "'Other Sheep not of this Fold': The Johannine Perspective on Christian Diversity in the Late First Century," *JBL* 97 (1978) 5–22.

19. Cf. Painter, 53–61 for a fuller description of the opponents' views.

20. I owe the following reconstruction of the literary and social history of Sethianism to J. D. Turner, "Sethian Gnosticism: A Literary History," *Nag Hammadi, Gnosticism, and Early Christianity*. (ed. C. W. Hedrick and R. Hodgson, Jr.; Peabody, Mass.: Hendrickson, 1986, 55–86). E. Pagels, *The Johannine Gospel in Gnostic Exegesis: Heracleon's Commentary on John* (SBLMS 17; Nashville: Abingdon, 1973) and A.F.J. Klijn, *Seth in Jewish, Christian, and Gnostic Literature* (Leiden: Brill, 1977) are basic studies in the general area of this essay.

figures of Seth and Christ (ca. 100–125 C.E.). From this period onwards Sethianism becomes increasingly estranged from the emerging Catholic orthodoxy, and from 300 C.E. it lived on chiefly in gnostic sects of late antiquity. It is thus in the formative period of the School of St. John (50–125 C.E.) that one can envision Sethianism as a vital force within the network of congregations and ideological tradition that has come to be called the School of St. John.

Reconstructing the common history of the School of St. John and Sethianism is beyond the scope of this essay, but certain chapters seem clear. A brief description of them will help set the stage for an evaluation of the kingdom in Sethian literature and life as well as an account of how the Sethian fascination with the kingdom may have accelerated its forfeiture by the Gospel and letters of John.

There is, in the first instance, the research of G. Schenke into the prologue of the Fourth Gospel and the Trimorphic Protennoia.[21] Schenke has unearthed in Jn 1:1–18 and the third discourse of Trimorphic Protennoia (XXII,1:46,5–50,20) a series of shared concepts (e.g., Word, Light, Tent) that build a case, if not for literary dependence of one upon the other, then at least for a heated contest over a fund of wisdom traditions which each wing of the School hoped to mine for its portrait of the drama of salvation.

Second, there are the three versions of an apocryphon or revelation discourse whose alleged author is John the Zebedee: Codex II,1, II1.1, and IV.1 in the Nag Hammadi Library (a fourth version is found in Papyrus Berolinensis Gnosticus 2). Culpepper and Strecker have identified the presence of a founding father figure in ancient literature as prima facie evidence for the existence of a school tradition. Thus on the strength of the Apocryphon of John alone one might wish to assign to Sethianism some role in the life of the School of St. John.

Third, a number of the Sethian themes listed above have counterpoints in the Fourth Gospel and the letters of John. The Sethian trinity of Sophia the Mother, God the Father, and Logos the Son (cf. *Ap. John* II,1:13,3–14, 15), or simply the simultaneous motherhood and fatherhood of Sophia (*Trim. Prot.* XIII,1:45,1–5) help account for the binitarian formula of the Fourth Gospel and 1 John in which the fatherhood of God and the sonship of Jesus leave no room for a mother figure (cf. Jn 10:30; 1 Jn 1:3, 8; 2:1, 22, 24; 3:23; 4:2, 9, 13). The Sethian reading of Gen 1–6 understood Gen 4:25–5:8 as an account of the origins of the Sethian race (cf. *Hyp. Arc.* II,4:91,

---

21. G. Schenke, "Die Dreigestaltige Protennoia (Nag Hammadi Codex XIII) herausgegeben und kommentiert," Th.D. Dissertation, Rostock, 1977; cf. James M. Robinson, "Sethians and Johannine Thought: the Trimorphic Protennoia and the Prologue of the Gospel of John," *The Rediscovery of Gnosticism* (ed. B. Layton; Leiden: Brill, 1981) 2: 643–62.

12–35): The fratricide of Cain moved God to give Adam a third son, namely Seth. Perhaps the attack upon Cain in 1 Jn 3:12, if not part of the widespread Cain and Abel legends of the period,[22] is a response to the Sethian exegesis of the Adam-Cain-Abel-Seth narratives.

Sethian baptism counted as a ritual of enlightenment. "Living water" (cf. Jn 4:7–15; *Trim. Prot.* XIII,1:41,23–25) transformed the faithful into the seed of Seth (cf. *Gos. Eg.* III,2:66,1–27), while a baptismal ritual called the Five Seals revealed salvific knowledge to the initiate and admitted one into the kingdom (cf. *Gos. Eg.* III,2:66,3; *Trim. Prot.* XIII,1:48,15–50:12; Jn 3:5; the reference to the kingdom in the Trimorphic Protennoia is a conjecture, filling a lacuna in the text). If the anointing (*chrisma*) by the holy one that leads to knowledge and truth in 1 Jn 2:20–21 is a rite of initiation into Christian faith,[23] then 1 Jn 2:20 could be emerging ortho- doxy's alternative to Sethian initiation.

One final point of contact between the School of St. John and Sethian- ism may be mentioned. The Gospel of John twice admits that its portrait of the heavenly redeemer Jesus is incomplete: "Now Jesus did many other things in the presence of his disciples not written in this book" (Jn 20:30; cf. 21:25). The Apocryphon of John concludes with the following state- ment of the resurrected Jesus to John:

> Now I will go to the perfect aeon. I have completed everything for you in your presence, and I have said to you everything that you shall write it down and give it secretly to your brethren in the spirit. (*Ap. John* II.1:31, 25–30)

This text defends the supplementary revelation in the Apocryphon of John, but it also issues a bold challenge to those who, like the author of 1 John, claim that their chain of tradition is the only one. To the same extent that the Fourth Gospel was vulnerable to a charge of incompleteness, the Apocryphon of John could insist upon its right to fill in the gaps with special revelations bequeathed to it not through the course of ordinary tradition but through exceptional interventions of the risen Lord.

The Kingdom of God in Sethian Gnosticism

Two probes into the literary history of Sethian texts will help uncover the meaning of the kingdom for Sethianism. The first example, from the Apocalypse of Adam, is designed to show how an important Sethian gnostic writing has transformed the kingdom into a symbol or idea that stands not for salvation but for an impediment to it. Such a recasting of

---

22. Cf. R. Brown, *The Epistles of John.* (AB 30; Garden City, New York: Doubleday 1982) 442–43.

23. Ibid., 341–48.

the concept of the kingdom makes it apparent why the Gospel of John and the letters of John found the concept no longer an appropriate religious concept.

In a penetrating analysis of the sources and literary history of the Apocalypse of Adam, C. W. Hedrick has identified 100 c.e. as the *terminus ad quem* for the combining of source A and B into the present form of the document.[24] Although Hedrick argues persuasively that the Apocalypse of Adam is a non-Christian writing, others have detected traces of a Christian hand in the document.[25] One of these Christianizing touches may well be the long description of the thirteen kingdoms which by Hedrick's reckoning stands as an independent unit of tradition within source B: *Apoc Adam* V,5: 77, 26–82, 18.[26]

> Then the angels and all the generations of the powers will use the name in error, asking: "Where did it (the error) come from?" or "where did the words of deception, which all the powers have failed to discover, come from?" [Now] the first kingdom [says of him] [that] he came [from . . .] (there follows a description of the remaining twelve kingdoms which then introduces the generation without a king, i.e., the Sethians). But the generation without a king over it says that God chose him from all the aeons. (*Apoc. Adam* V, 5: 77, 18–29; 82, 19–22)

In general, the Sethians held that their primeval history described in Gen 1–6 had disclosed to them all that was necessary for salvation. Any subsequent revelation, in the succeeding generations or kingdoms was at best a deficient statement of what they had already in hand.[27] In the thesis of this essay, the description of the thirteen kingdoms is aimed at a group for whom the concept of the kingdom symbolized the essential meaning of Jesus' preaching. Such a group might be churches organized around the synoptic portrait of Jesus, but it could also comprise Johannine churches in a period of their history that included a fuller appeal to the language of the kingdom (cf. Jn 3:3, 5). The depiction of the Sethians as a generation without a king, a text that follows upon the thirteen-kingdom passage (82:19–83:6) lends support to this view. In the internecine strife of the Johannine School the powerful party of the Sethians transformed the kingdom into a negative symbol so that eventually that wing of the school responsible for the writing and editing of the Fourth Gospel and letters of John dropped the idea of the kingdom almost entirely.[28]

24. C. W. Hedrick, *The Apocalypse of Adam.* (SBLDS 46; Chico, Calif.: Scholars Press, 1980) 214.

25. Turner, "Sethian Gnosticism," 75.

26. Cf. Hedrick, *Apocalypse of Adam*, 118–19. Text translated by G. MacRae in *Nag Hammadi Codices V*, 2–5 and VI with Papyrus Berolinensis 8502, 1 and 4 (NHS 11; ed. D. Parrott; Leiden: Brill, 1979) 181, 189.

27. Turner, "Sethian Gnosticism," 57–59.

28. Pace Hedrick, 199; cf. Parrott, 188. The likelihood of a link between the survival of the concept of the kingdom in the Apocalypse of Adam and its virtual disappearance in

In his study of the Christology of the Apocryphon of John, S. Arai has identified a number of interpolations intended to transform an originally non-Christian Sethian treatise into a Christian one.[29] While the most obvious redactional touch is the adding of a narrative frame in which the resurrected Christ reveals to John hitherto unknown truth, a series of deft insertions also contributes to the Christianizing of the Apocryphon of John. For example, II,1:6:23–7, 21a, introduces the figure of Christ who anoints with goodness (chrestos) into II,1:6,10–9,24, and thereby effects the identification of Christ with Autogenes.[30] The net result of these and other changes, which according to Turner reflect Sethian history around 100–125 C.E., would be to claim all of the Sethian mythological, astrological, and numerological lore in the now newly Christianized version of the Apocrypohon of John as essential elements of a Christian doctrine of salvation.

Thus, in the Sethian recounting of its universe at II,1:11,22–12,33 and in its record of humankind's creation at 15:15–29 the fifth power of the universe is the kingdom whose task is the creation of the blood-soul. Welburn[31] has spelled out the ancient astrological and cosmological traditions behind these texts, and it is not difficult to imagine that the kingdom in such a mythological framework would lose its relevance and meaning for the writers and editors of the Fourth Gospel and letters of John. After all, one of their chief benchmarks was the ability to describe the person and task of Jesus as a man and message from heaven without ever incorporating a full-length myth of such a heavenly figure and mission into literature.[32]

---

the Gospel of John and letters of John is increased if two other points are borne in mind. First, according to the Apocalypse of Adam the Sethian illuminator or savior is not born, while the Johannine savior and his followers must be born anew (cf. Jn 3:3, 5; 1 Jn 2:29; 3:9). Second, the Sethian savior does not advocate water baptism, while the Johannine savior does (Jn 3:5); cf. Hedrick, 201.

29. S. Arai, "Zur Christologie des Apokryphons des Johannes," NTS 15 (1969) 302–18. For an analysis of another Sethian treatise whose Christianization could reflect the Johannine ideological struggle cf. C. W. Hedrick, "Christian Motifs in the Gospel of the Egyptians," NovT 23 (1981) 242–60.

30. Arai, "Christologie," 305.

31. A. J. Welburn, "The Identity of the Archons in the 'Apocryphon of John,'" VC 32 (1978) 241–54.

32. C. Meeks, "Man from Heaven," 50. Meek's own investigation of the theme of kingship in John, The Prophet-King. Moses Traditions and the Johannine Christology (Leiden: Brill, 1967) speaks of a redefining of kingship in John through the introduction of the prophetic mission of Jesus. If kingship is being redefined—and not, as this essay argues, simply withdrawn from the theology of the Fourth Gospel and letters of John— then, to echo M. de Jonge, Jesus: Stranger from Heaven and Son of God. (SBLDS 11; Missoula: Scholars Press, 1977) 51, why does John not use the expression prophet in his redefinition? De Jonge, like Meeks, thinks that kingship is being redefined in John, though in a different direction.

Conclusion.

An analysis of other occurrences of the kingdom in Sethian literature (e.g., *Trim. Prot.* XIII,1:50, [8]; *Trim. Prot.* XIII,1:41,14) would strengthen the case for a symbol that lost its force and relevance for one wing of the School because another wing (the Sethians) transformed its meaning. In general it may be said that the standard theological accounts set out for the scarcity of references to the kingdom in the Fourth Gospel and letters of John do not adequately explain the virtual disapperance of a theme which both exegesis and dogmatic theology consider the central message of Jesus.

To the standard explanations for the apparent disinterest of the Fourth Gospel and the letters of John in the language of the kingdom this study proposes to add another. Johannine Sethianism claimed the kingdom for its mythological account of salvation, transforming thereby the kingdom into a symbol whose meaning was no longer acceptable to the School as a whole. In the later Johannine orthodoxy other symbols (eternal life, light, truth) came to stand for salvation, although remnants of the kingdom such as Jn 3:3, 5 and 18:36 recall, like lone crosses on a forgotten field of honor, a decisive engagement in the history of the early church.

13   The Kingdom of God in Paul

Karl Paul Donfried

Professor of Religion and Biblical Literature
Smith College

T O DEAL WITH THE KINGDOM AND KINGDOM OF GOD REFERENCES in the Pauline corpus is no simple task for it raises very profound and complicated issues with regard to the relationship of Paul to Jesus in general as well as Paul's use of the Jesus tradition in particular. While it is necessary to keep this larger issue in mind, methodologically one should deal first with the specific Pauline passages in which this terminology is used and only once that has been done will it be appropriate to return to the larger questions just raised.

Paul uses kingdom/kingdom of God language in seven passages: 1 Thess 2:10–12; Gal 5:21; 1 Cor 4:20; 1 Cor 6:9–10; 1 Cor 15:24; 1 Cor 15:50; and Rom 14:17. Although I do not consider 2 Thess as Pauline in the strict sense,[1] I will examine 2 Thess 1:5 briefly in connection with 1 Thess 2:10–12; some of the other deutero-Pauline passages will also be touched on briefly in the discussion of some of the above mentioned texts. I begin with 1 Cor 15:24 for a variety of reasons, not least of which is the fact that recent treatments of kingdom passages in Paul omit mention of this most significant reference,[2] as well as the fact that its formal structure is unique among the kingdom references in the Pauline letters. As I will show, 1 Cor 15:24 defines the kingdom as both present and future. In light of this I would wish to test the thesis whether Rom 14:17, 1 Cor 4:20–21, and 1 Thess 2:11–12 do not in fact have as their primary emphasis the pres-

---

1. See K. P. Donfried, "The Cults of Thessalonica and the Thessalonian Correspondence" NTS 31 (1985) 336–56.

2. For example, George Johnson, "'Kingdom of God' Sayings in Paul's Letters," in From Jesus to Paul: Studies in Honour of Francis Wright Beare, ed. Peter Richardson and John C. Hurd (Waterloo: Wilfrid Laurier University, 1984) 143–56 and G. Haufe, "Reich Gottes bei Paulus und in der Jesustradition" NTS 31 (1985) 467–72.

ence of the kingdom, and whether 1 Cor 15:50, 1 Cor 6:9–10 and Gal 5:21 do not have as their primary emphasis the kingdom as a still coming, future event. I also describe briefly their form and function in their respective contexts.

1 Corinthians 15:24

"Then comes the end, when he [Christ] delivers the kingdom to God the Father after destroying every rule and every authority and power."

This is a fascinating verse and yet one that has been virtually overlooked in the previous discussions of the kingdom in Pauline thought. The kingdom is closely associated with Christ; it is something which he will deliver to God at the end when even Christ will be subjected to God so "that God may be everything to every one" (15:28). If this is the case then clearly the concept of the kingdom for Paul is not an exclusively future one; in some sense the kingdom is present to those who are in Christ—it is a *present phenomenon* as well.

Conzelmann[3] shows Paul's indebtedness to the apocalyptic tradition in these verses of 1 Cor, particularly to the "Apocalypse of the Ten Weeks" in Eth. En. 91–93 and Sib Or 4:47–91. Although influenced by this tradition Paul transforms it and transposes the messianic kingdom

> into the present. For Christ is risen. His kingdom fills up the period between the resurrection and the consummation of the work of salvation after the parousia. It is not the kingdom of visible peace. This period is determined by the cross. Here the cosmological apocalyptic notions of the messianic kingdom disappear. It is Christologically speaking the time of the subjection of the powers, anthropologically speaking the time of the church, of the proclaiming of the death of Christ, of faith, of hope.[4]

Conzelmann is quite right when he asserts that "the kingdom of the messiah does not lie in the future for Paul. And the present state of believers is determined by the presence of the Spirit as ἀπαρχή [first portion] of what is to come, by transformation into a new creation, and by faith, hope and love as advance gifts of the eschatological existence."[5]

---

3. Hans Conzelmann, *A Commentary on the First Epistle to the Corinthians* (Hermeneia; Philadelphia: Fortress, 1975) 269–70.

4. Conzelmann, 270.

5. Conzelmann, 270, n. 63. Also in agreement with this position is Ernst Käsemann (*Commentary on Romans* [Grand Rapids: Eerdmans, 1980] 377) when he states that the coming kingdom of God in 1 Cor 15:24f. "is the consummation of the already present lordship of Christ and has dawned with it. . . . If Christ's reign is to be seen in the community, God's kingdom has already achieved anticipatory reality there. On earth this can take place only under assault." Both Conzelmann's and Käsemann's emphasis on Christology is important for only in this way can the kingdom of God be experienced in the present.

This understanding of Paul's eschatology differs markedly from the interpretations of such scholars as Lietzmann[6] and Schweitzer,[7] who argue that in 1 Cor 15:24 Paul means kingdom to refer to a "messianiche Zwischenreich" [messianic interim kingdom] which begins with the parousia and ends with the destruction of death. According to Lietzmann, Paul is referring precisely to this "messianische Zwischenreich" when he uses the term συμβασιλεύειν Χριστῷ [to reign together with Christ] and when he refers to the dead in 1 Thess 4:17 as reigning with Christ. That 1 Thess 4:17 has this meaning is highly unlikely;[8] further, συμβασιλεύειν is used only in 1 Cor 4:8. Not only must the precise context be understood, but also the connection with 1 Cor 15:24. We will return to this point shortly.

The context of Paul's advice on the kingdom in 1 Cor 15 is clear.[9] There are some in Corinth who have gotten their eschatological timetable mixed up. They believe that they have already received the fulness of God's eschatological gift in Christ in the present. The apostle wishes to show in 1 Cor 15:20–34 that there is an important eschatological reservation which these Corinthians overlook. Thus Paul writes in vv 23–24: "But each in his own order: Christ the first fruits, then at his coming those who belong to Christ. Then comes the end, when he delivers the kingdom to God the Father after destroying every rule and every authority and power." Although Christ has been raised, the resurrection of those in Christ is still *in the future*; although the kingdom is already present it will only reach its final goal in the future when "every rule and every authority and power" is destroyed. Until then the kingdom is in conflict with the kingdoms of this world and the mark of the Christian is the cross and not kingship.

In all likelihood Paul's clarification of the eschatological timetable in 1 Cor 15 is linked to certain assertions Paul makes in 1 Cor 4:8–13. What we have here is the apostle's sarcastic paraphrase of the Corinthian misunderstanding of the Christian life. "Already you are filled! Already you have become rich! Without us you have become kings (ἐβασιλεύσατε)! And would that you did reign, so that we might share the rule with you (καὶ ὄφελόν γε ἐβασιλεύσατε, ἵνα καὶ ἡμεῖς ὑμῖν συμβασιλεύσωμεν)"! Their understanding of the kingdom is that of eschatological fulfillment— already now they have been perfected and reign in the eschatological fulness of the kingdom. To all of this Paul issues a resounding "no"! Paul's overall answer to this problem in 1 Cor is not dissimilar to the hymn[10]

---

6. Hans Lietzmann, *An die Korinther I/II* (HNT 9; Tübingen: J.C.B. Mohr, 1959) 81.

7. Albert Schweitzer, *The Mysticism of the Apostle Paul* (New York: Holt, 1931) 90f.

8. See Donfried, "Cults," 349–52.

9. See the discussion in K. P. Donfried, *The Dynamic Word* (San Francisco: Harper & Row, 1981) 22–28.

10. See Martin Dibelius and Hans Conzelmann, *The Pastoral Epistles* (Hermeneia; Philadelphia: Fortress, 1972) 109.

(perhaps Pauline?)[11] cited in the deutero-Pauline 2 Tim: "If we have died with him, we shall also live with him; if we endure, we shall also reign with him (συμβασιλεύσομεν)" (2:11–12). Not unimportant is the fact that this correction is given in a situation quite similar to the distortion being described in 1 Cor 15: some "have swerved from the truth by holding that the resurrection is past already" (2 Tim 2:18).

To summarize: it is precisely to this wider problem of a misunderstood eschatological timetable that parts of 1 Cor are addressed and it is this situation that necessitates Paul's advice about the kingdom in chapter 15. It is present already, but not yet in its final, fulfilled eschatological sense; that is reserved for the end (τὸ τέλος, "when he delivers the kingdom to God the Father," 15:24). In the present the one in Christ lives under the sign of the cross not the sign of glory; the believer is called upon for the sake of the kingdom to endure.[12] It is precisely for this reason that Paul outlines the ignominy of his apostolic existence in 1 Cor 4:10–12.

Romans 14:17

"For the kingdom of God is not food and drink but righteousness and peace and joy in the Holy Spirit."

The Roman church is facing tension.[13] The strong and the weak have different attitudes toward what is proper food etiquette for the Christian. "One believes he may eat anything, while the weak man eats only vegetables" (Rom 14:2); as a result a dispute arises. Paul reminds them that the gift of the kingdom, the gift of life in Christ, is righteousness, peace and joy. It is this which stands at the center of the kingdom; not food and drink. Given the controversy in the present life of the Roman church it is only natural that Paul would be stressing the present dimension and characteristics of the kingdom.

Haufe characterizes both this reference to the kingdom as well as that found in 1 Cor 4:20 as an "antithetischer Definitionssatz" [antithetical definition formula] in which an negative assertion preceeds the positive one.[14] Both employ an οὐ γάρ . . . ἀλλά construction. Rom 14:17 replaces

11. For a general discussion of the problem see the discussion in C. K. Barrett, The Pastoral Epistles (Oxford: Clarendon Press, 1963) 7–12.

12. Note here our previous reference to 2 Tim 2:12: "if we endure, we shall also reign with him."

13. See K. P. Donfried, The Romans Debate (Minneapolis: Augsburg, 1977) 120–48.

14. Haufe, "Reich Gottes," 469. Haufe proceeds to indicate that this is not an antithetical definition formula in the strict sense since it is not giving a comprehensive definition of the kingdom, but one that is relevant and limited to the specific situation the apostle is addressing. Hans Conzelmann, 1 Corinthians 93, has pointed out the close parallels in 1 Macc 3:19, "The victory . . . standeth not in," and Epict., Diss. 2.1.4, etc. (Definitions: "The thing does not consist in").

the ἐν of 1 Cor 4:20 with a plain ἐστιν statement. Käsemann has suggested that we are dealing with a polemical declaration in Rom 14:17.[15] Haufe[16] challenges this and prefers to see the "pädagogisch-didaktische Interesse" (pedagogical-instructive interest) central on the basis that Paul is dependent on a "popularphilosophischen Schulbetriebes" [the activity of the popular philosophical school). If this is, in fact, the case, there is no reason why he could not modify that form to meet his needs. Given the overall polemical nature of Rom 14, Käsemann's interpretation is to be preferred.

We see no reason to accept here Johnson's[17] interpretation of δικαιοσύνη [righteousness] in a general sense and not in its technical Pauline usage. Once again we are inclined to Käsemann's interpretation.[18] He suggests that Paul is criticizing both the positions of asceticism and freedom which are opposing each other in Rome on this issue of food. Rather than set up a new set of Christian virtues, Paul reminds the Roman Christians that they have been placed "in the realm of eschatological grace. Righteousness is not right action but divine power. Peace is openness toward everyone. Joy is standing under an open heaven. Not feelings but realities are here described as the marks of the inaugurated lordship of God and Christian fellowship."[19] Käsemann also correctly reminds us that v 18 ("he who thus serves Christ is acceptable to God and approved by men") is closely connected with the preceeding verse. "'Serving Christ' sums up what has been said. It is the essence of the kingdom of God manifest in fellowship.[20]

---

1 Corinthians 4:20

"For the kingdom of God does not consist in talk (ἐν λόγῳ) but in power (ἐν δυνάμει)."

We have already had opportunity to comment on this verse in connection with our discussion of Rom 14:17. It can be described as an "antithetischer Definitionsatz," although understanding that this does not mean that it is intending to give an exhaustive definition of the kingdom of God; rather, as we shall see, it is concentrating on one dimension of that new reality in light of certain misunderstandings present in the Corinthian congregation.

15. *Commentary on Romans* (Grand Rapids: Eerdmans, 1980) 377.
16. "Reich Gottes," 469.
17. "Kingdom of God Sayings," 152.
18. *Romans,* 377.
19. *Romans,* 377. Note also the excellent discussion in C. E. B. Cranfield, *The Epistle to the Romans,* 2 vols., (ICC; Edinburgh: T. & T. Clark, 1979) 2:717–19.
20. *Romans,* 377.

A major problem in the Corinthian church is its members' arrogant boasting. Previously it was noticed how they claim already to be filled and to be reigning with Christ, viz., that already now they are living fully in an eschatological existence which, for Paul, in its finality is reserved for the future. The apostle indicates that during his forthcoming visit he "will find out not the talk of these arrogant people but their power" (1 Cor 4:19). Immediately thereafter follow the words that we are interested in: "For the kingdom of God does not consist in talk but in power."

Although δύναμις [power] is used by Paul in a variety of ways, here he appears to be referring to the powerful deeds which accompanied his apostolic preaching. This is certainly the case in 2 Cor 12:12: "The signs of a true apostle were performed among you in all patience, with signs and wonders and mighty words (δυνάμεσιν)." Our understanding is well stated by Victor Furnish: "Failing any indication to the contrary, Paul must be using the phrase *signs and wonders and deeds and power* in the way his readers would naturally take it—namely, with reference to some kind of miraculous occurrences, perhaps healings, which took place (despite the silence of Acts 18) when he was preaching the gospel to them."[21] This same intention appears also to be present in, for example, 1 Cor 2:4: "my speech (ὁ λόγος μου) and my message were not in plausible words of wisdom, but in demonstration of the Spirit and of power (δυνάμεως)"; in Rom 15:19: "For I will not venture to speak of anything except what Christ has wrought through me to win obedience from the Gentiles, by word and deed, by the power of signs (ἐν δυνάμει σημείων) and wonders, by the power of the Holy Spirit . . . so that I have fully preached the gospel of Christ"; and in 1 Thess 1:5: "for our gospel came to you not only in word (ἐν λόγῳ), but also in power (ἐν δυνάμει) and in the Holy Spirit and with full conviction." In his attempt to deal with those in Corinth who placed an excessive premium on sophisticated rhetoric and polished preaching, Paul makes clear that these are not the primary marks of the kingdom—it is not demonstrated by talk, in the sense just discussed, but by power. As the power of God is revealed in his kingdom by the gospel accompanied by signs demonstrating the authority of this new reality, so the Corinthians must give witness to the transformative power of the gospel not in their boasting but in the actuality of a new redeemed community living by and under the power of ἀγάπη [love] as an eschatological gift.[22]

If we have interpreted Paul's intention correctly, then there are a number of synoptic echoes of this theme. However one interprets Mk 9:1, it is noteworthy that the "kingdom of God has come ἐν δυνάμει [in power]." Paul's emphasis would be quite similar to the Matthean summary of

---

21. *II Corinthians* (AB 32A; Garden City: Doubleday, 1985) 556.
22. See esp. 1 Cor 12 and 13.

Jesus' activity in 9:35: "And Jesus went about all the cities and villages, teaching in their synagogues and preaching the gospel of the kingdom, and healing every disease and every infirmity." A similar emphasis is found in the Q passage Mt 12:28//Lk 11:20: "But if it is by the Spirit of God that I cast out demons, then the kingdom of God has come upon you."

According to in 1 Cor 4:20 the kingdom of God is present and provides the context for the life of the Corinthian church. In asserting this we need to remember what was said above: the presence of the kingdom of God through the Christ event in an anticipatory way does not in anyway reduce the eschatological nature of this kingdom.

---

1 Thessalonians 2:11–12

"We exhorted each one of you and encouraged you and charged you to lead a life worthy of God, who calls you into his own kingdom[23] and glory."

These verses follow Paul's defense of his motives and behavior during his initial visit to Thessalonica. Verse 10 summarizes much of Paul's appeal in vv 1–8, viz., that the Thessalonians should know "how holy and righteous and blameless was our behavior to you believers" precisely because Paul and his co-workers were not interested in pleasing men but God, the very God who entrusted his gospel to them. Since Paul's behavior results from that gospel which he preached to them, he reminds them of his proclamation when he was present among them, viz., "to lead a life worthy of God, who calls you into his own kingdom of glory." Paul refers (2:13) to their positive response to his proclamation as a way of confirming, at the very least, the integrity of the message he preached when he was among them. Two further points need to be emphasized in connection with this reminder. First, $\kappa\alpha\lambda\epsilon\hat{\iota}\nu$ [to call] is in the present. This stresses the present and continuing nature of the event in which they now participate and which will be consummated in the future. Secondly, just for clarity, we need to remind ourselves once again that Paul *orally communicated* this message about the kingdom during his presence in Thessalonica. In short, we have evidence that this term was rooted in his oral preaching.[24]

The point of Paul's original exhortation was this: since God has called

23. Paul does not use the more customary phrase, "kingdom of God," because he has just referred to God and obviously wishes to avoid redundancy.

24. Since 1 Thess 2:12 is found in the general context of the great thanksgiving and in the specific context of Paul's "apology" we cannot accept Haufe's ("Reich Gottes," 468) characterization of this verse as a "Drohwort (threatening word)." It simply does not function that way in 1 Thess 2.

and continues to call the Thessalonian Christians, they are expected to live a life that is being transformed continually by the gospel. In 5:5 Paul reminds them that already now "you are all sons of light and sons of the day"; thus the result is: "since we belong to the day, let us be sober, and put on the breastplate of faith and love, and for a helmet the hope of salvation" (5:8). By repeating the triadic formula "faith, love and hope" in 5:8[25] Paul indicates clearly his understanding of the Christian life as eschatological—as already, not yet. Already now, partially and proleptically, through Christ and his gospel, God's rule and glory[26] have broken into this transient world and are at work in them.[27] Thus the Thessalonian Christians have "turned to God from idols, to serve a living and true God, and to wait for his Son from heaven" (1:9–10).[28] The newness of their life in Christ has already begun and will be completed on the last day. As a result, "God has . . . destined us . . . to obtain salvation through our Lord Jesus Christ" (5:9).

The use in 1 Thess 2:12 of the adverb ἀξίως [worthy], more infrequent in the Pauline corpus, may well suggest that Paul is dependent on an early Christian baptismal tradition, a suggestion strengthened when one notes the similar use of this adverb in Phil 1:27, Eph 4:1, and Col 1:10.[29] Haufe[30] suggests that this same baptismal context lies behind the kingdom references in 1 Cor 4:20–21 and 1 Thess 2:11–12, except that in these two cases Paul develops them in a new way under the influence of the forms of popular philosophical schools.

As previously indicated, I shall comment briefly on 2 Thess 1:5, even though I do not hold it to be from the hand of Paul: "This is evidence of the righteous judgment of God, that you may be made worthy of the kingdom of God, for which you are suffering." The author of this document has just praised the congregation for its faith and love and offers support in all their "persecutions and in the afflictions" which they are enduring. Their steadfastness during these difficulties is a sign that they will be made worthy of the kingdom of God. Given both the change in language nuance between 1 Thess 2:12 and 2 Thess 1:5[31] and the strongly

25. Note 1 Thess 1:3.
26. Note, for example, the use of δόζα [glory] in 2 Cor 3:18; it is something which is already present in the Christian community.
27. Note 1 Thess 2:13.
28. Note the overall similarity with the deutero-Pauline Col 1:13: "He has delivered us from the dominion of darkness and transferred us to the kingdom of his beloved Son." We will discuss the baptismal context of these verse below.
29. So Rudolf Schnackenburg, Der Brief an die Epheser (EKK; Neukirchen-Vluyn: Neukirchener, 1982) 164. See also n. 59 below.
30. "Reich Gottes," 469.
31. The difference between εἰς τὸ περιπατεῖν ὑμᾶς ἀξίως τοῦ θεοῦ τοῦ καλοῦντος ὑμᾶς εἰς τὴν ἑαυτοῦ βασιλείαν καὶ δόξαν and εἰς τὸ καταξιωθῆναι ὑμᾶς τῆς βασιλείας τοῦ θεοῦ ὑπὲρ ἧς καὶ πάσχετε is quite substantial: "to lead a life worthy of God, who called you into his

apocalyptic language of 2 Thess 1:5–12, it is apparent that an eschatological shift has taken place in the understanding of the kingdom for the
author of 2 Thess. It is now strictly a future phenomenon and Wolfgang
Trilling is to be followed when he states: "Die strenge Zukünftigkeit steht
ausser Frage."[32] We now turn to those Pauline passages which view the
kingdom as primarily a future event.

---

1 Corinthians 15:10

"I tell you this, brethren: flesh and blood cannot inherit the kingdom of
God, nor does the perishable inherit the imperishable."

In his attempt to show that the resurrection is future and bodily, as
opposed to something already fully experienced spiritually, Paul attempts
to demonstrate that a future bodily transformation must precede entrance
into the kingdom of God.[33] In v 42f. the apostle argued that what "is sown
is perishable, what is raised is imperishable. . . . It is sown a physical body,
it is raised a spiritual body. . . . But it is not the spiritual which is first but
the physical, and then the spiritual." It is precisely to underscore this
point that he adds in v 50 that "flesh and blood," viz., the physical, cannot
inherit the future kingdom. Only when this physical body is transformed
on the last day, can one enter the kingdom. Thus, what characterizes
human existence in the present is the physical body; what characterizes
life in the future consummated kingdom is a transformed, spiritual body.

The phrase $\beta\alpha\sigma\iota\lambda\epsilon\acute{\iota}\alpha\nu$ $\theta\epsilon o\hat{\upsilon}$ $\kappa\lambda\eta\rho o\nu o\mu\hat{\eta}\sigma\alpha\iota$ [to inherit the kingdom of God]
here in 1 Cor 15:50 is virtually identical with the phrase found in 1 Cor
6:9–10 and Gal 5:21: $\beta\alpha\sigma\iota\lambda\epsilon\acute{\iota}\alpha\nu$ $\theta\epsilon o\hat{\upsilon}$ $o\vec{\upsilon}$ $\kappa\lambda\eta\rho o\nu o\mu\acute{\eta}\sigma o\upsilon\sigma\iota\nu$. In all likelihood
this expression is pre-Pauline[34] and derives from a baptismal-parenetic
context of the early church. In 1 Cor 6:9–10 and Gal 5:21 it is connected
with a list of negative conditions by which one is certain to be excluded
fron the kingdom.[35] In connection with these last two references, Haufe's
use of the category "Drohwort" [threatening word] is more accurate.
However, although the "Sprachmilieu" [language environment][36] of 1 Cor
15:50 is originally the same, its intention is quite different and therefore

---

own kingdom and glory" (RSV) and "That you may be made worthy of the kingdom of
God for which you are suffering" (RSV).

32. "There is no doubt about the radical futurity [of the kingdom]." *Der Zweite Brief an
die Thessalonicher* (EKK; Neukirchen-Vluyn: Neukirchener, 1980) 50.

33. Donfried, *Dynamic Word*, 22–28.

34. Note that only in these three kingdom references the article is omitted before
$\beta\alpha\sigma\iota\lambda\epsilon\acute{\iota}\alpha$, a phenomenon not found in the other kingdom references in Paul.

35. Note the modified form of this phrase in the deutero-Pauline Eph. 5:5.

36. Haufe, "Reich Gottes," 469.

1 Cor 15:50 cannot function as a "Drohwort."[37] Given the misunderstanding of the eschatological timetable in Corinth, the apostle takes up this traditional phrase as a teaching device and applies it to the misunderstandings at hand.[38] Against such a new threat Paul has to modify this common tradition which may originally stem from baptismal parenesis.[39]

---

1 Corinthians 6:9–10

"Do you not know that the unrighteous will not inherit the kingdom of God? Do not be deceived; neither the immoral, nor idolaters, nor adulterers, nor sexual perverts, nor thieves, nor the greedy, nor drunkards, nor revilers, nor robbers will inherit the kingdom of God (θεοῦ βασιλείαν οὐ κληρονομήσουσιν)."

As already intimated in our discussion of 1 Cor 15:50, these verses, together with v 11, are probably cited by Paul from a earlier tradition which is rooted in baptism and is then coupled with a post-baptismal list of vices which define, negatively, the requirements of the kingdom.[40] Hahn insists that the "kingdom of God" language as used here is derived from this earlier tradition, since only the references to the kingdom in the present (1 Cor 4:20; Rom 14:17) have a claim to authentic Pauline usage.[41] By use of this tradition, which reveals certain tensions with the apostle's theology,[42] Paul is making it clear that certain types of behavior will void the future inheritance of the kingdom even for those who have been baptized and justified. These actions are not magical and guarantee nothing in and of themselves. Although the original apocalyptic nature of the phrase kingdom of God is evident,[43] in this text it is placed in a parenetic context.[44] As Conzelmann[45] correctly recognizes, this raises the

---

37. Which Haufe, "Reich Gottes," 468–69, acknowledges.

38. There is a similarity between 1 Cor 15:50 and Jn 3:3–5 (and Mt 18:3) and it is fully possible that members of the Corinthian congregation were misunderstanding a Johannine-like tradition in the sense of eschatological fulfillment in the present.

39. See our discussion below and also the discussion in C. H. Dodd, *Historical Tradition in the Fourth Gospel* (Cambridge: University Press, 1963) 358–59, and R. E. Brown, *The Gospel According to John (I–XII)* (AB 29; Garden City: Doubleday, 1966) 143–44.

40. For a complete analysis of this tradition see Ferdinand Hahn, "Taufe und Rechtfertigung" in *Rechtfertigung: Festschrift für Ernst Käsemann* [ed. J. Friedrich, W. Pöhlmann, P. Stuhlmacher; Tübingen: J. C. B. Mohr, 1976] 104–9; and, Udo Schnelle, *Gerechtigkeit und Christusgegenwart* (Göttingen: Vandenhoeck & Ruprecht, 1983) 37–44.

41. A statement such as this requires caution, since Paul in many cases will take up traditions and use them to express his theological or ethical purpose. Hahn, "Taufe," 105, n. 41.

42. See Hahn, "Taufe," 104.

43. See Conzelmann, *1 Corinthians*, 106.

44. Schnelle, *Gerechtigkeit*, 38.

45. *1 Corinthians*, 107.

whole question of the relationship of indicative and imperative in Pauline thought. Precisely because justification for Paul is not simply a point
in past time but is a continuing event,[46] he makes it clear that the one who
is in Christ must now lead a life congruent with the gift that has been
given in baptism and which continues to be given in the Spirit through the
congregation. His intention in citing this tradition becomes especially
evident in v 18: "Shun immorality." Those who participate in prostitution[47] will be excluded from the future kingdom.[48]

This pre-Pauline tradition is consistent with the words attributed to
Jesus in Mk 1:15: "The time is fulfilled, and the kingdom of God is at hand;
repent, and believe in the gospel." There also appears to be a close
proximity with the M tradition, especially as formulated in Mt 25:34:
"Then the King will say to those at his right hand, 'Come, O blessed of my
Father, inherit ($\kappa\lambda\eta\rho\text{ο}\nu\alpha\mu\acute{\eta}\sigma\alpha\tau\epsilon$) the kingdom prepared for you from the
foundation of the world." Not only do we have the same verb as in 1 Cor
6:10, but also the fact that such inheritance is dependent on a certain type
of ethical behavior. But before we discuss these parallels more extensively it will be well to review the kingdom reference in Gal 5:21 first and
then return to this issue.

Galatians 5:21

"I warn you, as I warned you before, that those who do such things shall
not inherit the kingdom of God ($\beta\alpha\sigma\iota\lambda\epsilon\acute{\iota}\alpha\nu\ \theta\epsilon\text{ο}\hat{\upsilon}\ \text{ο}\hat{\upsilon}\ \kappa\lambda\eta\rho\text{ο}\nu\text{ο}\mu\acute{\eta}\sigma\text{ο}\upsilon\sigma\iota\nu$)."

The first part of this verse, which serves as a "quotation formula" for the
remainder, suggests that Paul's advice about the kingdom is not a novelty
but was included in his previous communications with this congregation,
a fact also paralleled in 1 Thess 2:12.[49] Both in its present form and in its
previous oral form, this kingdom reference as well as the wider context
appear to come from a tradition including early Christian baptismal
instruction.[50] The tension with Pauline theology can be seen at several
points, perhaps most pointedly in the use of $\kappa\lambda\eta\rho\text{ο}\nu\text{ο}\mu\epsilon\hat{\iota}\nu$ (inherit) which is
in tension with the use of that term elsewhere in Galatians.[51]

---

46. See Hahn, "Taufe," 117–24; Donfried, *Dynamic Word*, 50–64.

47. Probably temple prostitution, although for a different perspective see the discussion in Jerome Murphy-O'Connor, "The Corinth that Saint Paul Saw," BA 47 (1984)
147–59.

48. Here, contrary to Schnelle (see n. 41), we see the section beginning with 1 Cor 6:9
as looking forward to the issue of prostitution rather than backward to the issue of
Christians involved with lawsuits against one another.

49. For a further discussion of this see Hans Dieter Betz, *Galatians* (Hermeneia;
Philadelphia: Fortress, 1979) 284.

50. Betz, *Galatians*, 284.

51. Gal 3:18, 29; 4:1, 7, 30.

Given the strong possibility that some Galatian Christians misunderstood Paul's use of the term "freedom,"[52] Paul uses this traditional material in a parenetic context to warn the Galatian Christians that certain types of activity, viz. "works of the flesh," are not only inappropriate for those who are now in Christ but that those who do them shall not inherit the kingdom of God. Indisputably the apocalyptic dimension of the kingdom is being stressed in this verse. As we noted previously there are parallels to this use of kingdom language in M and to this we shall now turn.

The "inherit the kingdom of God" formula found in 1 Cor 6:9–10 and Gal 5:21[53] finds it most striking parallel in Mt 25:34, a passage which is unique to the M tradition.[54] Although Mt 25:34 is a positive reference to those who will enter the kingdom, its opposite is found, although in a substantially modified form, in 25:41. Obviously if one is to be thrown into the eternal fire one will not inherit the kingdom. Also related to this tradition are those synoptic references about not entering the kingdom of God (Mk 10:15 and parallels; Mt 5:20; 7:21; 18:3).[55] Haufe[56] rightly shows the practical interchangeability of εἰσέρχομαι [to enter] and κληρονομεῖν [to inherit] in the Septuagint.[57] This, too, points to a common early Christian tradition. The fact that this language about "inheriting the kingdom" is found neither in its negative nor positive form in Q once again suggests that we are dealing with an early Christian baptismal-parenetic tradition in which this material was first used for catechetical instruction. Thus it was the needs of the earliest Christian communities which necessitated the transformation of Jesus' proclamation of the kingdom to meet the requirements of its baptismal and post-baptismal instruction and other parenetic necessities. That is not to say that the original message of Jesus was lost sight of; rather it was taken up, expanded, and applied in new situations.

Conclusion

What tentative conclusions may be reached? Let us attempt to divide our summary into three parts: Paul's use of kingdom language; Luke's description of Paul's proclamation in Acts; the relationship of Paul's use of kingdom language to that of Jesus and the synoptic tradition.

52. Note Gal 5:13.
53. In modified form also in 1 Cor 15:50.
54. Note similar but not exact uses of "to inherit" in Mt 5:5 and 19:29.
55. Note in this connection our previous discussion of Jn 3:5.
56. "Reich Gottes," 470.
57. Dt 4:1; 6:18; 16:20.

1. With regard to Paul's use of kingdom language it can be concluded that Paul understands that the kingdom of God is consummated in the future but that it has already achieved anticipatory reality in the present through the resurrection and reign of Christ. The "already-not yet" nature of the kingdom is especially evident in 1 Cor 15:50. Further, we found that Rom 14:17, 1 Cor 4:20–21, and 1 Thess 2:12 stressed the presence of the kingdom and that 1 Cor 15:50, 1 Cor 6:9, and Gal 5:21 emphasized its futurity. With regard to those texts stressing the presence of the kingdom we noted that they stem from a baptismal context, although Rom 14:7 and 1 Cor 4:20–21, with their οὐ γὰρ . . . ἀλλά structure characteristic of an "antithetischer Definitionsatz" [antithetical definition formula] reveal a further development through the influence of the popular philosophical schools. Those texts stressing the apocalyptic nature of the kingdom, 1 Cor 15:50, 1 Cor 6:9, and Gal 5:21 also stem from a baptismal context, although they are all marked by a specific tradition using the verb κληρονομεῖν (to inherit). At this point we noticed some noteworthy relationships with M and other parts of the synoptic tradition, but not with Q.

Since all these texts, with the possible exception of 1 Cor 15:50, derive from a baptismal context,[58] how can one describe their differences, especially the οὐ γὰρ . . . ἀλλά construction, on the one hand, and the κληρονομεῖν construction, together with the absence of the article before βασιλεία, on the other? Perhaps one might suggest that Rom 14:17, 1 Cor 4:20–21, and 1 Thess 2:12 are modified for their present contexts from a more kerygmatic tradition and that 1 Cor 15:50, 1 Cor 6:9, and Gal 5:21 derive from a tradition that was originally intended to offer specific, perhaps post-baptismal, ethical instruction.

2. As we turn our attention to Acts, we notice that in Acts 14:22, 19:8, 20:25 and 28:23, 31 Luke describes Paul as preaching the kingdom of God. While in the first reference there is a clearly future reference to the kingdom ("through many tribulations we must enter the kingdom of God"), the other three verses, while not excluding a future reference, are not oriented to a particular time and might well be emphasizing the present nature of the kingdom.[59] While not wishing to deny Luke's theological intention in shaping his view of Paul, we would disagree with Jürgen Roloff,[60] for example, when he understands the kingdom references in Acts as merely Luke's way of summarizing the teaching of Jesus.

---

58. "Baptismal context" is a somewhat vague term although it is widely used in the literature. Such a context can involve both indicative and imperative elements. Perhaps one should refer to the former as "baptismal" (viz. kerygmatic) and to the latter as "post-baptismal" (viz., parenetic). One should not overlook the fact that the former can easily be transformed to fit the needs of the latter; precisely because this happens it becomes more important to attempt the isolate the original Sitz im Leben of each.

59. So. e.g., F. F. Bruce, *The Acts of the Apostles* (Grand Rapids: Eerdmans, 1960) 480.

60. *Die Apostelgeschichte* (NTD; Göttingen: Vandenhoeck & Ruprecht, 1981) 283.

The fact remains that Paul used this term both in his oral preaching and parenesis as well as in his written letters. One must be a bit more cautious before one assigns every instance of such terminology to the hand of Luke, as Roloff apparently does.

One other passage in Acts needs to be reviewed briefly in light of our discussion of Paul and his use of kingdom language: Acts 17:6-7. The scene is Thessalonica and the accusers of Paul and his followers argue before the city authorities that these "men who have turned the world upside down have come here also, and Jason has received them; and they are all acting against the decrees of Caesar, saying that there is another king, Jesus." Paul's categorical statement in 1 Thess 2:12 that he did speak to the Thessalonians about the kingdom during his presence in the city should help us to understand the relative accuracy of the Acts 17 account, not only with regard to Paul's use of king/kingdom language but also with regard to the fact that this language may well have served as the catalyst for the animosity he and his co-workers aroused in Thessalonica.[61]

3. Finally we come to the question whether our study can offer some assistance in helping us understand the relation of Paul's proclamation about the kingdom of God to that of Jesus and the synoptic tradition. There are obvious points of contact between them, the most evident being that both Paul and Jesus used the phrase kingdom of God. Beyond this there are some more substantive relationships as well. We divided the Pauline references to the kingdom of God into present and future. This accords well with the synoptic tradition. The apocalyptic notion of the kingdom is found both in the triple tradition (Mk 14:25 par.) and in Q (Mt 6:10//Lk 11:2) as well as in various single traditions. The present nature of the kingdom is especially evident in the Q tradition (Mt 12:28//Lk 11:20). Additionally the references to $\grave{\epsilon}\nu$ $\delta\nu\nu\acute{a}\mu\epsilon\iota$ [in power] in 1 Cor 4:20 may well be influenced by the triple tradition (Mk 9:1 par) and this is not unrelated to the theme expressed in Mt 9:35 concerning the teaching and healing ministry of Jesus. We also observed a specific relationship to the M tradition and its use of $\kappa\lambda\eta\rho o\nu o\mu\epsilon\hat{\iota}\nu$ (e.g., Mt 25:34 and 5:19). This verb appears to be used almost synonymously with $\epsilon\grave{\iota}\sigma\acute{\epsilon}\rho\chi o\mu\alpha\iota$ [to enter] not only in the M tradition (5:20) but also in the triple tradition (Mk 10:14 par; Mk 10:15 par; Mk 10:23-25 par) and in the Markan tradition as well (9:47).

For the most part these observations are in agreement with the conclusions reached by F. Neirynck.[62] We would agree fully when he states that there "is no trace . . . in the Pauline letters of a conscious use of a saying of Jesus. Possible allusion to such sayings (on the basis of similarity

61. For a more complete discussion of this position see K. P. Donfried, "Cults," 342-48.
62. "Paul and the Sayings of Jesus," delivered at Colloquium Biblicum Lovaniense 1984 and forthcoming in the publication of that meeting (Bibliotheca Ephemeridum Theologicarum Lovaniensium).

of form and content with gospel sayings) also show significant differences, and a direct use of a gospel saying in the form it has been preserved in the synoptic gospels is hardly provable."[63] One can also concur with Neirynck when he states that "Paul's knowledge of the Q tradition or pre-Q collection . . . cannot be demonstrated"[64] since the paucity and anonymity of such possible allusions make it most doubtful whether Paul was specifically referring to them as sayings of Jesus.

Reference must also be made to Nikolaus Walter's insightful study.[65] In general he agrees with Neirynck's conclusions: Paul quotes no sayings of Jesus but he is familiar with the Jesus tradition. Walter shows that in the extant Pauline letters the Jesus tradition is used primarily in parenetic contexts,[66] but also in sections in which Paul defends his apostolic ministry.[67] Walter cites 1 Cor 4:11–13 and 9:14; we would add 1 Thess 2:1–12. Further, when Paul cites the Jesus tradition it is usually without reflection and it is used with enormous freedom, viz., he can refer to it and yet not be bound by it (e.g. 1 Cor 9:1–18).

The Jesus-Paul debate is an enormously complex one and cannot be reviewed here.[68] However, our study does show that Paul is dependent on the teaching of Jesus as reflected in the synoptic tradition, particularly with regard to the concept kingdom of God. Thus we would agree with S. G. Wilson that references to Jesus' teachings are rare;[69] however, we would add the kingdom of God references to his short list of such teachings. Further, we would suggest that Paul's use of the phrase kingdom of God supports those scholars who would wish to show that a fundamental unity and continuity between Jesus and Paul can be detected in the several central themes which are common to both.[70] Some

---

63. Neirynck, "Paul," 31.

64. Neirynck, "Paul," 31.

65. "Paulus und die urchristliche Tradition," *NTS* 31 (1985) 498–522.

66. The following statement of Walter ("Paulus," 515) seems to interpret the parenetic context quite broadly: "Der von Paulus aktiv 'gepflegte' Ausschnitt aus dem Bestand von Jesustradition, den er möglicherweise gekannt hat, hat es meist in der einen oder anderen Weise mit der Grundlegung und den Grunderkenntnissen seiner Verkündigung und Theologie (aber nicht mit den zentralen christologisch-soteriologischen Aussagen . . .) oder aber mit seiner apostolischen Existenz zu tun." (That regularly preserved selection from the survival of the Jesus tradition, which he possibly knew, has in one way or another something to do with the fundamental and basic understandings of his proclamation and theology [but not with the central christological-soteriological assertions] or have something to do with his life as an apostle.)

67. Walter, "Paulus," 508–13.

68. See the useful review by S. G. Wilson "From Jesus to Paul: The Contours and Consequences of a Debate," in *From Jesus to Paul: Studies in Honour of Francis Wright Beare* (ed. Peter Richardson and John C. Hurd; Waterloo: Wilfrid Laurier University, 1984) 1–21.

69. S. G. Wilson, "From Jesus to Paul," 7.

70. For example, eschatology. See Wilson, "From Jesus to Paul," 10, and the literature cited there.

may object to our citing the kingdom of God references in this context because of their brevity and their fragmentary nature. To this we would respond, by way of summary, with the helpful conclusion reached by Nikolaus Walter: "Aber jene Auffassung von der sachlichen Übereinstimmung des paulinischen Evangeliums mit der Botschaft Jesu kann auch bestehen, wenn der—natürlich nicht entbehrliche—Traditionszusammenhang sich sehr viel indirekter oder (um es mit Bildern aus dem Bereich der Optik zu sagen) mit Strahlenbündelungen, -brechungen, -spiegelungen, auch mit partiellem Strahlenausfall und andererseits mit Anreicherungen von fremder Herkunft vollzogen hat."[71]

71. Walter, "Paulus," 518. A translation of this sentence, worked out in conjunction with Prof. Walter, might read as follows: "But such an understanding of the substantial agreements of the Pauline gospel with the message of Jesus can also exist when the continuity of traditions has taken place quite indirectly, through (to use images from the realm of optics) the emission and common focusing, refraction, and reflection of rays. This continuity of tradition can take place even though there may be a partial 'fading-out' of certain traditions and the embellishment of others through materials of foreign origin, such as certain non-Jesus, for example, Jewish-Hellenistic, traditions."

14   The Kingdom of God in Early Patristic Literature*

Everett Ferguson

Professor of Bible
Abilene Christian University

WHETHER THE KINGDOM OF GOD is future or present has dominated discussion of Jesus' proclamation since Albert Schweitzer.[1] The treatment of the early patristic usage of the terminology of the kingdom must be set in the broader terms of the discussion of the meaning of kingdom in the NT. Although the temporal question may not always be the most helpful category to apply to the NT material, it does seem to have been a significant concern in the early Christian development. Most of the second-century references to the kingdom of God can be classified according to a temporal outline. The principal options may be outlined as follows:

   I. The Kingdom as Present—Realized Eschatology
     A. Interior—the kingdom within the believer
     B. Soteriological/Ecclesiastical—the kingdom as meaning salvation or realized in the church
  II. The Kingdom as Future—Consistent Eschatology
     A. Millennial—the kingdom as earthly before the end
     B. Heavenly—the kingdom as the world to come
 III. The Kingdom as Both Present and Future—Inaugurated Eschatology
    In Process of Being Realized—the present kingdom as leading to consummation
 IV. Symbolic—the kingdom as a literary symbol

---

*This contribution is a rewriting of a paper read at the Eighth International Conference on Patristic Studies at Oxford in 1979. Parts of that paper incorporated in this article are reprinted with permission from *Studia Patristica* XVIII (ed. E. A. Livingstone), E. Ferguson, "The Terminology of the Kingdom in the Second Century," Copyright 1982, Pergamon Press.

1. A history of research and selections from some major interpretations may be found in Bruce Chilton, ed., *The Kingdom of God* (Issues in Religion and Theology 5; Philadelphia: Fortress, 1984).

These views are not mutually exclusive. Some examples of kingdom in each of these senses may be found in second-century Christian literature, but the great majority of passages will be found to represent a consistent eschatological reference.

The basic meaning of kingdom in biblical usage was kingship, "reign." From this came the secondary meaning of realm, kingdom in its modern sense.[2] The secondary sense definitely predominates in early patristic literature, but is not the exclusive meaning. This shift in emphasis from the active sense of kingly power to the static sense of realm illustrates the shift in thinking from the dynamic biblical concepts to the more static concepts of Greco-Roman thought. In that regard the patristic view of the future and heaven differed from the consistent eschatology advocated by Schweitzer in interpreting the NT texts.

Biblical Citations and Allusions

Many occurrences of the word kingdom in early patristic literature are found in biblical quotations and allusions. These have been largely omitted, for reasons of space, from the collection of quotations in the appendix. Some observations, however, are in order because of the insights which these quotations give to the concerns of the authors.

The use of a particular verse was sometimes thrust upon an author by reason of special circumstances. The refutation of Gnosticism by Irenaeus, bishop of Lyons (ca. 180–200), required extensive treatment of 1 Cor 15:50.[3] Paul's statement that "Flesh and blood cannot inherit the kingdom of God" accorded well with the Gnostic dualism of body and soul, with its corollaries of the salvation of the soul and denial of a resurrection of the flesh. Irenaeus interpreted "flesh and blood" as referring to the sinful works of the flesh, the flesh without the Spirit of God.

2. K. L. Schmidt, "βασιλεύς," *TDNT* (ed. G. Kittel; Grand Rapids: Eerdmans, 1964) 1:549–93; B. Klappert, "King, Kingdom," *NIDNTT* (ed. Colin Brown; Grand Rapids: Zondervan, 1976) 2:372–90.

G. W. H. Lampe, "Some Notes on the Significance of *Basileia Tou Theou, Basileia Christou* in the Greek Fathers," *JTS* 49 (1948) 60 makes a generalization which holds for the second century when he says that patristic usage differs from the Synoptic Gospels in that kingdom bears a less "dynamic" meaning and as a rule does not suggest the irruption of the divine into human history. Exceptions to this generalization will be noted in the discussion below.

Treatments of the kingdom of God in the post-canonical literature are not nearly so numerous as those dealing with the Bible, but in addition to works cited in the notes following mention may be made of A. Robertson, *Regnum Dei* (London, 1901); Robert Murray, *Symbols of Church and Kingdom* (London: Cambridge Univ. Press, 1975); and the works cited in John E. Groh, "The Kingdom of God in the History of Christianity: A Bibliographical Survey," *Church History* 43 (1974) 257–67.

3. *Against Heresies* 5.9–14; cf. 1.30.13.

Irenaeus' eschatological understanding of the kingdom is shown in his special fondness for Mt 25:34.[4] Likewise other authors indicate their viewpoint by their favorite texts. Irenaeus' eschatological understanding was reinforced by Dan 2 and 7; Dan 7:27 was important also to Justin Martyr (ca. 150–160) in his argument against Judaism. Daniel 7:27 (supported by 2 Sam 7:12–16; Ps 132:12; cf. 2 Pet 1:11) furnished him with the set phrase "eternal kingdom" in order to contrast Christ's kingdom with the temporal kingdom of Israel.[5] Justin, as other Christians, also found Ps 45 useful in exalting Jesus as the anointed King.[6] From the NT, Justin quotes Mt 8:11f. with some frequency.[7] Clement of Alexandria (ca. 190–200) most frequently cites Mt 11:12 (Lk 16:16), emphasizing the human effort which must be exerted in order to enter the kingdom.[8] The Pseudo-Clementine *Recognitions* show their moral concern by the special interest in Mt 6:33.[9]

The biblical phrases which really caught the attention of the second century were "inherit the kingdom of God" (1 Cor 6:9; Gal 5:21; cf. Eph 5:5; Mt 25:34; Js 2:5) and especially Jesus' "enter the kingdom of heaven [God]" (frequently in Matthew and Luke), phrases occurring too often to cite examples and both understood the same way—eschatologically.

Factors Influencing Christian Usage

Debate with the Jews

The polemic against Judaism made it necessary for Christians to affirm that the kingdom had been taken from the Jews and that the followers of Jesus were its true heirs (Nos. 55, 62, 64, 75; Mt 8:11f. was important here). Thus Justin declares that the eternal kingdom belongs to Jesus (No. 49; cf. 46 and 48 and Tertullian, *Against Marcion* 4.33), and Irenaeus asserts that Christ has the eternal kingdom (Nos. 65, 69, 72). Of course, neither Jews nor Christians in the second century were permitted a "political" expression of their kingdom claims.

Political Situation

"Kingdom" occurs occasionally in second-century Christian literature as a neutral term for the secular kingdoms in human history (Nos. 11, 20, 57, 58; cf. 56). Of more significance was its use for the Roman Empire in

---

4. *Against Heresies* 4.18.6; 28.2; 40.2; 5.27.1.
5. *Dialogue* 31; 79.2; 118:2; 68.5; 76.1; and see 65.
6. *Dialogue* 56; 63; 86.
7. *Dialogue* 76.4; 120.5f; 140.2.
8. *Miscellanies* 4.2; 5.2; *Who Is the Rich Man that Is Saved* 21; 31.
9. Appendix No. 109; *Recognitions* 2.21; 46; 3.20; 37; 41.

conscious relation or even contrast to God's kingdom. The *Martyrdom of Polycarp* (155 ?) employs a dating formula at its conclusion which deliberately substitutes a reference to the eternal reign of Christ in place of the year of the reigning emperor (No. 27; cf. 24 and 25). The Apologists were particularly aware that the biblical word for "kingdom" was the ordinary word for the empire (Nos. 45, 58) or any kingship (No. 68). They stressed that the source of earthly rule was God (No. 58; cf. 11 and Justin, *II Apology* 2.19 for God as king in contrast to the emperor) and could even make a parallel between the origins and growth of Christianity and the development of the Roman Empire (No. 59). More typically, Christians made a contrast between the earthly human kingdoms and the heavenly kingdom of God (Nos. 45, 106; cf. Jn 18:36). Hegesippus summed up the characteristic second-century understanding of the kingdom of God saying that it was no threat to Rome because it was heavenly, angelic, and altogether future (No. 61).

Controversy with Gnosticism

The Gnostics emphasized the present realization of the blessings of salvation and the immediate passage of the soul at death into the heavenly realm. Therefore, their emphasis was on the interior kingdom (Nos. 113, 114).[10] The debate between the Gnostics and their opponents within the church may be seen in the contrasting interpretations of a saying attributed to Jesus found in the *Gospel of Thomas* 22 (No. 112) and *2 Clement* 12 (No. 16).[11] According to the wording of the latter, the saying was this: "Whenever the two shall be one, and outside as the inside, and the male with the female, neither male nor female." The *Gospel of Thomas* does not offer an interpretation of the saying but formulates it in terms of conditions for entry into the kingdom. The interpretation of the saying as referring to the interior kingdom is explicit in the Naassenes

10. Cf. *Gospel of Thomas* 3; 113. In some passages from Nag Hammadi the kingdom appears to be heavenly without being eschatological—e.g. *Tripartite Tractate* (I,5) 96, 17–37; 101, 29–102, 22; 131, 35–132, 20; *Eugnostos* (V,1) 8, 19–23; (III,3) 81, 13–16; (III,3) 85, 15–17; 85, 21–86, 2.

11. It may be deduced from Clement of Alexandria, *Miscellanies* 3.13.92; 6.45; and 9.36 that the quotation comes from the *Gospel of the Egyptians*. A similar statement is found in the *Martyrdom of Peter with Simon* 9, 94. The passage in *2 Clement* 12 is discussed in K. P. Donfried, *The Setting of Second Clement in Early Christianity* (Leiden: Brill, 1974) 73–77, 152–54, who sees in 2 Clement 12 an Anti-gnostic polemic, and by T. Baarda, *Early Transmission of Words of Jesus* (Amsterdam: VU Uitgeverij, 1983) 261–88, who concludes that 2 Clement 12 preserves the earliest form of a saying independently attested also in the Gosp. Egy, and in the Gosp. Thomas 22. For the kingdom in *Gospel of Thomas* see L. Cerfaux, "Les paraboles du royaume dans l'Evangile de Thomas," *Muséon* 70 (1957) 307–27; D. Mueller, "Kingdom of Heaven or Kingdom of God?" *VC* 27 (1973) 266–76; B. F. Miller, "Study of the Theme of 'Kingdom'; The Gospel According to Thomas: Logion 18," *Nov T* 9 (1967): 52–60.

(Ophites), who used a variant of this logion. Hippolytus sandwiches his quotation of this saying among the Naassenes between two other sayings which expressly interpret the kingdom as within, a treasure hidden inside a person waiting to be discovered (Nos. 113, 114). *Second Clement* puts the logion attributed to Jesus in the context of the question of the time when the kingdom comes. The author gives a consistently moral interpretation to the several parts of the saying. This moral interpretation and the eschatological understanding of the time of the coming of the kingdom were characteristics of the second-century "orthodox" and were in marked contrast to Gnostic understandings.[12]

Interpretations of the Kingdom of God

Apostolic Fathers

Some of the earliest noncanonical documents seem to preserve a duality of present and future that may be interpreted along the lines of inaugurated eschatology. The *Epistle of Barnabas* 8:5f. (No. 7) refers to the reign of Christ from the cross and says that "in his kingdom there will be evil and foul days in which we will be saved." Similarly, ch 4 (No. 5) may be understood as present. The section at the end, based on the "Two Ways" (No. 8), however, speaks in eschatological tones, and the reference in ch 7 (No. 6) is apparently future.

Ignatius, bishop of Antioch at the beginning of the second century, implies, along with a future kingdom (Nos. 18, 21), a present dynamic kingdom by declaring the old kingdom of evil destroyed at the coming of Christ (No. 19). He seems to make a Johannine-like association of kingdom and eternal life (No. 19).

Hermas, a prophet at Rome in the first half of the second century, has a clearly future view of the kingdom (Nos. 32, 32), and he emphasizes the ethical conduct required in order to enter it (Nos. 30, 31, 33, 35). Although he does not make the kingdom present, his thought brings the church and kingdom more closely together than does that of any of his contemporaries.[13] Hermas had a great fondness for the phrase "enter the kingdom of God," and from Jn 3:5, or some statement behind that verse, associated entrance into the kingdom with baptism and taking the name of the Son of God (Nos. 30, 32). The church and the kingdom are in close association, for through Christ one enters the kingdom, and Christ is the

12. *Second Clement* also gives an eschatological interpretation to 1 Cor 2:9 (No. 15), a statement which appears as a saying of Jesus in *Gospel of Thomas* 17. This accords with the general eschatological usage of kingdom in *2 Clement*. (Nos. 12–17).

13. Robert Frick, *Die Geschichte des Reich-Gottes-Gedankens in der alten Kirche bis zu Origenes und Augustin* (Giessen, 1928) 32.

rock on which the church (tower) is built (No. 30), so that entrance into the church is entrance into the kingdom and failure to enter the church excludes one from the kingdom.

The other earliest noncanonical documents have a predominantly futuristic understanding of the kingdom.[14] The *Didache* (from Syria, perhaps ca. 100) includes two prayers for the church to be gathered into the (eschatological) kingdom (Nos. 2, 3). The petition for grace to come and this world pass away (No. 3) is equivalent to a prayer for the kingdom to come.[15] Is it significant that this document, which provides the earliest attestation for the addition of the doxology to the Lord's Prayer (No. 1; cf. 3), does not include "Yours is the kingdom"?

Clement of Rome (ca. 96 C.E.) transferred the proclamation by Jesus of the coming kingdom, as reported in the Synoptic Gospels, to the apostles after the resurrection (No. 9), only without the sense of imminence and urgency. The kingdom of God (No. 9) and the kingdom of Christ (No. 10) appear to be the same, as is common in early Christian writings.[16]

Papias of Hierapolis in the early second century gave expression to the hope for a millennial kingdom on earth (No. 36).

Apologists

The Apologists of the second century, in writings addressed to pagans, made infrequent use of kingdom terminology.[17] The *Epistle to Diognetus* refers to God sending his Son as a king (No. 41), but his kingdom is placed in heaven (No. 43), so the kingdom which Christians enter through the power of God (No. 42), although not unambiguous, is probably to be understood also as in heaven. The other references in the Apologists (Nos. 44, 58) or writings influenced by apologetic concerns (No. 60) also follow a futurist understanding.

Among the Apologists, Justin Martyr (mid-second century) made the most frequent use of the word kingdom (Nos. 45–55), but most of these occurrences are in the *Dialogue with Trypho*, which records the Christian debate with Jews. Although Justin most often speaks of the "eternal kingdom," he also believed in an intermediate millennium.[18] His kingdom language puts the emphasis on eschatology.[19]

---

14. Ibid., 27ff.
15. Ibid., 47.
16. Schmidt, 581; H. M. Herrick, *The Kingdom of God in the Writings of the Fathers* (Chicago: University Press, 1903) 10, 105.
17. Frick, 35ff.
18. *Dialogue* 80, without use of the word kingdom.
19. Herrick, 21. L. W. Barnard, "Justin Martyr's Eschatology," 19 (1965) 87–87 states that Justin preserves the "already" and "not yet" of NT eschatology. I would agree with this as a general assessment, but it is not true of his kingdom terminology.

Irenaeus

Irenaeus has the most fully articulated doctrine of the kingdom of any second-century author. For him "kingdom" was equivalent to heaven in a routine way (Nos. 66, 70, 73, 78, 82, 83), and his usual phrase was "kingdom of heaven" (Nos. 63, 71, 76, 77, 80, 85), not "kingdom of God" (but cf. Nos. 66, 76, 84). Irenaeus also believed there would be an earthly millennial kingdom at the second coming of Christ before the worthy entered into their abode in heaven (Nos. 79, 86–92). Irenaeus integrated this millennial kingdom into his total theology by presenting it as a time when the righteous become accustomed to partake of God's glory (Nos. 87, 90).

Although Irenaeus' use is predominantly eschatological, either millennial ("earthly kingdom") or heavenly, there are exceptions. After all, God possesses a kingdom without end (No. 70) and has committed the kingship of all that is to Christ (No. 65). Thus the heavenly kingdom is not altogether future: Those who die in innocence go immediately into the kingdom (No. 73). This thought may be a corollary of Irenaeus' identification of the kingdom and heaven. The meaning of kingship is preserved in the statement that even the law of Moses showed that death did not properly have the kingship (No. 74). The context of some passages where the prevailing usage of Irenaeus might make one think of the future kingdom (Nos. 76, 82, 84) at least implies the possibility of a present understanding of the kingdom.[20] In these passages the kingdom is in some sense the state of salvation.[21]

Miscellaneous Writings

Poetic language is often ambiguous, and the *Odes of Solomon*, conventionally dated to the early second century,[22] share that characteristic. The *Odes* preserve the Semitic meaning, "*kingship*" (Nos. 38, 40). In one passage the kingdom may be equivalent to the church (No. 39).

The apocryphal *Acts of John* (No. 111) speaks about "joint-heirs and partners in the kingdom." It is not clear whether the gospel ministry or heaven is the meaning.[23]

20. Giorgio Jossa, *Regno di Dio e Chiesa. Ricerche sulla concezione escatologica ed ecclesiologica dell' Adversus haereses di Ireneo di Lione* (Naples, 1970) 246–48, finds the kingdom of God purely future in Irenaeus.

21. Herrick, 22f.; however, the "earthly kingdom" in Irenaeus is the millennial kingdom, not the church, as Herrick supposes.

22. A third-century date has been argued by Han J. W. Drijvers, "Facts and Problems in Early Syriac-Speaking Christianity," *The Second Century* 2 (1982) 166–69.

23. Chapter 78 carries a variant reading "his kingdom" for "his own rest and renewal of life." The association of kingdom and rest is to be noted; cf. Nos. 12, 86, and in Gnosticism the *Tripartite Tractate* (I,5) 101, 29–102, 22 and *Second Apocalypse of James* (V,4) 56, 2–5.

The *Pseudo-Clementines* have a striking formulation of "two kingdoms"—the kingdom of the kings of the earth and the kingdom of heaven, the devil's kingdom and God's kingdom, the present kingdom and the future kingdom (Nos. 106, 107). Although there are passages where the idea of "kingship" is present, the prevailing usage is future (Nos. 108, 109).[24] The Jewish-Christian *Epistle to James* has a beautiful picture of the church as a ship bearing people through the storms of life into the kingdom (No. 110).

The *Sentences of Sextus* (No. 105) draws on the Stoic principle that the wise person is the true king in order to affirm that "the wise person shares in the kingdom of God." The philosophical background indicates that the kingdom in this statement is present and interior. This metaphorical, philosophical sense is symbolic but unlike either the biblical image or the Gnostic usage.

Clement of Alexandria (late second century)

For an author so influenced by Greek thought it is notable that Clement's use of kingdom "is limited to the eschatological sense and depends on biblical conceptions of entrance into the kingdom."[25] For Clement kingdom was primarily a biblical word, and that part of the biblical usage which he appropriated was the future, heavenly aspect (Nos. 93–95, 97–98, 101–104). Clement was concerned with the moral life, and he emphasized the connection between inheriting or entering the kingdom and present moral conduct and spiritual qualities (Nos. 93, 95–102). Clement's identification of "seeing God" with entering the kingdom (No. 102) has a parallel in *Gospel of Thomas* 27. At one place Clement associates the church with the kingdom without identifying them: the earthly assembly is a copy of the heavenly church (No. 96).[26]

Origen (185–254)

Origen marks the change in Christian usage of "kingdom" to the interior meaning of the rule of God in the heart.[27] He was able to integrate the "Gnostic" dimension of the kingdom, the inward rule of God in the soul, into his total thought (No. 115). Origen frequently used future language for the kingdom, but the kingdom's eschatological character

---

24. Herrick, 31–34 concludes that the kingdom is always eschatological in the *Homilies* whereas the *Recognitions* wavers as to whether the righteous are now in God's kingdom. My impression is that one sees the "kingship" idea in the *Homilies* and the meaning "kingdom" with reference to the future more in the *Recognitions*. The different layers in this literature from different dates, now extremely difficult to determine, make pursuit of this question unprofitable.

25. Frick, 92, who gives a sympathetic treatment of Clement's kingdom ideas.

26. Herrick, 26.

27. Lampe, 58–73, and see n. 30.

allowed room for the immanent also. Luke 17:21 and 1 Cor 15:24 were favorite verses with him. In the deepest sense what Origen meant by the kingdom of God was the rule of the divine Spirit in the world of spirits. This rule is not only at the beginning and end of the development but continues throughout. The creation awaits the fulfillment not as a sudden breaking-in, but as the inner progress of the kingdom growing within.[28]

Origen's interpretation of the Lord's Prayer prepared the way for later fathers to emphasize the reign of God in the soul.[29] This understanding of the kingdom permitted Origen to speak more frankly of the kingdom in his apologetic work *Against Celsus* (No. 116) than did other apologists, unless Celsus' comments on the kingdom in the Gospels made a response necessary. Accompanying the interiorization of the kingdom was a change in emphasis from a general eschatology to an individual eschatology, also evident in Gnosticism. Origen achieved a synthesis of the present and future, the dynamic and static features of the kingdom, but he did so in the framework of a philosophy and world view quite different from the thought world of Jesus and the earliest church.

Summary and Evaluation

Apart from the Gnostics (Nos. 112–114), the interpretation of the kingdom as an interior, present possession hardly occurs before Origen (Nos. 105, 115). There are a few passages in early noncanonical Christian literature which relate the kingdom to the present salvation or the church (Nos. 7, 19, 30, 32, 39, 82, 84). The affirmation that the kingship belongs to Jesus could be understood to support this view (Nos. 49, 65, 69, 72). Inaugurated eschatology might be invoked to account for the kingdom seeming to be both present and future in the same author (Nos. 5–8, 18–21, 65–66), and one might even cite an occasional instance of a symbolic meaning (Nos. 105, 41.)

Otherwise, the overwhelming usage of "kingdom" in second-century Christian literature is eschatological. G. W. H. Lampe states that although the variety of meanings given the phrase "kingdom of God" in patristic literature is great, most common of all is the idea of the kingdom as a present spiritual reality.[30] This may be true for patristic literature as a

---

28. Frick, 95–103. Walter Nigg, *Das Ewige Reich* (Zurich, 1954) 61–77 notes the importance of Origen in building up a new theology to take the place of apocalyptic.

29. Herrick, 26. Actually Tertullian had already combined the eschatological interpretation of "thy kingdom come" with an inward interpretation, "come in us"—*On Lord's Prayer* 5. But Tertullian's references to kingdom are on the whole eschatological and Origen's not so much so.

30. Lampe, 62. The article is similar to the entry in the *Patristic Greek Lexicon*

whole, but it is clearly wrong for the second century, where this meaning is rare. The kingdom for second-century authors is almost uniformly future (Nos. 2, 3, 9, 10, 12, 15, 78 ,106, 108, 109, etc.), heavenly (Nos. 29, 58, 63, 67, 71, 77, 95, 106, etc.), and eternal (Nos. 26, 44, 47, 48, 51, 52, 53, 70, 106, etc.). For several writers in the second century the future kingdom will be earthly and millennial: Cerinthus (No. 37), Papias (36), Justin (*Dialogue* 80), Irenaeus (Nos. 79, 86–92), and others. The Montanist movement had as one of its characteristics an expectation of the imminent appearance of the kingdom.[31]

Corollaries of the eschatological perspective were emphases on the conduct necessary to gain entrance into the heavenly kingdom (Nos. 13–15, 18, 21, 31, 33–35, 44, 63, 85, 98–100, 107) and upon the kingdom as a reward for such conduct (Nos. 8, 12, 80, 103, 109). This very strong correlation of the kingdom with moral conduct may be seen as a reflection of the meaning of the "rule of God." It was characteristic of the second century to emphasize that aspect of the Gospels' account of Jesus' proclamation which demanded conduct worthy of the kingdom. Nevertheless, some authors did not fail to remind their readers that the kingdom is God's gift and activity, and entrance into it is by grace (Nos. 24, 26, 42, 43, 66, 71, 95).

The debate with Jews could have favored an emphasis on the church as a replacement of Judaism as the realm in which God's kingship is presently exercised. The references to the kingdom of Christ (or Christ possessing the kingdom) occur primarily in an anti-Judaic context. On the other hand, since the Jews no longer had a kingdom and Christians were in a precarious political situation in the empire, the debate with Judaism could also have shifted attention to the heavenly nature of the kingdom.

The other principal factors influencing Christian thought in the second century—the external difficulties from the "kingdom" of Rome and internal controversies with Gnosticism—definitely favored an eschatological interpretation of the kingdom. The church's troubles with the Roman Empire gave it reason to play down the kingdom idea, especially any indication of its present manifestation. Thus in political contexts Christians emphasized that Christ's kingdom is otherworldly and heavenly (Nos. 45, 61).

The controversy with Gnosticism was also a significant factor in the church choosing to focus on the eschatological nature of the kingdom. The Gnostics emphasized the present aspect of the NT teaching about the kingdom. A radically realized eschatology was already encountered in the NT (1 Cor 15; 2 Tim 2:18). The second-century Gnostics seem to have

(Oxford: Clarendon, 1962), 289–92, although I find the classification and especially the references chosen to illustrate it unsatisfactory.

31. Nigg, 47ff. on early writers in general and pp. 78ff. on Montanism.

gone further in interiorizing the kingdom. Just as NT authors drew on apocalyptic ideas to counter an overly realized eschatology (cf. 2 Thess 2), so the second-century church emphasized a future eschatology.

The kingdom terminology was no longer capable in the second century of carrying as much freight as it did in the NT. Of course, history and human beings rarely stay in neat compartments; in the same way, the alternatives are not absolute in the second century, but the broad outline seems clear: The "orthodox" church took the futuristic side of the NT proclamation of the kingdom, and the "Gnostics" took the present aspect.

Appendix: Kingdom Language in the Second Century[32]

1. "Your kingdom come" quoted from the Lord's Prayer (Did 8:2).
2. "May your church be gathered from the corners of the earth into your kingdom" (Did 9:4).
3. "Remember, Lord, your church to deliver her from all evil and to perfect her in your love, and to gather her from the four winds when she has been sanctified into your kingdom which has been prepared for her. Yours is the power and the glory for ever. May grace come and this world pass away" (Did 10:5f.).
4. "'I am a great king, says the Lord'" (Did 14:3 quoting Mal 1:11, 14).
5. "Let us never relax on the basis of being the elect and fall asleep in our sins, lest the wicked ruler gain power over us and thrust us out from the kingdom of the Lord" (Barn 4:13).
6. "'Even so,' he says, 'those who want to see me and touch my kingdom must receive me through tribulations and suffering'" (Barn 7:11).
7. "Why was the wool put on the wood? Because the kingdom of Jesus is on the wood, and because those who hope on him shall live forever.[33] Why are the wool and the hyssop together? Because in his kingdom there will be evil and foul days in which we shall be saved" (Barn 8:5f.).
8. "He who does these things shall be glorified in the kingdom of God, and he who chooses the others shall perish with his works" (Barn 21:1).
9. "The apostles went forth in the assurance of the Holy Spirit preaching the good news that the kingdom of God is going to come" (1 Clem 42:3).
10. "Those who have been perfected in love according to the grace of God have a place among the pious who shall be manifested at the visitation of the kingdom of Christ" (1 Clem. 50:3).
11. "You, Master, gave the authority of kingship to rulers and governors" (1 Clem. 61:1).
12. "The promise of Christ is great and marvellous and is the rest of the coming kingdom and of eternal life" (2 Clem 5:5).
13. "If we do not keep our baptism pure and undefiled, with what confidence shall we enter into the royal house [kingdom] of God?" (2 Clem 6:9).

---

32. I have been greatly assisted in compiling these passages by Herrick's list, pp. 109ff., but his list is no longer sufficient.

33. Based on a variant reading of Ps. 96:10; cf. Justin, *Dialogue* 73:1; *I Apology* 41.4

14. "Let us love one another in order that we all may enter into the kingdom of God" (2 Clem 9:6).
15. "If we do righteousness before God, we shall enter into his kingdom and receive the promises 'which ear has not heard nor eye seen nor entered into the heart of man'" (2 Clem 11:7).
16. "Let us then wait for the kingdom of God hour by hour in love and righteousness, since we do not know the day of God's appearing. For when the Lord himself was asked when his kingdom would come, he said: 'Whenever the two shall be one, and the outside as the inside, and the male with the female, neither male nor female.' 'The two is one' when we speak the truth to each other and one soul may be in two bodies with no insincerity. And 'the outside as the inside' means this: he calls the inside the soul and the outside the body. In what way your body appears, even so let your soul be manifest in good works. And 'the male with the female, neither male nor female' means this: when a brother sees a sister he thinks nothing concerning her femaleness nor does she think anything concerning his maleness. 'When you do these things,' he says, 'the kingdom of my Father will come'" (2 Clem 12).
17. "Unbelievers shall be astonished when they see the royal house [kingdom] of the world in Jesus" (2 Clem 17:5).
18. "Those who corrupt families 'shall not inherit the kingdom of God.'" (Ign Eph 16:1). (Cf. 1 Cor 6:9f.; Eph 5:5).
19. "The old kingdom was destroyed, for God was manifest as man for the newness of eternal life" (Ign Eph 19:3).
20. "The kingdoms of this age will profit me nothing. It is better for me to die in Christ Jesus than to rule over the ends of the earth" (Ign Rom 6:1).
21. "'Be not deceived,' my brothers, if any one follows a schismatic, 'he shall not inherit the kingdom of God'" (Ign Phld 3:3).
22. "Theirs is the kingdom of God" quoting Mt 5:10 (Lk 6:20) (Pol Phil 2:3).
23. "Shall not inherit the kingdom of God" (Pol Phld 5:3, referring to Galatians 5:17–21).
24. "How can I blaspheme my king who saved me?" (Mart Pol 9:3).
25. "We rightly love the martyrs as disciples and imitators of the Lord on account of their unsurpassable affection to their king and teacher" (Mart Pol 17:3).
26. "To him who is able to bring us all by his grace and gift into his eternal kingdom" (Mart Pol 20:2).
27. "When our Lord Jesus Christ was reigning for ever" (Mart Pol 21:2).
28. "In whose footsteps may we be found in the kingdom of Jesus Christ" (Mart Pol 22:1, =Epilogue 1).
29. "In order that the Lord Jesus Christ may gather me with his elect into his heavenly kingdom" (Mart Pol 22:3, =Epilogue 5).
30. "'What is the rock and the gate?' 'This rock and the gate,' he said, 'is the Son of God.' 'How is it, Sir,' I said, 'that the rock is old but the gate is new?' . . . 'The Son of God is older than all his creation . . . therefore the rock is old. . . . Because he was manifested at the consummation of the last days the gate is new, that those who are going to be saved may enter through it into the kingdom of God. . . . No one shall enter into the kingdom of God unless he take his holy name. . . . A man is not able to enter into the kingdom of God otherwise than through the name of his Son who was beloved by him. . . . Whoever does not receive his name shall not enter into the kingdom of God.' I said, 'What is the tower?' He said, 'This tower is the church.' 'And what are these maidens?' He said, 'These are holy spirits, and a man cannot be found

in the kingdom of God in any other way except they clothe him with their clothing. For if you receive the name alone but do not receive the clothing from them, you will benefit nothing'" (Herm Sim 9.12.3, 4, 5, 8; 13.1, 2).

31. "He who bears these names [faith, self-control, power, longsuffering, etc.] and the name of the Son of God will be able to enter the kingdom of God. . . . The servant of God who bears these names [unbelief, impurity, disobedience, etc.] shall see the kingdom of God but shall not enter it" (Herm Sim 9.15.2, 3).

32. "'They had need,' said he, 'to come up through the water that they might be made alive, for they could not otherwise enter into the kingdom of God unless they put away the mortality of their former life. So these also who had fallen asleep received the seal of the Son of God and entered into the kingdom of God. For before a man bears the name of the Son of God he is dead. But when he receives the seal he puts away mortality and receives life. The seal then is the water. They go down then into the water dead and come up alive. This seal, then, was preached to them also, and they made use of it to enter into the kingdom of God'" (Herm Sim 9.16.2–4).

33. "The rich cleave with difficulty to the servants of God, fearing that they will be asked for something by them. Such with difficulty enter into the kingdom of God. For just as it is difficult to walk with naked feet among thistles, so it is also difficult for such men to enter into the kingdom of God" (Herm Sim 9.20.2, 3).

34. "Such then shall live without doubt in the kingdom of God, because by no act did they defile the commandments of God but remained in innocence all the days of their lives" (Herm Sim 9.29.2).

35. "This world and the vanities of their riches must be cut away from them, and then they will be suitable for the kingdom of God. For it is necessary for them to enter into the kingdom of God. . . . Therefore not one of this kind shall perish" (Herm Sim 9.31.2).

36. "[Papias] says that there will be a millennium after the resurrection of the dead, when the kingdom of Christ will be set up in material form on this earth" (Eusebius *Church History* 3.39.12).

37. "Cerinthus . . . says that after the resurrection the royal house of Christ will be on earth" (Gaius of Rome from Eusebius *Church History* 3.28.2).

38. "Because his kingdom is firm" (Odes Sol 18:3).

39. "And the foundation of everything is Thy rock. And upon it Thou hast built Thy kingdom, And it became the dwelling-place of the holy ones" (Odes Sol 22:12).

40. "And with it, was a sign of the kingdom and of providence" (Odes Sol 23:12).

41. "As a king sending a son, he sent him as King, he sent him as God" (Diog 7:4).

42. "When we made it plain that we were unable to enter the kingdom of God by ourselves, we became able through the power of God" (Diog 9:1).

43. "To mankind God sent his only Son, to them he promised the kingdom in heaven, and he will give it to them who loved him" (Diog 10:2).

44. "This is the way of the truth which leads those who travel therein to the everlasting kingdom promised through Christ in the life to come." Aristides, *Apology* 16 (late Greek text only, missing from the Syriac, so probably not original).

45. "You, when you heard we expected a kingdom, uncritically understood us to say a human when we speak of the one with God. . . . If we were expecting a

human kingdom, we should also deny our Christ that we might not be killed" Justin *I Apology* 11.

46. "Trypho said, 'These and such like scriptures, sir, compel us to wait for him who, as Son of man, receives from the Ancient of days the eternal kingdom'" Justin *Dialogue* 32. (Dan 7 quoted in ch 31; cf. chs 76 and 79.)

47. "Christ is preached at first made subject to suffering, then returning to heaven, and coming again with glory and having the eternal kingdom" (*Dialogue* 34). (Cf. selection 108.)

48. "Trypho replied . . . 'That the Christ is to come again in glory and to receive the eternal kingdom of all the nations when every kingdom is subjected to him is sufficiently shown by the scriptures recounted by you'" (*Dialogue* 39).

49. "The eternal kingdom is Jesus'" (*Dialogue* 46).

50. Jesus preached, "that the kingdom of heaven is near" (*Dialogue* 51; cf. Ps. Clement, *Homilies* I.6; *Recognitions* I.6).

51. "If we keep his commandments, he has promised to provide an eternal kingdom" (*Dialogue* 116).

52. "He shall raise all men from the dead and appoint some to be incorruptible, immortal, and free from sorrow in the everlasting and imperishable kingdom, but he shall send others away to the everlasting punishment of fire" (*Dialogue* 117).

53. "Those worthy of the eternal kingdom to come" (*Dialogue* 120).

54. "All powers and kingdoms feared his name" (*Dialogue* 121; same in 131).

55. "They deceive themselves and you supposing that the eternal kingdom will be given to those of the dispersion who are of Abraham after the flesh, although they are sinners, faithless, and disobedient towards God" (*Dialogue* 140).

56. "The brothers of Zeus, who shared the kingdom with him. . . . Kronos was ejected from his kingdom. . . . How, too, can he give kingdoms who no longer reigns himself?" (Tatian, *Oration* 9).

57. Earthly kingdoms as chronological periods—four times in (*Oration* 39).

58. "May you, by considering yourselves, be able to have the heavenly kingdom also. For all things are subservient to you . . . who have received the kingdom from above." Athenagoras, *Plea* 18. (He uses 'kingdom' for the kingship of the Roman emperor in 1.3; 6.3; 37.1 [twice].)

59. "If you protect the philosophy which grew up with the empire [kingdom] and began with Augustus. . . . Our doctrine flourished for good along with the empire in its beginning" (Melito, *Apology* from Eusebius *Church History* 4.26.7, 8).

60. "And I pray thee, let me rest a little from my song, Holy Giver of manna, king of a great kingdom" Sib Or 2:347 (in the context of describing the parousia and judgment).

61. "[The grandsons of Judas, the brother of Jesus according to the flesh] were asked [by the authorities] concerning the Christ and his kingdom, its nature, origin, and time of appearance, and they explained that it was neither of the world nor earthly, but heavenly and angelic, and it would be at the end of the world, when he would come in glory to judge the living and the dead" (Hegesippus from Eusebius, *Church History* 3.20.4).

62. "Tell my people that I will give to them the kingdom of Jerusalem which I would have given to Israel. . . . The kingdom is already prepared for you: watch!" (4 Ezra 2:10–13).

63. "The former road leads to the kingdom of heaven by uniting man with God" (Irenaeus *Proof of the Apostolic Preaching* 1).

64. Many prophecies written "about our Lord Jesus Christ and about the people and about the calling of the Gentiles and about the kingdom" (*Proof of the Apostolic Preaching* 28).

65. To Christ God "has committed the kingship of all that is" (*Proof of the Apostolic Preaching* 41; cf. 36).

66. Jesus "takes us and bears us into the kingdom of the Father" (*Proof of the Apostolic Preaching* 46).

67. Gen 49:10f., "For 'whom lies in store' a kingship in heaven. . . . He is the expectation of the nations' . . . because we expect him to re-establish the kingdom" (*Proof of the Apostolic Preaching* 57).

68. Herod was frightened lest he be ousted by Christ from the kingship (*Proof of the Apostolic Preaching* 74).

69. The Jews denied the eternal king and acknowledged the temporal Caesar as king (*Proof of the Apostolic Preaching* 95). (On Christ as eternal king cf. 47; 52; 56; 58; 61; 64; 84.)

70. God "possesses a kingdom without end" (Irenaeus *Against Heresies* 2.28.3).

71. The covenant "which renovates man, and sums up all things in itself by means of the Gospel, raising and bearing men upon its wings into the heavenly kingdom" (*Against Heresies* 3.11.8).

72. Christ "has received from his Father an eternal kingdom in Israel (*Against Heresies* 3.12.13).

73. (Referring to the slaughter of the innocents in Mt 2) "He suddenly removed those children belonging to the house of David, whose happy lot it was to have been born at that time, that he might send them on before into his kingdom." (*Against Heresies* 3.16.4).

74. The law of Moses "did truly take away death's kingdom showing that he was no king but a robber (*Against Heresies* 3.18.7).

75. Jeconiah and his descendants were "excluded from the kingdom" (*Against Heresies* 3.21.9 [twice]).

76. "Those who frame the idea of another God besides him who made the promises to Abraham are outside the kingdom of God . . . setting at naught and blaspheming God, who introduces through Jesus Christ Abraham to the kingdom of heaven" (*Against Heresies* 4.8.1).

77. "For God shall be seen as Father in the kingdom of heaven" (*Against Heresies* 4.20.5; cf. 5.23.2).

78. "Abraham believed in things future as if they were already accomplished, because of the promise of God; and in like manner do we also, because of the promise of God, behold through faith that inheritance in the kingdom" (*Against Heresies* 4.21.1).

79. "He shall at his second coming first rouse from their sleep all [righteous persons] and shall raise them up, as well as the rest who shall be judged, and give them a place in his kingdom" (*Against Heresies* 4.22.2).

80. "They who believe in him . . . shall receive the kingdom of heaven" (*Against Heresies* 4.24.2).

81. "In order that both the sower and the reaper may rejoice together in the kingdom of Christ" (*Against Heresies* 4.25.3).

82. Solomon "prefigured the kingdom of Christ." "We ought to fear lest . . . we obtain no further forgiveness of sins but be shut out from his kingdom" (*Against Heresies* 4.27.1, 2, citing a "certain presbyter.").

83. "The beauty and splendor which exist in his kingdom" (*Against Heresies* 4.23.11).
84. They are ignorant "of the ineffable Father, of his kingdom, and of his dispensations" (*Against Heresies* 4.34.3).
85. "Inasmuch, then as in this world some persons betake themselves to the light, and by faith unite themselves with God . . . on this account he says that those on the right hand are called into the kingdom of heaven" (*Against Heresies* 5.38.1).
86. "Bringing in for the righteous the times of the kingdom, that is the rest, the hallowed seventh day, and restoring to Abraham the promised inheritance [the kingdom]" (*Against Heresies* 5.30.4 [which clarifies the similar statement in 4.16.1; cf. also 5.33.2]).
87. "They are ignorant of . . . the [earthly] kingdom which is the commencement of incorruption, by means of which kingdom those who shall be worthy are accustomed gradually to partake of the divine nature" (*Against Heresies* 5.32.1).
88. "The predicted blessing, therefore, belongs unquestionably to the times of the kingdom, when the righteous shall bear rule upon their rising from the dead" (*Against Heresies* 5.33.3).
89. The promise of the Old Testament indicates "the feasting in the kingdom of the righteous which God promises that he himself will serve" (*Against Heresies* 5.34.3).
90. "The righteous shall reign on earth . . . and shall become accustomed to partake of the glory of God the Father, and shall enjoy in the kingdom association and communion with holy angels" (*Against Heresies* 5.35.1; (called "the times of the kingdom" in 5.35.3).
91. "For in the times of the kingdom the righteous man who is upon the earth shall then forget to die" (*Against Heresies* 5.36.2).
92. "John foresaw the first resurrection of the just and the inheritance in the kingdom of the earth. . . . For the Lord also taught these things, when he promised that he would have the mixed cup new with his disciples in the kingdom. . . . The same God the Father . . . fulfills at the resurrection of the just the promises for the kingdom of his Son" (*Against Heresies* 5.36.3).
93. "Then shall he be deemed worthy to be made his heir, then will he share the kingdom of the Father with his own dear Son" (Clem Alex *Exhortation* 9).
94. "And they shall rejoice in the kingdom of their Lord forever. Amen" (*Exhortation* 10).
95. "By his blood and by the word he has gathered the bloodless host of peace and assigned to them the kingdom of heaven. . . . Both [work and grace] are necessary that the friend of Christ may be rendered worthy of the kingdom and counted worthy of the kingdom" (*Exhortation* 11).
96. "He who eats of this meal [righteousness, peace, joy] shall possess the kingdom of God, fixing his regards here on the assembly of love, the heavenly church" (Clem Alex *Instructor* 2.1).
97. "Wealth, when not properly governed, is a stronghold of evil, casting their eyes about which many will never reach the kingdom of heaven" (*Instructor* 2.3; cf. 3.7).
98. "He who has this wealth [the true riches of the Word] shall inherit the kingdom of God" (*Instructor* 3.7).
99. "If we are called to the kingdom of God, let us walk worthily of the kingdom, loving God and our neighbor. . . . When the kingdom is worthily proved, we

dispense the affection of the soul by a chaste and closed mouth, by which gentle manners are expressed" (*Instructor* 3.11).

100. "The good man who has become an heir of the kingdom" (Clem Alex, *Miscellanies* 2.19).

101. "This is he who is blessed by the Lord, and called poor in spirit, a meet heir of the kingdom of heaven" (Clem Alex, *Who Is the Rich Man That Is Saved?* 16).

102. "Becoming pure in heart you may see God, which is another way of saying 'enter the kingdom of heaven'" (*Who Is the Rich Man That Is Saved?* 19).

103. "The kingdom of heaven is [the apostles'] recompense" (*Who Is the Rich Man That Is Saved?* 21).

104. "Spare not perils and toils that you may purchase here the heavenly kingdom. . . . This kingdom God will give you" (*Who Is the Rich Man That Is Saved?* 32).

105. "The wise person shares in the kingdom of God" (*Sentences of Sextus* 311). (Cf. Clem Alex *Miscellanies* 2.4 on the Stoic principle that the wise man possesses kingship.)

106. "God appointed two kingdoms and established two ages, determining that the present world should be given to the evil one . . . but he promised to preserve for the good one the age to come, as it will be great and eternal. . . . Two kingdoms have been established—the one called the kingdom of heaven and the other the kingdom of those who are now kings upon earth" (Ps. Clement, *Homilies* 20.2).

107. "God instituted two kingdoms and has given to each man the power of becoming a portion of that kingdom to which he shall yield himself to obey" (Ps. Clement, *Recognitions* 5.9; see 8, 10–12 and cf. 1.24).

108. "For two advents of him are foretold: one in humiliation, which he has accomplished; the other in glory, which is hoped to be accomplished, when he shall come to give the kingdom to those who believe in him and who observe all things which he has commanded. And when he had plainly taught the people concerning these things, he added this also: That unless a man be baptized in water in the name of the threefold blessedness . . . he can neither receive remission of sins nor enter the kingdom of heaven" (*Recognitions* 1.69). (Cf. on the two comings 1.49 and on baptism 6.9; *Homilies* 11.26; 13.21.)

109. "The first duty of all is to inquire into the righteousness of God and his kingdom; his righteousness that we may be taught to act rightly, his kingdom that we may know what is the reward appointed for labor and patience, in which kingdom there is indeed a bestowal of eternal good things upon the good" (*Homilies* 2.20).

110. "For the whole business of the church is like a great ship bearing through a violent storm men who are of many places and who desire to inhabit the city of the good kingdom" (Ps. Clement, *Epistle to James* 14).

111. "My brethren . . . joint-heirs and partners with me in the kingdom of God" (*Acts of John* 106).

112. "Jesus saw infants being suckled. He said to his disciples, 'These infants being suckled are like those who enter the kingdom.' They said to him, 'Shall we then, as children, enter the kingdom?' Jesus said to them, 'When you make the two one, and when you make the inside like the outside and the outside like the inside, and the above like the below, and when you make the male and the female one and the same, so that the male not be male nor the

female female; and when you fashion eyes in place of an eye, and a hand in place of a hand, and a foot in place of a foot, and a likeness in place of a likeness; then will you enter'" (Gospel of Thomas 22).[34]

113. "A happy nature which, the Naassene says, is the kingdom of heaven to be sought for within a man" (Hippolytus Refutation of All Heresies 5.2).

114. "[The Naassene said the miracle at Cana] manifested the kingdom of heaven. This is the kingdom of heaven that reposes within us as a treasure, as leaven hidden in the three measures of meal" (Refutation of All Heresies 5.3; cf. also 5.4).

115. "It is evident that he who prays that the kingdom of God should come prays with good reason that the kingdom of God should spring up and bear fruit and be perfected in him. For every saint who takes God as his king and obeys the spiritual laws of God dwells in himself as in a well-ordered city, so to speak. Present with him are the Father and Christ who reigns with the Father in the soul that has been perfected. . . . But every sinner is under the tyranny of 'the prince of this world.' . . . As we advance unceasingly the kingdom of God that is in us will reach its highest point when [1 Cor. 15:28]. . . . The kingdom of God cannot co-exist with the kingdom of evil. If therefore it is our will to be under the reign of God, let not sin in any wise reign in our mortal body" (Origen On Prayer 25).

116. "But we desire not only to understand the nature of that divine kingdom of which we are continually speaking and writing, but also ourselves to be of those who are under the rule of God alone, so that the kingdom of God may be ours" (Origen, Against Celsus 8.11).

34. Other references to the kingdom in Gospel of Thomas include logia 3, 20, 27, 46, 49, 54, 57, 76, 82, 96–99, 107, 109, 113, 114. See n. 10 and 11.